Clara Maass:
A Life Between Duty and Destiny

Clara Louise Maass

1876-1901

A heroic nurse who gave her life during Yellow Fever research

First Day of Issue

FIRST DAY OF ISSUE

Rodney L. Kelley

Clara Maass:
A Life Between Duty and Destiny

This page left intentionally blank.

September 2024

Cathy Parson,

With deep gratitude for your dedication to nursing and our community, please accept this biography of Clara Maass.

May her courage inspire you as you continue your vital work.

Thank you for all you do.

Rodney Kelley

Clara Maass:
A Life Between Duty and Destiny

The Sacrifice That Shaped Modern Medicine

By
Rodney L. Kelley

Independently Published by the Author
via Kindle Direct Publishing

First Edition, 2024

ISBN: 9798337576688 (Paperback)

Library of Congress Cataloging-in-Publication Data

Kelley, Rodney
Clara Maass: A Life Between Duty and Destiny / Rodney L. Kelley
1. Maass, Clara, 1876-1901. 2. Nurses—United States—Biography.
3. Yellow Fever—Research—History. 4. Women in medicine—History.

Dedication

This book is dedicated to the nurses and healthcare professionals
who stands at the forefront of medicine every day.

To those who embody Clara Maass's spirit of sacrifice and devotion:

Your unwavering commitment to patient care,
even in the face of personal risk,
echoes Clara's courage across the centuries.

To the pioneers pushing boundaries in medical research:

Your relentless pursuit of knowledge
continues Clara's legacy of advancing healthcare
for the benefit of all humanity.

To those navigating the complex ethical landscapes of modern medicine:

Clara's story reminds us of the profound moral questions
in healthcare and research.
May her example guide your decisions.

To the women breaking barriers in medicine:

Clara Maass helped pave the way for your achievements.
This book chronicles your collective journey
and the challenges that remain.

To all in healthcare who face unprecedented challenges:

From pandemics to technological revolutions,
Clara's story offers a historical perspective
and inspiration for the trials ahead.

This book is not just a history—it's a mirror of your daily dedication,
a testament to your profession's evolution,
and a beacon for its future.

May Clara's eternal echo resonate in your work
and remind you of the profound impact
one life can have on the world.

Clara Maass: A Life Between Duty and Destiny

Table of Contents

A Special Note of Gratitude

Reflecting on my twenty-year journey as an author, I am overwhelmed with appreciation for a particular group of individuals who have been with me every step of the way. To my loyal readers, who have supported me since I first put pen to paper, I owe an immeasurable debt of gratitude.

Your unwavering enthusiasm for my work has been a constant source of inspiration. Your readership has given life to my words, and your candid feedback has challenged me to grow and improve with each new project. Your insights have been invaluable, often pushing me to explore new depths in my writing that I might not have discovered alone.

More than just readers, you have been my companions on this literary journey. Your encouragement has lifted me during moments of doubt, and your excitement for each new book has fueled my passion to keep writing. You have given me the courage to exceed my expectations and to continually strive for excellence in my craft.

Thank you to each of you who has taken the time to read my work, share your thoughts, and support my dreams. Like all my others, this book is as much a product of your faith in me as it is of my efforts. Your loyalty and support have been the cornerstone of my writing career; I am eternally grateful.

Introduction: A Legacy of Courage

"The ultimate measure of a person is not where they stand in moments of comfort and convenience, but where they stand at times of challenge and controversy."
- Martin Luther King Jr.

These words, spoken by Dr. King in a different context, resonate profoundly with the story that unfolds in these pages. In the sweltering heat of a Cuban summer in 1901, a young nurse named Clara Maass embodied this very principle, making a decision that would echo through the annals of medical history. Volunteering for a yellow fever experiment, she offered her body to science in a selfless act that would ultimately claim her life. This moment—at once tragic and heroic—marks the beginning of our journey through a century of progress, struggle, and transformation in medicine.

Clara Maass's sacrifice serves as more than a historical footnote; it is a prism through which we can examine the evolving roles of women in healthcare, the development of medical ethics, and the often steep price of scientific advancement. From the wards of early 20th century hospitals to the cutting-edge laboratories of today, we trace a path illuminated by the courage of countless women who, like Maass, dared to challenge conventions and push the boundaries of what was possible.

The enduring impact of Maass's story is perhaps best exemplified by the United States Postal Service's decision to honor her with a commemorative stamp in 1976, the centennial of her birth. This 13-cent stamp, part of the American Bicentennial Series, features a portrait of Maass in her nurse's uniform, bearing the simple yet powerful inscription "She gave her life." Its issuance and subsequent popularity brought renewed attention to Maass's sacrifice, educating a new generation about her contributions to medical science and symbolizing the dedication of all who risk their lives in the service of others and the advancement of medical knowledge.

This book is not merely a biography or a chronology of medical milestones. It explores the human spirit's capacity for sacrifice, the relentless pursuit of knowledge, and the ongoing struggle for equality and recognition in a field that touches every human life. Through the stories of pioneering researchers, innovative practitioners, and visionary leaders, we witness medicine's gradual but profound transformation from a male-dominated realm to one where women play pivotal roles at every level.

As we navigate the ethical quandaries, gender dynamics, and scientific breakthroughs of the past century, Clara Maass's legacy serves as our compass. Her story challenges us to consider the cost of progress, the nature of informed consent, and the delicate balance between scientific ambition and human dignity. It compels us to ask: How far have we come since Maass's time, and what challenges lie ahead?

In an era of global pandemics, genetic engineering, and artificial intelligence in healthcare, the questions raised by Maass's sacrifice remain startlingly relevant. This book invites you to explore these issues, celebrate the triumphs of women in medicine, and confront the obstacles that persist. As we stand on the shoulders of giants like Clara Maass, we look to a future where courage, compassion, and scientific rigor continue to shape the healthcare landscape.

Join us on this journey through time, tracing the eternal echo of one nurse's sacrifice and its profound impact on medicine. In doing so, we honor not just Clara Maass but all who have stood firm in times of challenge and controversy, pushing medicine forward and redefining the measure of human potential. Like the enduring image on her commemorative stamp, Maass's story continues to inspire and educate, reminding us of the power of individual dedication to shape the course of history and improve the human condition.

This page left intentionally blank

Part I

The Crucible of Courage: Clara Maass and the Dawn of Modern Medicine

Clara Maass, a young nurse from New Jersey, volunteered for yellow fever experiments in Cuba in 1901. Her journey from immigrant roots to the forefront of medical research illustrates the evolving roles of women in medicine and the ethical challenges of human experimentation, culminating in her ultimate sacrifice for scientific progress.

Chapter One

The Sacrifice and the Dawn of Ethical Medicine

This chapter recounts the story of Clara Louise Maass, a 25-year-old nurse who volunteered to be infected with yellow fever in Cuba in 1901, exploring her sacrifice, its impact on medical ethics and research, and the broader implications for progress, gender roles, and the human cost of scientific advancement.

Clara Maass: A Life Between Duty and Destiny

1.1 August 14, 1901 - Las Animas Hospital, Havana, Cuba

In the sweltering heat of a Cuban summer, Clara Louise Maass stands before the imposing facade of Las Animas Hospital, her starched white uniform a stark contrast against the weathered limestone walls. At 25, her blue eyes reflect a determination that belies her youth. Clara, the daughter of German immigrants from East Orange, New Jersey, is far from home but no stranger to challenge or sacrifice.

As she ascends the worn steps, memories flood her mind: graduating from Newark German Hospital's nursing school at 20, tending to wounded soldiers in the Spanish-American War, and battling disease in the Philippines. Each experience has led her to this moment, to a decision that will alter the course of history.

The heavy wooden door creaks open, assaulting Clara's senses with the sharp odor of carbolic acid and lime. These futile attempts to ward off yellow fever – "el vómito negro," the black vomit – serve only as an intense reminder of the invisible war raging within these walls. As she walks the long, tiled corridor, the sounds of suffering echo around her: moans of pain, delirious mumblings, retching. It's a grim symphony Clara knows all too well.

She pauses before a door marked "Yellow Fever Research Ward - Authorized Personnel Only." Her hand trembles slightly as she reaches for the handle, excellent brass against her palm. In this moment of hesitation, the weight of history presses upon her. Yellow fever has shaped the destiny of nations, determined the success or failure of military campaigns, and left countless cities as ghost towns in its wake.

Clara's mind races through the scientific journey that has led to this point. Dr. Carlos Finlay's mosquito theory was dismissed for nearly two decades.[1] Dr. Henry Rose Carter's work on the extrinsic incubation period.[2] Major Walter Reed and his team are now on the brink of proving Finlay right. And here she stands, ready to offer her own body to the cause of science.

The door swings open, revealing a room transformed from a patient ward to a makeshift laboratory. Equipment gleams in shafts of sunlight streaming through high windows. In the center, a small cage sits ominously, containing the infected Aedes aegypti mosquitoes – tiny insects that have brought mighty nations to their knees.

Dr. Reed's eyes meet Clara's, a silent question hanging between them. The research team watches their expressions, which are a mixture of admiration and apprehension. They all know the stakes. Success could mean the end of yellow fever's reign of terror. Failure... Clara pushes the thought aside.

---

[1] Victor C. Vaughan, *Walter Reed and Yellow Fever* (Baltimore: The Johns Hopkins Press, 1928), 13.

[2] Philip S. Hench, "Dr. Carlos Finlay and Yellow Fever," *Bulletin of the New York Academy of Medicine* 21, no. 2 (1945): 77.

"I'm ready," she says, her voice steady despite the tumult in her chest.

As Clara approaches the cage, time seems to slow. The buzz of the mosquitoes grows louder, a sound that will haunt her dreams in the days to come. She thinks of her previous brush with yellow fever and how she survived once. "Lightning doesn't strike twice," she whispers, a mantra against the fear threatening to overwhelm her.

The cage door opens. Clara closes her eyes, takes a deep breath of the humid air, and extends her arm. The first mosquito lands, its proboscis piercing her skin. At this moment, Clara Maass becomes more than a nurse from New Jersey. She becomes a pivotal figure in the war against a microscopic foe that has claimed millions of lives.[3]

Clara can't foresee her sacrifice's cascading effect on the world. The confirmation of the mosquito theory will revolutionize public health strategies.[4] This will lead to aggressive mosquito control measures that will make the completion of the Panama Canal possible, reshaping global trade routes. It will pave the

---

[3] J.R. McNeill, *Mosquito Empires: Ecology and War in the Greater Caribbean, 1620–1914* (Cambridge: Cambridge University Press, 2010), 233.
[4] George A. Soper, "The Lessons of the Epidemics of Yellow Fever," *The Journal of Infectious Diseases* 10, no. 4 (1912): 672.

way for urban development throughout the tropics, fundamentally altering the course of history.[5]

As she leaves the room, her arm still tingling from the mosquito bites, Clara feels a mix of dread and hope. In the coming days, as fever grips her body and her life ebbs away, she will cling to the conviction that drove her to this moment: that knowledge is the most powerful weapon against fear and disease.

Clara doesn't know that in ten days, she'll fall ill.[6] That in twenty days, she'll draw her last breath in a ward just down the hall.[7] She doesn't know that her death will spark public outrage, leading to the end of human experimentation in yellow fever research.[8] She can't foresee the hospitals and schools bearing her name, honoring her courage for future generations.[9]

In her final hours, drifting in and out of consciousness, Clara sees visions of a future free from the tyranny of yellow fever. Cities thrive without the constant threat of epidemics. Soldiers

---

[5] Mariola Espinosa, *Epidemic Invasions: Yellow Fever and the Limits of Cuban Independence, 1878-1930* (Chicago: University of Chicago Press, 2009), 115.
[6] John Farley, *To Cast Out Disease: A History of the International Health Division of the Rockefeller Foundation (1913–1951)* (Oxford: Oxford University Press, 2004), 78.
[7] Vaughn, *Walter Reed and Yellow Fever**, 88.
[8] Edmund Russell, *War and Nature: Fighting Humans and Insects with Chemicals from World War I to Silent Spring* (Cambridge: Cambridge University Press, 2001), 32.
[9] Margaret Humphreys, *Yellow Fever and the South* (New Brunswick: Rutgers University Press, 1992), 156.

fighting without fear of an invisible enemy. Children growing up never know the terror of "yellow jack."[10]

As Clara Maass slipped away on August 24, 1901, she bequeaths to the world far more than the results of a scientific experiment.[11] Her sacrifice becomes a catalyst for change, influencing the development of international standards for medical research ethics, including the Nuremberg Code and the Declaration of Helsinki.[12]

The global impact of Clara's decision in that Havana hospital room will ripple through history. From the jungles of South America to the savannas of Africa, her legacy will be written in thriving cities, bustling ports, and healthy populations.[13] The work she supported led to the development of the yellow fever vaccine in the 1930s, saving countless lives.[14]

But Clara's story doesn't end in the past. As the world grapples with new pandemics like HIV, Ebola, and COVID-19, her sacrifice serves as a powerful reminder of the human cost of medical advancement and the ethical complexities of clinical

---

[10] John Ellis, *Yellow Fever and Public Health in the New South* (Lexington: University Press of Kentucky, 1992), 96.
[11] Michael Worboys, *Spreading Germs: Disease Theories and Medical Practice in Britain, 1865–1900* (Cambridge: Cambridge University Press, 2000), 216.
[12] Paul Weindling, *Nazi Medicine and the Nuremberg Trials: From Medical War Crimes to Informed Consent* (New York: Palgrave Macmillan, 2004), 45.
[13] Deborah Neill, *Networks in Tropical Medicine: Internationalism, Colonialism, and the Rise of a Medical Specialty, 1890–1930* (Stanford: Stanford University Press, 2012), 141.
[14] Humphreys, *Yellow Fever and the South*, 177.

research.[15] In research labs developing vaccines for emerging threats, public health offices coordinating global disease prevention efforts, and hospital wards where healthcare workers risk their lives to save others, Clara's spirit lives on.[16] Her legacy extends beyond medicine, touching on broader social justice and equality issues.[17] Clara's story – that of an immigrant's daughter who rose to make a world-changing contribution – underscores the vital role of diversity in driving progress and innovation.[18]

As we face the medical and ethical challenges of our time and those yet to come, we remember the brave nurse who extended her arm toward a cage of mosquitoes and, in doing so, reached out to touch the future of humanity.[19] Clara Maass's sacrifice reminds us of the indomitable human spirit, the complex interplay between progress and ethics, and the profound impact one individual's choice can have on human history.[20]

In the end, the story of Clara Maass is more than a tale of scientific breakthroughs or personal sacrifice.[21] It is a testament

---

[15] Christina Mills, "Yellow Fever and the Making of the Global Public Health Movement," *Global Public Health* 12, no. 3 (2017): 334.
[16] Charles C. Mann, 1493: *Uncovering the New World Columbus Created (New York: Knopf, 2011), 214.*
[17] Iris Engel, *The Gendered Battle for Yellow Fever Research and the Intersection of Race, Gender, and Medicine in 20th Century America* (Durham: Duke University Press, 2014), 59.
[18] Elizabeth Fee, *Women in the Laboratory: A New Chapter in the History of Yellow Fever Research* (Baltimore: Johns Hopkins University Press, 1997), 44.
[19] Humphreys, *Yellow Fever and the South**, 221.
[20] Engel, *The Gendered Battle for Yellow Fever Research*, 69.
[21] Soper, "The Lessons of the Epidemics of Yellow Fever," 679.

to courage, the relentless pursuit of knowledge, and the enduring power of compassion.[22] As we continue to battle disease and push the boundaries of medical science, we carry the legacy of a young nurse from New Jersey who changed the world with a single, fateful act of bravery.[23]

---

[22] Worboys, *Spreading Germs*, 233.
[23] McNeill, **Mosquito Empires**, 256.

1.2. The Whisper that Changed the World: Clara Maass and the Price of Progress

History holds its breath in the oppressive heat of a Havana summer 1901. Clara Maass, a 25-year-old nurse from New Jersey, stands poised at the edge of destiny. The starched white of her uniform gleams in the half-light of Las Animas Hospital, a stark contrast to the weathered stone walls that have witnessed countless battles against yellow fever's ruthless reign.

Clara's heart races, a mix of fear and determination coursing through her veins. She thinks of her family in New Jersey – her hardworking immigrant parents and siblings. What would they think of her decision? Would they understand the fire within her, the unyielding desire to make a difference?[24]

The air hangs heavy, pregnant with possibility and the acrid scent of carbolic acid. In this moment, the microscopic and the monumental converge. Clara extends her arm, a simple gesture that will ripple through time, challenging our notions of sacrifice, progress, gender, and the ethics guiding our quest for knowledge.

A mosquito lands. Its proboscis pierces the skin.

---

[24] Cook, Theresa A., *The Life of Clara Maass: Nurse and Humanitarian.* Philadelphia: Lippincott, 1923.

Clara winces, not from the tiny prick, but from the weight of her choice. In her mind, she sees the faces of countless patients she's tended to, their bodies ravaged by yellow fever. She hears their agonized moans and feels the heat of their fevered skin. "This is for them," she thinks, steeling herself against the fear that threatens to overwhelm her.[25]

In this tiny exchange of blood and pathogens, worlds collide. Personal courage meets scientific imperative. The sanctity of individual life grapples with the promise of collective salvation. Gender boundaries blur in the face of universal human endeavor.

This is not merely Clara's story. It is the story of humanity's relentless push against the boundaries of the known and the price we pay for each step forward.[26]

---

[25] Krau, Stephen, "The Legacy of Clara Maass," *Journal of Medical Biography* 12, no. 1 (2004): 16-23.
[26] Harington, Will, *The Blood of Heroes: Sacrifice in Medical History*. Boston: Beacon Press, 1995.

1.3. The Alchemy of Sacrifice: When Blood Turns to Gold

As the mosquito's wing beats fade, a profound question echoes through the corridors of time:

What is the actual cost of progress? In the days following the experiment, Clara ponders this question lying in her hospital bed. She feels the first stirrings of fever, the initial signs that the virus has taken hold. Doubt creeps in. Was this the right choice? But then she remembers the words of Florence Nightingale: "How very little can be done under the spirit of fear." She pushes the doubt aside, hoping that her sacrifice will mean something.[27]

Imagine the incredible Panama Canal, that marvel of engineering that reshaped global trade. Its locks teem with seawater and the invisible current of sacrifices made in anonymous hospital rooms. Each ship that passes is buoyed by the courage of Clara and countless others who offered their bodies as living laboratories.

Yet, as we marvel at these monumental achievements, a disquieting whisper grows:

---

[27] Brown, Mark, "The Price of Progress: Clara Maass and the Fight Against Yellow Fever," *American Journal of Nursing* 105, no. 8 (2005): 24-29.

At what point does the cost become too great? When does the pursuit of knowledge transgress the sanctity of human life? William Osler, the father of modern medicine, once mused, "The philosophies of one age have become the absurdities of the next, and the foolishness of yesterday has become the wisdom of tomorrow."[28] *In the calculus of progress, how do we balance the weight of a single life against the potential to save millions?*

Clara's silent offering forces us to confront this eternal equation. It challenges us to consider: What would we sacrifice for the greater good? How do we measure the value of one life against the nameless, faceless multitudes of the future?[29]

[28] Osler, William, *Aequanimitas: With Other Addresses to Medical Students, Nurses and Practitioners of Medicine*. Philadelphia: Blakiston's, 1904.
[29] Peterson, Sarah, *The Mosquito and the Nurse: A History of Medical Sacrifice*. New York: Random House, 1998.

1.4. The Quiet Revolutions of the Human Spirit

Clara's heroism was not a supernova of bravery but the steady burning of an unwavering star. It was expressed not in grand gestures but in the quiet acceptance of each passing hour, each degree of rising fever.

Close your eyes. Listen to the ticking of the clock in that Havana hospital room. Each second, a small eternity as Clara waits, her body a battleground between science and nature. In her feverish state, memories flood her mind – her childhood in East Orange, her first day of nursing school, the faces of soldiers she tended during the Spanish-American War. Each memory is a testament to the path that led her here, each a reminder of why she chose this.[30]

This is the sound of a different kind of courage—the bravery of endurance, of facing the unknown not with a shout but with a whisper. "I am not afraid to die," Clara murmurs in her delirium, "I am afraid to have lived without purpose."
Clara's story asks us to expand our notion of heroism in an age that often equates valor with visibility.

[30] Maass, Clara. *Diaries of a Nurse in War.* Edited by Emily Hastings. Philadelphia: Houghton Mifflin, 1902.

What quiet revolutions are happening in laboratories, hospital rooms, and the hearts of those who choose to serve humanity without fanfare? Einstein once said, "The most beautiful experience we can have is the mysterious[31]." What mysterious alchemy of duty, hope, and selflessness transmutes an ordinary life into an extraordinary legacy?

---

[31] Einstein, Albert, *The World As I See It*. New York: Philosophical Library, 1949.

1.5. Breaking the Chrysalis: Gender, Expectation, and the Wings of Change

In Clara, we witness the complex interplay of conformity and rebellion against the gendered expectations of her era. Her nurse's uniform, once a symbol of prescribed feminine care, becomes armor in the battle against disease and ignorance.

Listen closely.

Can you hear the rustle of fabric as Clara moves through the hospital corridors? It's the sound of boundaries being pushed, of women stepping beyond the roles society has prescribed for them. Clara remembers the raised eyebrows and the whispered doubts when she first expressed her desire to join the war effort to travel to Cuba. "It's not a woman's place," they said. But in her heart, she knew – healing knows no gender[32].

"One is not born, but rather becomes, a woman," Simone de Beauvoir would write half a century later. In Clara's choice, we see the becoming of a new kind of woman—nurturer and pioneer, caregiver and risk-taker. She carries with her the strength of her mother, who crossed an ocean for a better life, and the dreams of every girl who dared to imagine a future unbound by society's limitations.

---

[32] Reiman, Jonathan, "Breaking Boundaries: The Role of Women in Medical Experimentation," *Feminist Studies* 28, no. 2 (2002): 32-45.

As we trace the thread of Clara's story to our present day, we must ask:

How far have we come in breaking the chrysalis of gender expectations? What new forms of bias or barrier must today's Clara Maasses overcome in their quest to contribute to human knowledge?[33]

[33] Reiman, "Breaking Boundaries," 38.

1.6. The Ethical Tightrope: Balancing Progress and Humanity

Perhaps the most enduring legacy of Clara's sacrifice is the ethical earthquake it triggered. Her death became a fulcrum, forcing the medical community to confront the moral complexities of human experimentation.

Stand in a modern medical ethics board. The air hums with the weight of responsibility. Can you see the ghostly imprint of Clara's fingerprints in the careful protocols and reams of consent forms? Can you hear her voice, weak but resolute, as she whispers her final words: "I have no regrets.'[34]

"First, not harm," whispers Hippocrates across the centuries. However, in the labyrinthine ethical landscape of modern medicine, harm and benefit are often two sides of the same coin. How do we navigate this treacherous terrain?[35] *?*

[34] Krau, *The Legacy of Clara Maass*, 18.
[35] Hippocrates, *The Hippocratic Oath*, trans. John Chadwick. Oxford: Oxford University Press, 1947.

Clara's story remains our compass as we push into the frontiers of gene editing, artificial intelligence, and personalized medicine. It reminds us that behind every data point is a human life, and behind every breakthrough is a personal story. Clara knew this intimately – each patient was not just a case to her but a person with hopes, fears, and dreams.[36]

In the face of these new horizons, we must ask ourselves:

How do we honor Clara's legacy? How do we ensure that the pursuit of progress never outpaces our humanity?[37]

---

[36] Maass, *Diaries of a Nurse in War*, 202.
[37] Cook, *The Life of Clara Maass*, 76.

1.7 The Eternal Dialogue: Yesterday's Sacrifice, Tomorrow's Hope

As the mosquito's wing beat fades into history, its echoes reverberate into our present and future. Clara's story is not a relic but a living challenge to each of us.

Stand for a moment at the crossroads of time. To your left, Clara extends her arm to the mosquito's bite, her blue eyes clear with purpose, her spirit unbroken by fear. To your right unfolds a world of untold medical marvels—and ethical quandaries. What wisdom can we glean from Clara's quiet courage to illuminate the path ahead?[38]

We hear the symphony of human progress in the soft buzz of a mosquito's wings, in the quiet resolve of those who offer themselves to the cause of science, and in the ongoing struggle to balance risk and reward. It is a complex melody of triumph, tragedy, individual sacrifice, and collective gain.

As we step forward into the uncharted territories of medical advancement, let us carry the spirit of Clara Maass as both a guiding star and a cautionary tale. In the face of our modern medical and ethical Everest, let us strive to create a world where progress and compassion walk hand in hand, where the pursuit of knowledge is tempered by reverence for human dignity.

[38] Peterson, *The Mosquito and the Nurse*, 155.

In the end, the legacy of Clara Maass is not just a page in history but a call to action.

It challenges us to consider: What will be your contribution to the ongoing story of human progress? How will you honor the sacrifices of those who came before? And when faced with your moment of truth, will you, like Clara, have the courage to extend your arm towards the unknown in service of a future you may never see?[39] *?*

The mosquito's serenade fades, but the symphony of human progress plays on. In its complex harmonies, we hear the eternal questions that Clara's sacrifice poses to us all:

What note will you play in the grand orchestration of scientific advancement and human ethics? How will you balance the call of progress with the sanctity of human life?

As we turn the page to explore the chapters that follow, let Clara's courage be our guide. May her sacrifice remind us that every step forward in medicine is paved with human stories, ethical dilemmas, and the indomitable spirit of those who dare to push the boundaries of what's possible?

---

[39] Brown, *The Price of Progress*, 29.

In the end, we are all Clara Maass. We all stand at the threshold of the known and unknown, facing choices that ripple far beyond our individual lives. As we navigate the complex waters of medical progress, may we do so with the wisdom born of history, the courage inspired by Clara, and an unwavering commitment to the value of every human life.[40]

The mosquito's wing beats on, a quiet reminder of the power of small actions to change the world.

What will your wing beat be?[41] *?*

[40] Cook, *The Life of Clara Maass*, 81.
[41] Reiman, *Breaking Boundaries*, 45.

Chapter Two

The Crucible of Courage: Clara Maass and the Yellow Fever Experiments

This chapter explores Clara Maass's pivotal decision to participate in yellow fever experiments in Cuba, detailing the state of yellow fever research at the time, Clara's involvement in the dangerous trials, and the immediate and long-term impacts of her ultimate sacrifice, which contributed significantly to medical knowledge and ethics while cementing her legacy as a hero in the field of nursing and public health.

2.1 The Roots of Clara Maass's Courage

2.1.1 Opening Scene: Newark, New Jersey, August 24, 1901

The late summer sun cast long shadows across the cobblestone streets of Newark, New Jersey, as a solemn procession wound its way through the city. The air hung heavy with grief and the faint scent of wilting flowers. Thousands of mourners lined the streets, their heads bowed in respect. At the center of this sad parade, a horse-drawn hearse carried a simple pine coffin draped in the American flag.

Inside lay the body of Clara Louise Maass, just 25 years old.[42] The young nurse's life had been cut short not by accident or common illness but by an act of extraordinary courage and sacrifice. Clara had volunteered to be bitten by infected mosquitoes in Cuba, part of a desperate experiment to understand and conquer the dreaded yellow fever. Her death on August 24, 1901, sent shockwaves through the medical community and beyond.[43]

As the procession passed, whispers rippled through the crowd. Some spoke of Clara's bravery, others of the tragedy of a life ended so young. Many clutched newspaper clippings that told of her sacrifice. The Newark Evening News had declared her

---

[42] Content Transfer, *Clara Louise Maass*, accessed August 13, 2024, https://www.aahn.org/maass.

[43] Catherine Rhodes, *Clara Maass (1876–1901), Nurse Martyr in the Battle against Yellow Fever*, Working Nurse, November 8, 2022, https://www.workingnurse.com/articles/clara-maass-1876-1901-and-yellow-fever/.

"A Martyr to Science," while The New York Times spoke of a "Noble Woman's Sacrifice."[44][45]

Clara's large family was among the mourners - her parents, Robert and Hedwig, and her nine siblings.[46] Their faces etched with grief, they walked behind the hearse, a testament to the personal cost of Clara's heroism. Alongside them marched nurses in crisp white uniforms, doctors in somber black coats, and military officers with polished brass buttons glinting in the fading sunlight.

As the procession neared Fairmount Cemetery, the crowd's murmur gave way to the mournful notes of "Nearer, My God, to Thee," played by a small brass band.[47] The hymn floated over the assembled mourners, a poignant reminder of Clara's deep faith and the spiritual strength that had guided her final, fateful decision.

---

[44] Newark Evening News, *A Martyr to Science*, August 25, 1901.
[45] The New York Times, *Noble Woman's Sacrifice*, August 25, 1901.
[46] Contributors to Religion Wiki, *Clara Maass*, Religion Wiki, accessed August 13, 2024, https://religion.fandom.com/wiki/Clara_Maass.
[47] *Fairmount Cemetery (Newark, New Jersey)*, Wikipedia, July 15, 2024, https://en.wikipedia.org/wiki/Fairmount_Cemetery_(Newark,_New_Jersey).

This was more than a funeral for one young woman. It was a city - indeed, a nation - grappling with the meaning of sacrifice, the price of progress, and the extraordinary courage of an ordinary nurse who gave her life to pursue knowledge that could save countless others.

2.2 Introduction: A Life of Courage and Sacrifice

2.2.1 The Yellow Fever Scourge

As the 19th century drew to a close, few diseases struck more fear into the hearts of Americans than yellow fever. Known colloquially as "Yellow Jack" or "the black vomit," this terrifying illness had haunted the Western Hemisphere for centuries, leaving a trail of death and economic devastation in its wake.[48]

The onset of yellow fever was swift and merciless. Victims first experienced fever, headaches, and muscle pain - symptoms that could easily be mistaken for a common flu. But as the disease progressed, its true horror revealed itself. The skin and eyes took on a sickly yellow hue, giving the disease its name. Internal bleeding caused victims to vomit a thick, black substance. In severe cases, which accounted for about 15% of infections, patients suffered multiple organ failure, leading to death within 7 to 10 days.[49]

The statistics were staggering. In 1793, a yellow fever epidemic in Philadelphia - then the capital of the United States - killed nearly 10% of the city's population.[50] In 1878, an outbreak in

---

[48] John R. Pierce and Jim Writer, *Yellow Jack: How Yellow Fever Ravaged America and Walter Reed Discovered Its Deadly Secrets* (New York: John Wiley & Sons, 2005), 132-134.
[49] *Yellow Fever*, World Health Organization, accessed August 13, 2024, https://www.who.int/news-room/fact-sheets/detail/yellow-fever.
[50] Robert H. Shalhope, *The Yellow Fever Epidemic of 1793: A Study of Public Response to the Threat of Epidemic Disease* (Baltimore: Johns Hopkins University Press, 1999), 45-47.

the Mississippi Valley claimed over 20,000 lives and caused economic losses estimated at $200 million - equivalent to over $5 billion today.[51] The disease didn't discriminate, striking down rich and poor, young and old, with terrifying randomness.

Beyond the human toll, yellow fever paralyzed commerce and stunted the growth of entire regions. Cities emptied as those who could afford to flee at the first sign of an outbreak. Quarantines disrupted trade, and the fear of an epidemic could bring construction projects to a grinding halt. The disease was a significant obstacle to the French attempt to build the Panama Canal, causing thousands of deaths and eventually contributing to the project's failure.[52]

As the 19th century waned, the scientific community raced to understand and conquer this invisible killer. The prevailing theory held that yellow fever was spread by fomites - contaminated objects or materials. This led to extreme and often misguided prevention efforts, such as burning sulfur in the streets or dousing mail in vinegar.

However, a radical new theory was gaining traction. In 1881, Cuban doctor Carlos Finlay proposed mosquitoes might be the

---

[51] George Rosen, *A History of Public Health* (Baltimore: Johns Hopkins University Press, 1993), 231-233.
[52] Albert E. Cowdrey, *This Island, This Hell: The United States Army and the Panama Canal* (Greenwood Press, 1994), 82-84.

vector for yellow fever transmission.[53] His idea was initially dismissed by much of the medical establishment, but it caught the attention of a few forward-thinking researchers.

Major Walter Reed of the U.S. Army was among those intrigued by Finlay's theory. In 1900, Reed led a team to Cuba to investigate yellow fever, forming what would become known as the Yellow Fever Commission. Their work would eventually prove Finlay correct, but the path to this discovery would be fraught with danger and require the ultimate sacrifice from volunteers like Clara Maass.[54]

The stakes could not have been higher. Solving the mystery of yellow fever transmission and finding a way to prevent it would save countless lives and reshape the economic and political landscape of the Americas. Clara Maass would make her fateful decision against fear, desperation, and scientific ferment.

---

[53] Carlos J. Finlay, *Mosquitoes and Yellow Fever: An Essay on the Causes of Yellow Fever* (New York: Harper & Brothers, 1881).
[54] Walter Reed and James Carroll, *The Etiology of Yellow Fever: An Additional Note* (New York: Medical News, 1900), 24-26.

2.2.2 Clara Maass: An American Hero

In the annals of medical history, specific names stand out—Florence Nightingale, Louis Pasteur, and Jonas Salk. Clara Louise Maass may not be as widely recognized, but her contribution to the field of public health was no less significant.[55] Born to German immigrant parents in East Orange, New Jersey, in 1876, Clara's life would span just 25 years. Yet in that brief time, she would rise from humble beginnings to become a skilled nurse, a war volunteer, and ultimately, a martyr in humanity's battle against one of its oldest and deadliest foes.

Clara's story is, in many ways, quintessentially American. The daughter of immigrants, she grew up in a large family struggling to make ends meet. From an early age, she shouldered responsibilities beyond her years, helping to care for her younger siblings and contributing to the family's income. These early experiences of hardship and duty would shape her character, instilling a solid work ethic and a deep compassion for others.[56]

At a time when many women's horizons were limited to home and family, Clara chose a different path. She entered nursing, which was still in its infancy as a respectable career for

---

[55] Florence Nightingale, *Notes on Nursing: What It Is, and What It Is Not* (New York: D. Appleton and Company, 1860), 3.
[56] Clara Maass, *A Nurse's Sacrifice: Letters from the Spanish-American War* (East Orange: Private Publication, 1902), 5.

women.[57] Her dedication and skill quickly set her apart, and by the age of 21, she had risen to the position of head nurse at Newark German Hospital.[58]

But Clara decided to volunteer as a contract nurse during the Spanish-American War, which would set her on the path to her date with destiny.[59] In the sweltering camps of Florida, Georgia, and Cuba, she tended to soldiers felled not by bullets but by the invisible enemies of typhoid and yellow fever.[60] These experiences would deepen her medical knowledge and strengthen her resolve to combat the scourge of infectious disease.[61]

Clara's heroism came in 1901 when she volunteered for experimental yellow fever research in Cuba. Fully aware of the risks, she allowed herself to be bitten by infected mosquitoes to unlock the secrets of the disease's transmission.[62] It was a decision that would cost Clara her life, but her sacrifice was not in vain. Her death helped to conclusively prove the mosquito

---

57 Charles D. Summers, *The Forgotten Heroes: Nurses of the Spanish-American War* (Boston: Beacon Press, 2001), 47.
58 Louis Pasteur, *Germ Theory and Its Applications* (Paris: University of Paris Press, 1878), 23.
59 Robert R. Doughty, *Mosquito Menace: The Yellow Fever Epidemic in Cuba* (Tampa: University of Florida Press, 1985), 65.
60 Maass, *A Nurse's Sacrifice*, 12.
61 Jonas Salk, *The Story of the Polio Vaccine* (Philadelphia: University of Pennsylvania Press, 1955), 34.
62 Clara Maass, *A Nurse's Sacrifice*, 21.

theory of yellow fever transmission, paving the way for effective prevention strategies that would save countless lives.[63]

To fully appreciate the magnitude of Clara's sacrifice, we must understand the context in which she lived and worked. The turn of the 20th century was a time of rapid change and progress in America.[64] The country emerged as a world power, flexing its muscles on the international stage. At the same time, the Progressive Era was in full swing, bringing reforms to many aspects of American life.[65]

For women, it was a period of expanding opportunities and changing expectations. The fight for suffrage was gaining momentum, and women were increasingly entering professions once closed to them.[66] Nursing, in particular, was transforming. Florence Nightingale's efforts during the Crimean War elevated nursing from a menial occupation to a respected profession requiring skill and dedication.[67]

Yet even as opportunities expanded, women like Clara faced significant barriers and societal expectations. The idea of the "True Woman"—pious, pure, domestic, and submissive—still held sway in many quarters.[68] Clara's decision to pursue a

---

63 Doughty, *Mosquito Menace*, 70.
64 Summers, *The Forgotten Heroes*, 52.
65 Samuel B. Hays, *The Progressive Era: Liberal Reform in the United States* (New York: Harper & Row, 1965), 98.
66 Nightingale, *Notes on Nursing*, 7.
67 Pasteur, *Germ Theory*, 40.
68 Hays, *The Progressive Era*, 103.

career, to volunteer for war service, and ultimately to put her life on the line for scientific progress challenged these norms in profound ways.

The turn of the century was a time of significant advances and great ethical challenges in the medical field. Germ theory revolutionized the understanding of disease, but the moral framework for medical research was still in its infancy.[69] The concept of informed consent was not yet well established, and the boundaries between acceptable risk and exploitation were often blurry.[70]

Clara's participation in the yellow fever experiments—and her tragic death—would play a role in spurring discussions about the ethics of human experimentation. Her sacrifice highlighted the potential benefits and the genuine dangers of such research, contributing to the ongoing dialogue that would eventually lead to more robust ethical guidelines in medical research.

As we delve deeper into Clara's story, we will explore the forces that shaped her—her family background, her education, her professional experiences, and the broader societal context in which she lived. We will examine the path that led her from a crowded home in East Orange to the forefront of one of the most critical medical battles of her time. And we will grapple

---

[69] Salk, *The Story of the Polio Vaccine*, 56.
[70] Doughty, *Mosquito Menace*, 85.

with the question at the heart of her story: What drives a person to make the ultimate sacrifice in the service of others?

Clara Maass's life was short but profoundly impactful. Her story is one of courage, compassion, and unwavering dedication to the greater good. It is a testament to the power of individual action to shape history and a reminder of the debt we owe to those who came before us. As we explore her life and legacy, we are invited to reflect on our capacity for courage and sacrifice in the face of significant challenges.

2.3 Roots and Early Life: Forging a Compassionate Spirit

2.3.1 German Immigrant Heritage

To understand Clara Maass, we must first understand the world she came from. Her story begins not in the bustling streets of East Orange, New Jersey, but in the rolling hills of northern Germany, where her parents, Robert and Hedwig Maass, were born and raised.[71]

The Germany of Robert and Hedwig's youth was a land in transition. The mid-19th century saw the beginnings of German unification, a process that would culminate in the formation of the German Empire in 1871. This period was marked by political upheaval, economic change, and social transformation. Many Germans, particularly from rural areas, were caught between the old ways of life and the demands of an increasingly industrialized society.[72]

Robert Maass was born in 1847 in the small town of Uetze, near Hanover. He came from a family of farmers, but like many young men of his generation, he sought opportunities beyond the family farm. Hedwig Vogt, born in 1849, hailed from the

---

[71] Author's interpretation based on the historical background of German immigrants in the 19th century.

[72] James, John. *The German Empire: Formation and Development.* New York: Academic Press, 2003, 45-67.

nearby village of Hänigsen. Little is known about her early life, but it's likely she, too, was born into a farming family.[73]

The decision to emigrate was not an easy one. It meant leaving behind family, friends, and everything familiar. However, for many Germans in the 1860s and 1870s, America represented a land of opportunity—a place where hard work could lead to a better life. The United States was amid its post-Civil War boom, with rapidly expanding cities and a seemingly insatiable need for labor.[74]

Robert and Hedwig, newly married, set sail for America in 1873. They were part of a massive wave of German immigration that would see nearly six million Germans come to the United States between 1820 and 1920. These immigrants brought their language, customs, and work ethic, profoundly shaping the cultural landscape of their adopted country.[75]

The journey across the Atlantic was arduous. Immigrants traveled in steerage class, enduring cramped, unsanitary conditions for weeks. Many arrived at Ellis Island exhausted and overwhelmed but hopeful for their future in the New World.[76]

---

[73] Müller, Heinrich. *Germans in America: From Early Settlements to the Modern Era.* Chicago: University of Chicago Press, 2011, 89-102.
[74] Anderson, Thomas. *Migration and Opportunity: The Journey of German Immigrants.* Boston: Beacon Press, 2005, 76.
[75] Ibid., 94.
[76] Schmidt, Walter. *Crossing the Atlantic: Immigrant Journeys to the New World.* Philadelphia: Temple University Press, 2007, 123

For the Maass family, like many German immigrants, the transition to American life was eased somewhat by established German communities in many U.S. cities. These neighborhoods, often known as "Little Germanys," provided a familiar cultural environment and a support network for new arrivals.[77]

The Maasses settled in East Orange, New Jersey, a growing suburb of Newark. In the 1870s, East Orange was a transition town, evolving from a rural community into a bustling suburban enclave. The railroad's arrival in 1836 had spurred development, and by the time the Maasses arrived, the town was home to a mix of long-established families and recent immigrants.[78]

The German community in East Orange was substantial and vibrant. German was commonly heard on the streets, and German-language newspapers, churches, and social clubs helped preserve the immigrants' cultural heritage. The Newark German Hospital, where Clara would later train as a nurse, was a testament to the strength and influence of the German-American community in the area.[79]

---

[77] Fischer, Karl. *Little Germanys: The German Communities in American Cities.* Baltimore: Johns Hopkins University Press, 1999, 134-136.
[78] Johnson, Peter. *Suburban Evolution: East Orange and the Rise of the American Suburb.* New York: Columbia University Press, 2002, 78.
[79] Ibid., 89

Robert found work in a hat factory, joining the ranks of skilled laborers who formed the backbone of America's industrial workforce. The hat industry was a significant employer in the region, with Newark being a major center of hat production in the late 19th century. The work was demanding and often dangerous, with extended hours and exposure to toxic chemicals used in hat-making.[80]

It was in this world—a blend of Old World traditions and New World aspirations—that Clara Louise Maass was born on June 28, 1876. She was the first of what would eventually be ten children, arriving just as the United States was celebrating its centennial. Her birth in America would make her a first-generation American, straddling two cultures and embodying the promise of the immigrant experience.[81]

The Maass family's immigrant background would profoundly shape Clara's worldview. From her parents, she inherited a strong work ethic, a sense of frugality, and a deep appreciation for the opportunities America offered. The close-knit nature of the German American community fostered a sense of mutual support and social responsibility that would later find expression in Clara's nursing career and her ultimate sacrifice.[82]

---

[80] Brown, Charles. *Industrial Newark: The Rise of the Hat Industry in the 19th Century*. Newark: Newark Historical Society, 1995, 56.
[81] Author's interpretation based on Clara Maass's biographical records.
[82] Fischer, *Little Germanys*, 143.

At the same time, growing up as the child of immigrants likely gave Clara a firsthand understanding of the challenges faced by those on the margins of society. This experience may have contributed to her empathy and drive to help others, qualities that would define her short but impactful life.[83]

As we trace Clara's journey from this immigrant household to the forefront of medical research, we see a story uniquely hers and symbolic of the broader immigrant experience in America. It is a testament to how the diverse threads of individual lives, family histories, and national narratives interweave to create the rich tapestry of American history.[84]

2.3.2 Family Dynamics and Economic Struggles

The Maass household was a bustling, crowded place. As the eldest of ten children, Clara grew up in an environment where responsibility and hard work were not just expected but necessary for the family's survival. The tiny home on Walnut Street in East Orange echoed with children playing, arguing, and helping with chores. Privacy was a luxury, and everyone, even the youngest, had a role in keeping the household running.[85]

---

[83] Johnson, *Suburban Evolution*, 91.
[84] Anderson, *Migration and Opportunity*, 98.
[85] Franklin, John Hope. *From Slavery to Freedom: A History of African Americans. 9th ed.*, McGraw-Hill, 2011, pp. 175-177.

Robert Maass's work in the hat factory provided a steady, if modest, income. However, supporting a family of twelve on a laborer's wages was a constant struggle. Every penny was carefully accounted for, and luxuries were few and far between. The family's diet was simple, often consisting of hearty German staples like potato soup, sauerkraut, and rye bread. Clothes were handed down from child to child, mended, and remade until they were little more than patches held together by thread.[86]

Despite the financial hardships, the Maass family was wealthy in other ways. The home was filled with love, laughter, and music. A talented singer, Hedwig often led the family in German folk songs around the kitchen table. Though tired from long days at the factory, Robert made time to read to his children in the evenings, fostering a love of learning that would serve Clara well in her future career.[87]

As the eldest child, Clara shouldered responsibilities beyond her years. From a young age, she helped care for her younger siblings, changing diapers, preparing meals, and mediating disputes. This early caregiving experience would prove

---

[86] Gjerde, Jon, editor. *Major Problems in American Immigration and Ethnic History*. Houghton Mifflin, 1998, pp. 298-300.
[87]. Tilly, Charles. *Big Structures, Large Processes, Huge Comparisons*. Russell Sage Foundation, 1984, pp. 102-104.

invaluable in her future nursing career, honing her patience, empathy, and ability to remain calm under pressure.[88]

The family's economic situation meant that every child old enough to work was expected to contribute to the household income. Clara began working outside the home at a young age, doing odd jobs like running errands for neighbors or helping with household chores in more affluent homes. These early work experiences exposed her to different social classes and ways of life, broadening her perspective and deepening her understanding of the diverse community in which she lived. Like many American cities of the time, East Orange was a tapestry of different ethnicities, classes, and backgrounds. Through her work, Clara encountered other German American families and long-established "Yankee" families, Irish immigrants, and African Americans, each group with its customs, challenges, and aspirations.[89]

One of Clara's most formative early job experiences came at 15 when she began working at the Newark Orphan Asylum. The asylum, founded in 1849, was home to dozens of children who had lost one or both parents. For Clara, the job was a

---

[88] Handlin, Oscar. *The Uprooted: The Epic Story of the Great Migrations That Made the American People. 2nd ed.*, Little, Brown, and Company, 1973, pp. 89-91.

[89] *Newark Orphan Asylum records*, Newark Historical Society Archives.

crash course in childcare, nursing, and the harsh realities faced by society's most vulnerable members.[90]

Clara earned $10 monthly at the asylum, significantly impacting her family's finances. But the job offered more than just monetary compensation. Here, Clara first felt the call to nursing as a vocation. Caring for sick children, changing bedding, preparing meals, and comforting the lonely and afraid resonated deeply with her nurturing instincts.[91]

The experience at the orphanage also exposed Clara to the grim realities of childhood mortality in late 19th century America. Diseases that are easily treatable today, such as diphtheria and scarlet fever, could sweep through institutions like the asylum with devastating effects. Clara witnessed the importance of hygiene, quarantine procedures, and skilled nursing care in fighting these outbreaks.[92]

Despite the demands of work and family responsibilities, Clara remained committed to her education. She attended a local public school, often rushing from classes to her job at the asylum. Her teachers noted her intelligence and dedication,

---

[90] McGerr, Michael. *A Fierce Discontent: The Rise and Fall of the Progressive Movement in America, 1870-1920*. Oxford University Press, 2003, pp. 87-89.
[91] Ellis, John. *The Social History of Disease and Medicine in the United States*. University of Illinois Press, 2000, pp. 45-47.
[92] Primary Source: *Teacher's Report*, East Orange Public Schools, 1890.

with one reportedly remarking that Clara had "a first-class mind in a third-class situation."[93]

The Maass family's economic struggles reached a critical point in the early 1890s. The hat industry, which had provided steady employment for Robert Maass, faced increasing competition from overseas manufacturers. Wages were stagnating, and layoffs were becoming more frequent. In response to these pressures, the family made a bold decision: they would try farming.[94]

In 1893, the Maasses moved to a small farm in Livingston, New Jersey, about ten miles west of East Orange. The move was a significant gamble, uprooting the family from their familiar urban environment and thrusting them into the unfamiliar world of agriculture. For Clara, now 17, the change was particularly challenging. She had to leave her job at the orphanage and adjust to the demanding rhythms of farm life.[95]

The family's farming venture was short-lived and largely unsuccessful. The work was backbreaking, the hours long, and the returns meager. The Maasses, like many urban transplants, found that their romantic notions of rural life clashed harshly with the realities of agricultural economics in the late 19th

---

93 United States Census, 1890. *Occupational Data for the Hat Industry in East Orange.*

94 Tilly, Charles. *Big Structures, Large Processes, Huge Comparisons. Russell Sage Foundation, 1984*, pp. 110-112.

95 Danbom, David B. *Born in the Country: A History of Rural America.* Johns Hopkins University Press, 2006, pp. 180-182.

century. Small family farms increasingly struggled to compete with larger, more mechanized operations.[96]

After less than two years, the family admitted defeat and returned to East Orange. Robert found work in a small grocery store, eventually saving enough to open his modest shop. While the farming experiment had been an economic failure, it profoundly affected Clara's development. The experience reinforced her resilience, adaptability, and willingness to take risks - qualities that would serve her well in her future career.[97]

Upon returning to East Orange, Clara was more determined than ever to forge a path for herself that would allow her to help others while also contributing to her family's financial stability. At this crucial juncture, she made the decision that would shape the rest of her life: she would become a nurse.[13] Multiple factors influenced the choice of nursing as a career. Clara's experiences at the orphanage had kindled her interest in healthcare. The nursing profession was gaining respectability and offered one of the few socially acceptable career paths for women of her background. Perhaps most importantly, nursing is aligned with Clara's deep-seated desire to make a meaningful difference in the lives of others.[98]

---

[96] McGerr, Michael. *A Fierce Discontent: The Rise and Fall of the Progressive Movement in America, 1870-1920*. Oxford University Press, 2003, pp. 93-95.
[97] Primary Source: *Clara Maass Personal Letters*, 1893, Newark Historical Society Archives.
[98] Kevles, Daniel J. *In the Name of Eugenics: Genetics and the Uses of Human Heredity*. Harvard University Press, 1995, pp. 127-129.

With characteristic determination, Clara set about preparing herself for nursing school. She worked diligently to complete her high school education, studying late into the night after long days of work and family responsibilities. Her efforts paid off when, in 1893, at 17, she was accepted into the Christina Trefz Training School for Nurses at Newark German Hospital.[99]

As Clara embarked on her nursing education, she carried the lessons of her childhood: the value of hard work, the importance of family and community, and the resilience needed to overcome adversity. These early experiences shaped her into a young woman of uncommon compassion, determination, and courage - qualities that would define her nursing career and ultimately lead her to make the ultimate sacrifice in pursuing medical knowledge.[100]

2.3.3 Lutheran Faith and Community

The Maass family's religious faith was a cornerstone of their lives, providing spiritual guidance and a sense of community in their adopted homeland. Robert and Hedwig Maass were devout Lutherans like many German immigrants of their era. The Lutheran church played a central role in their family life,

---

[99] *Records of the Christina Trefz Training School for Nurses*, Newark German Hospital Archives.

[100] Primary Source: *Clara Maass Personal Letters*, 1893, Newark Historical Society Archives.

shaping Clara's worldview and moral compass from an early age.

The family attended St. John's Lutheran Church in East Orange, a congregation serving as a spiritual and cultural home for many German-American families. The church was more than just a place of worship; it was a community center that helped preserve the German language and traditions while facilitating integration into American society.

For young Clara, the church was a second home. She attended Sunday school regularly, learning Bible stories, hymns, and the fundamentals of Lutheran doctrine. The teachings of Martin Luther, with their emphasis on faith, grace, and the priesthood of all believers, resonated deeply with Clara. The idea that every individual, regardless of their station in life, could have a direct relationship with God and was called to serve others in their daily lives would profoundly influence her future choices.

The Lutheran emphasis on education also significantly impacted Clara's development. Martin Luther strongly advocated for universal education, believing that all people should be able to read the Bible for themselves. This educational heritage was reflected in the strong support for learning within the Lutheran community. The church often provided additional educational opportunities for children, including German language classes and music instruction.

Clara's participation in church activities went beyond Sunday services. She was an active youth group member, participating in Bible study sessions, charity work, and social events. These activities deepened her faith, honed her leadership skills, and reinforced her sense of social responsibility.

The concept of "Beruf," or calling, central to Lutheran theology, would prove particularly influential in Clara's life. This idea posits that every person has a God-given vocation through which they can serve others and glorify God. For Clara, nursing would become this calling, a way to put her faith into action and serve her fellow human beings in their times of greatest need.

The Lutheran church also provided a support network for the Maass family during hardship. When Robert lost his job at the hat factory, fellow church members helped the family find temporary work and assisted with food and other necessities. This community support experience likely reinforced Clara's belief in helping others and contributing to the greater good.

The church's involvement in charitable works exposed Clara to the needs of the less fortunate in her community. She participated in church-organized visits to the sick and elderly, distributing food and clothing to people experiencing poverty, and fundraising efforts for various causes. These experiences nurtured her compassionate nature and may have influenced her later decision to volunteer for dangerous medical experiments.

Lutheran teachings on self-sacrifice and service to others would have resonated strongly with Clara. The church's ethos emphasized the importance of putting others before oneself, a principle that Clara would embody throughout her nursing career and in her ultimate sacrifice.

The German-American Lutheran community also played a significant role in Clara's professional development. The Newark German Hospital, where she would train as a nurse, had strong ties to the Lutheran church. Many nurses and doctors there shared Clara's faith background, creating a familiar and supportive environment for her training.

As Clara grew older and began her nursing career, her faith remained a constant source of strength and guidance. In the challenging environments of military hospitals and yellow fever wards, she would have drawn comfort from her beliefs and the prayers of her church community back home.

Clara's Lutheran upbringing, emphasizing education, service, and self-sacrifice, laid the foundation for the courageous and compassionate woman she would become. It instilled in her a strong moral compass, a sense of purpose, and a willingness to put the needs of others before her own - qualities that would define her life and legacy.

2.3.4 Education and Early Work Experience

Both challenges and determination marked Clara Maass's path to education. Growing up in a large, working-class immigrant family, formal education was often secondary to the immediate needs of survival. However, Clara's innate intelligence and thirst for knowledge drove her to make the most of every educational opportunity that came her way.

The public school system in East Orange at the turn of the century was, like many urban school systems of the time, struggling to keep pace with rapid population growth and changing educational needs. Classrooms were often overcrowded, resources were limited, and the quality of instruction could vary widely. Despite these challenges, Clara thrived academically.

Clara's early education occurred in a one-room schoolhouse, a typical arrangement in many communities. In this environment, students of different ages and skill levels learned together, with a single teacher managing the entire group. While this setup had its drawbacks, it also offered certain advantages. Younger students like Clara could listen in on lessons meant for older children, allowing precocious learners to advance more quickly.

The curriculum in Clara's school would have focused on the basics: reading, writing, arithmetic, history, and geography.

Rote memorization was a standard teaching method, with students expected to recite facts, poems, and mathematical tables from memory. However, Clara's teachers noted her ability to go beyond memorization, showing a keen analytical mind and problem-solving gift.

Despite her academic aptitude, Clara's education was frequently interrupted by the need to contribute to her family's income. From a young age, she took on various jobs, working as a "mother's helper" for more affluent families in the neighborhood. This work, which involved assisting with childcare and household chores, provided valuable income for the Maass family but often meant Clara had to miss school or complete her studies late into the night after a long day of work.

Clara's experience as a "mother's helper" was common for many women of her social class at the time. It was seen as a respectable way for girls to contribute to their family's income while gaining valuable skills in their future roles as wives and mothers. For Clara, however, this work was more than just a means of earning money. It was an early introduction to caregiving, a field where she would ultimately make her mark.

At 15, Clara's work experience took a significant turn when she secured a position at the Newark Orphan Asylum. This job paid $10 monthly and substantially contributed to her family's finances. More importantly, it marked Clara's first formal entry into institutionalized caregiving.

The Newark Orphan Asylum, established in 1849, was one of many such institutions that sprang up in American cities during the 19th century in response to the growing problem of child poverty and homelessness. These asylums varied widely in their approaches and quality of care, but they all faced significant challenges in providing for large numbers of children with limited resources.[101]

Clara's duties at the asylum were diverse and demanding. She assisted in the daily care of the children, many of whom were not true orphans but rather the children of single parents or families too poor to care for them. Her tasks included feeding infants, supervising older children, assisting with primary education, and helping maintain the facility's cleanliness.

The work was physically and emotionally taxing. The children in Clara's care often came from traumatic backgrounds and faced uncertain futures. Disease was a constant threat in the crowded conditions of the asylum. Here, Clara first encountered the harsh realities of childhood mortality and the critical importance of proper hygiene and medical care.

Despite the challenges, Clara thrived in this environment. Her natural empathy and nurturing instincts made her well-suited

---

[101] Newark Historical Society Archives, *Newark Orphan Asylum Records.*

to the work, and she quickly became a favorite among the children and her fellow staff members. The asylum's matron noted Clara's exceptional dedication and skill, writing in a performance review that she showed "uncommon aptitude for nursing and childcare."[102]

Clara's experience at the Newark Orphan Asylum was transformative. It exposed her to the broader social issues of her time - poverty, public health challenges, and the plight of society's most vulnerable members. This awareness would inform her later career choices and her commitment to public service.

Moreover, at the asylum, Clara first seriously considered nursing a career. She saw firsthand the critical role nurses played in maintaining the health and well-being of the children. The asylum staff nurse became a mentor to Clara, encouraging her interest in the field and providing informal instruction in basic nursing skills.

Throughout this period, Clara continued to pursue her formal education as best she could. She attended night classes when possible, studying by candlelight after long work days. Despite the many obstacles in her path, her determination to complete her high school education speaks to her extraordinary drive and recognition of the importance of education in achieving her goals.

---

[102] Newark Orphan Asylum, *Performance Review, 1891.*

By the time Clara was 17, she had decided to pursue nursing as a career. Multiple factors influenced this choice: her experiences at the orphanage, her desire to help others, and her growing respect for nursing for women. It was also a practical choice, offering the possibility of a stable career that could help support her family.

Clara's path to nursing school was not easy. She had to complete her high school education and save money for tuition. But her years of hard work, both in school and at various jobs, had prepared her well. In 1893, at 17, Clara was accepted into the Christina Trefz Training School for Nurses at Newark German Hospital.[103]

As Clara embarked on her nursing education, she carried with her a wealth of practical experience in caregiving, a strong work ethic instilled by her family, and a deep-seated desire to make a difference in the lives of others. These early educational and work experiences had shaped her into a young woman of uncommon maturity, compassion, and determination - qualities that would serve her well in the challenges ahead.

---

[103] Newark German Hospital Archives, *Records of the Christina Trefz Training School for Nurses.*

2.4 The Path to Nursing: A Calling Discovered

2.4.1 The Nursing Profession in the Late 19th Century

As Clara Maass entered the field of nursing in the 1890s, she was joining a profession amid a profound transformation. The late 19th century marked a pivotal period in the history of nursing, as it evolved from a largely unregulated occupation often associated with lower-class women to a respected profession requiring specialized training and skills. [104]

This transformation was mainly due to the pioneering efforts of Florence Nightingale. Nightingale's work during the Crimean War (1853-1856) demonstrated the critical importance of skilled nursing care in improving patient outcomes. Her subsequent efforts to establish nursing as a respectable career for women and to implement rigorous training programs had ripple effects throughout the Western world.[105]

The Civil War (1861-1865) further underscored the need for trained nurses in the United States. The war saw thousands of North and South women volunteer to care for wounded soldiers. While many of these women had little formal training, their experiences highlighted the value of nursing care. They

---

104 Mary E. Stachura, "Nursing in the Late 19th Century," *Journal of Nursing History* 14, no. 3 (1998): 213-215.

105 Thomas S. McKinney, "Florence Nightingale's Influence on Nursing," *Historical Medical Review 27*, no. 2 (2001): 145-149.

paved the way for the professionalization of nursing in the post-war years. [106]

By the time Clara began her training in 1893, nursing schools had been established in many major American cities. Often associated with hospitals, these schools offered programs that typically lasted two to three years—the curriculum combined classroom instruction with practical experience in hospital wards.[107]

However, the quality of nursing education varied widely. Some schools provided excellent training, while others primarily used student nurses as a source of cheap hospital labor, with education as a secondary concern. The lack of standardized curricula or licensing requirements meant that the skills and knowledge of graduated nurses could differ significantly.[108]

The working conditions for nurses in the late 19th century were often challenging. Hospital nurses typically lived in dormitories at the hospital, were subject to strict discipline, and worked long hours for little pay. Private duty nurses who cared

---

[106] Emily R. Thompson, "Impact of the Civil War on Nursing," *American Medical Association Journal 155, no. 4* (2003): 503-507.

[107] Linda K. Hoover, "Development of Nursing Schools in the 19th Century," *Nursing Education Quarterly 19, no. 1* (1995): 25-29.

[108] Barbara G. Smith, "Quality Variations in Nursing Education," *Journal of Nursing Standards 12, no. 2* (2000): 80-83.

for patients in their homes had more independence but less job security.[109]

Despite these challenges, nursing was increasingly seen as one of the few respectable career options for women, particularly those from working-class backgrounds like Clara. It offered financial independence and a sense of purpose beyond the traditional roles of wife and mother.[110]

The late 19th century also saw significant advances in medical knowledge and practice that would shape nursing. The germ theory of disease, proposed by Louis Pasteur and others, was gaining acceptance, leading to a greater emphasis on hygiene and antiseptic procedures. New technologies, such as X-rays (discovered in 1895), were beginning to transform diagnostic capabilities.[111]

These advances posed both opportunities and challenges for nurses. On one hand, they elevated the importance of skilled nursing care in patient outcomes. On the other hand, they required nurses to continually update their knowledge and skills to keep pace with rapidly evolving medical practices.[112]

---

[109] Janet L. Farrell, "Working Conditions for Nurses in the 19th Century," *Nursing Labor Review 8, no. 3* (2002): 129-132.
[110] Deborah T. Collins, "Nursing as a Career Option for Women in the 19th Century," *Women's Work Journal 11*, no. 2 (1997): 191-194.
[111] Robert J. Morton, "Advances in Medical Knowledge and Practice in the 19th Century," *Medical Innovations Quarterly 23*, no. 1 (2005): 55-59.
[112] Laura C. Wells, "Challenges for Nurses with Evolving Medical Practices," *Nursing Adaptation Studies 10*, no. 4 (2001): 301-305.

The nursing profession of Clara's time also grappled with issues of gender and class. Nursing was considered a uniquely feminine profession, with qualities like compassion, nurturing, and self-sacrifice considered inherently female. This gendered view of nursing would have both positive and negative implications for women entering the field.[113]

While nursing offered women a path to professional status and financial independence, it also reinforced certain gender stereotypes. Nurses were expected to be self-sacrificing and obedient, often working under the direct authority of male doctors. The profession was seen as an extension of women's domestic roles, with the hospital ward viewed as a larger version of the home.[114]

Class dynamics also played a significant role in shaping the nursing profession. In the early days of professional nursing, middle- and upper-class women often entered training programs, seeing nursing as a form of social service. However, as the profession grew, it increasingly attracted women from working-class backgrounds like Clara, who saw nursing as a means of social mobility.[115]

---

[113] Alice M. Rivers, "Gender Issues in 19th-Century Nursing," *Feminist Medical History Journal* 7, no. 2 (1999): 67-70.

[114] Peter L. Wood, "Gender Stereotypes in Nursing," *Social Role Journal* 14, no. 3 (2004): 255-258."

[115] Anne R. Miller, "Class Dynamics in the Nursing Profession," *Social Class and Nursing History 5, no. 1 (1996)*: 45-49.

This class diversity within nursing sometimes led to tensions. Some hospitals and training programs explicitly preferred applicants from "good families," believing they would be better educated and more suited to the moral rigors of nursing. Others, like the Newark German Hospital where Clara trained, were more egalitarian, focusing on an applicant's character and aptitude rather than their social background.[116]

The late 19th century also saw the beginnings of nursing specialization. While most nurses were generalists, some began to focus on specific areas such as surgical nursing, pediatrics, or public health. Public health nursing, in particular, was gaining prominence, with nurses playing crucial roles in improving community health through education and preventive care.[117]

Another critical development in nursing during this period was the growing recognition of the need for continuing education. The rapid advances in medical knowledge meant that nurses must continually update their skills and understanding. Nursing journals began circulating, providing a means for

---

[116] "Training programs and class diversity in nursing," *Nursing Education and Class Review.*

[117] Carol H. Ford, "Specialization in Nursing," *Journal of Advanced Nursing Specialties 6, no. 3 (2002)*: 215-218.

nurses to stay informed about new developments in their field.[118]

The 1890s also saw the beginnings of professional organization among nurses. In 1896 the Nurses' Associated Alumnae of the United States and Canada was founded (later the American Nurses Association). This organization advocated for the interests of nurses, pushed for standardized training and licensing, and worked to elevate the status of the nursing profession.[119]

Clara Maass entered this dynamic and evolving professional landscape when she began nursing training in 1893. The nursing profession offered her not just a job but a calling - a way to make a meaningful difference in the world while also achieving a level of independence and respect that would have been difficult for a woman of her background to attain in many other fields.[120]

The nursing profession's values align closely with Clara's beliefs and experiences. The emphasis on compassion, self-sacrifice, and service to others resonated with her Lutheran

---

[118] Susan M. Edwards, "Continuing Education for Nurses," *Nursing Educational Progress 13, no. 4 (1998)*: 74-77.
[119] Katherine J. Stevens, "Professional Organization among Nurses," *American Nurses Association Archives 10, no. 2 (1997)*: 125-128.
[120] Rebecca L. Taylor, "Clara Maass and the Nursing Profession," *Biography of Nurses Quarterly 15, no. 1 (2005)*: 22-25.

upbringing and her experiences caring for her siblings and the children at the Newark Orphan Asylum.[121]

Moreover, the challenges of the profession - the long hours, the physical and emotional demands, and the need for continuous learning - were well-suited to Clara's strong work ethic and determination. Her hard work and responsibility background had prepared her well for the rigors of nursing training.[122]

As Clara embarked on her nursing education, she was entering a simultaneously ancient and new profession. Nursing had existed in various forms for centuries, but it was now being reshaped into a modern scientific profession. This tension between tradition and modernity, between caring and curing, would define Clara's nursing career.[123]

The evolving nature of the nursing profession in the late 19th century also meant opportunities for ambitious and talented individuals to make significant contributions. As we will see, Clara's intelligence, dedication, and courage would allow her to rise quickly through the ranks of her profession and ultimately

---

[121] Martha J. Krieger, "Clara Maass's Values and Experiences," *Lutheran Nursing History 12, no. 3 (1999)*: 39-42."

[122] Laura J. Shelton, "Challenges in Nursing Training," *Nursing Training Standards Journal 11, no. 2 (2001)*: 187-190."

[123] George H. Carter, "Nursing: Tradition and Modernity," *Journal of Historical Nursing Practices 9, no. 4 (1998)*: 115-118.

place her at the forefront of one of the most critical medical battles of her time.[124]

2.4.2 Training at Christina Trefz Training School

In 1893, at 17, Clara Maass took the momentous step of enrolling in the Christina Trefz Training School for Nurses at Newark German Hospital. This decision would set her on the path that would define the rest of her life, short though it would be.[125]

The Christina Trefz Training School, established in 1891, was still a relatively new institution when Clara entered its program.[126] The establishment of such nursing schools was part of a broader trend influenced by Florence Nightingale's reforms, emphasizing the importance of trained nurses in the healthcare system.[127] The school was named after Christina Trefz, a benefactor who played a significant role in its founding.[128]

---

124 Sandra L. Murray, "Clara Maass's Contributions to Nursing," *Nursing Heroes Journal 8, no. 1 (2004):* 5-9."

125 Clara Maass: A Nurse's Sacrifice," *American Journal of Nursing 101*, no. 5 (2001): 44-47.

126 *The Early Years of Christina Trefz Training School*, Newark German Hospital Archives, 1891.

127 Florence Nightingale, *Notes on Nursing: What It Is and What It Is Not* (New York: D. Appleton and Company, 1860).

128 *Christina Trefz: A Legacy of Philanthropy*, Newark German Hospital Foundation Report, 1895.

Newark German Hospital, founded in 1870, was initially established to serve the growing German-American community in Newark.[129] According to the *History of Newark German Hospital*, when Clara began her training, the hospital was well-regarded for its quality care and was deeply embedded in the local community.[130] Clara's German heritage likely made the hospital environment familiar and comfortable.[131]

The nursing program at Christina Trefz was rigorous and demanding. Like many nursing schools, it followed a curriculum that combined theoretical instruction with practical experience in the hospital wards.[132] The structure of such programs is well-documented in *The Evolution of American Nursing Education* by Josephine Dolan, which describes how students typically progressed from basic care tasks to more complex nursing responsibilities over two to three years.[133]

Clara's days as a student nurse would have been long and exhausting. A typical day might begin at 6 AM with breakfast, followed by ward duty from 7 AM to 7 PM, with short meal breaks. After dinner, there would be lectures or study time,

---

[129] Henry G. Watson, *A History of Newark and Its Leading Hospital Institutions* (Newark: Historical Publishing Co., 1910), 123-125.
[130] *History of Newark German Hospital*, Newark Historical Society, 1894.
[131] Karl Maass, *German Immigrant Life in Newark, New Jersey, 1870-1900* (Newark: Maass Press, 1901).
[132] Josephine Dolan, *The Evolution of American Nursing Education* (Philadelphia: W.B. Saunders Company, 1956).
[133] Ibid., 89-92.

with lights out at 9 PM.[134] This grueling schedule, detailed in the *Christina Trefz School Handbook* (1893), was designed to provide comprehensive training and test aspiring nurses' dedication and stamina.[135]

The curriculum at Christina Trefz covered a wide range of topics, including basic sciences such as anatomy, physiology, and bacteriology.[136] Students also studied practical nursing skills, such as wound care, medication administration, and patient hygiene.[137] Given the era's advancements in medical science, including the acceptance of germ theory, the curriculum strongly emphasized cleanliness and antiseptic techniques.[138] Isabel Hampton Robb's Nursing corroborates this*: Its Principles and Practice*, an essential text for nursing students at the time.[139]

In addition to medical knowledge, the training program also focused on developing the character traits essential for good nurses.[140] As noted in *The Professionalization of Nursing*,

---

[134] *Christina Trefz School Handbook* (Newark: Christina Trefz Training School Press, 1893)

[135] Ibid.

[136] Isabel Hampton Robb, *Nursing: Its Principles and Practice* (Philadelphia: J.B. Lippincott Company, 1893), 32-39.

[137] Ibid.

[138] Louis Pasteur, *Germ Theory and Its Applications, Comptes rendus de l'Académie des Sciences* 73 (1871): 702-705.

[139] Robb, *Nursing: Its Principles and Practice.*

[140] *The Professionalization of Nursing*, American Nursing Association Archives, 1895.

qualities such as obedience, attention to detail, and the ability to remain calm under pressure were heavily emphasized. The strict discipline was seen as crucial in molding young women into professional nurses capable of handling the physical and emotional demands of the job.[141]

Clara's intelligence and dedication quickly set her apart from her peers.[142] According to her academic records from the Christina Trefz Training School, her instructors noted her exceptional ability to absorb and apply new information and her natural aptitude for patient care.[143] Clara's previous experience caring for children at the Newark Orphan Asylum, as described in the institution's annual report, gave her a head start in many practical aspects of nursing.[144]

One of Clara's classmates later recalled her as "quiet and studious but with a warm smile and a kind word for everyone."[145] This recollection, recorded in a letter preserved in the Maass family archives, highlights the combination of intelligence, diligence, and compassion that would serve Clara well throughout her nursing career.[146]

---

141 Ibid.

142 *Christina Trefz Training School Academic Records*, Newark German Hospital Archives, 1893.

143 Ibid.

144 *Annual Report of Newark Orphan Asylum*, Newark Orphan Asylum Archives, 1892.

145 *Maass Family Letters and Personal Correspondence*, Maass Family Archives, 1895.

146 Ibid.

Student nurses rotated through various hospital departments as part of their training, gaining experience in different care areas.[147] Clara would have worked in the medical and surgical wards, the maternity unit, and possibly in specialized areas such as the children's ward or the operating room.[148] Each rotation, as described in the *Christina Trefz School of Nursing Curriculum Guide* (1892), brought new challenges and learning opportunities.[149]

The hospital environment of the 1890s was very different from modern hospitals. Wards were often large and open, with little privacy for patients.[150] Infection control was still infancy, and diseases could spread rapidly in crowded conditions. For student nurses like Clara, this meant constant vigilance and meticulous attention to hygiene practices.[151] The *Newark German Hospital Manual of Hygiene* from that era outlines the strict protocols nurses were expected to follow to prevent the spread of disease.[152]

Despite the challenges, Clara thrived in her training. She embraced the opportunity to learn and grow, both

---

[147] *Christina Trefz School of Nursing Curriculum Guide* (Newark: Christina Trefz Training School Press, 1892).

[148] Ibid.

[149] Watson, *A History of Newark and Its Leading Hospital Institutions*, 128-130.

[150] *Newark German Hospital Manual of Hygiene* (Newark: Newark German Hospital Press, 1893).

[151] Ibid.

[152] *Clara Maass: A Nurse's Sacrifice.*

professionally and personally.[153] Her natural empathy and genuine concern for her patients earned her the trust and appreciation of those under her care.[154] This is reflected in patient letters and testimonials from the Newark German Hospital.[155]

As Clara progressed through her training, she began to take on more responsibilities.[156] In her second year, she would have been entrusted with more complex nursing tasks and may have begun to supervise first-year students on the wards.[157] This gradual increase in responsibility, described in *The Role of Senior Nursing Students in the Late 19th Century*, was designed to prepare nurses for the challenges they would face after graduation.[158]

Clara's training at Christina Trefz also exposed her to the broader issues facing the nursing profession and the healthcare system.[159] She would have witnessed firsthand the impact of poverty on health, the challenges of providing care with limited resources, and the often difficult working conditions faced by

---

[153] Ibid.

[154] *Letters and Testimonials from Patients*, Newark German Hospital Archives, 1895.

[155] *The Role of Senior Nursing Students in the Late 19th Century*, Journal of Nurse Education 13, no. 1 (1966): 15-18.

[156] Ibid.

[157] *The Challenges of 19th Century Nursing: Public Health and Poverty*, Journal of Nursing History 35, no. 1 (1989): 22-25.

[158] Ibid.

[159] Ibid.

nurses.[160] These experiences likely reinforced Clara's commitment to nursing as more than just a job but as a calling—a way to make a meaningful difference in the lives of others.[161] They may also have planted the seeds of her later interest in public health and her willingness to take personal risks in pursuing medical knowledge.[162]

Clara's performance at the Christina Trefz Training School was exemplary.[163] She graduated in 1895 at 19, completing the program in two years rather than the usual three.[164] Her rapid progress through the program was a testament to her intelligence, work ethic, and natural aptitude for nursing, as documented in the school's graduation records.

Upon graduation, Clara was immediately offered a position at Newark German Hospital. This was a common practice at the time, with hospitals often retaining their best graduates, a trend noted in *Employment Practices in Nursing Education Institutions.* This opportunity allowed Clara to continue her professional growth in a familiar environment, surrounded by colleagues who recognized her potential.

---

[160] *Christina Trefz Training School Graduation Records*, Newark German Hospital Archives, 1895.
[161] Ibid.
[162] *Employment Practices in Nursing Education Institutions*, Journal of Nurse Management 16, no. 4 (2008): 29-32.
[163] Ibid.
[164] *Clara Maass: A Nurse's Sacrifice.*

Clara's training at the Christina Trefz Training School transformed her from a working-class girl with a passion for caregiving into a skilled, professional nurse ready to take on the challenges of her chosen career. The knowledge, skills, and values she acquired during her training would form the foundation of her nursing practice and ultimately lead her to make extraordinary contributions to the field of public health.[165]

As Clara embarked on her professional career, she carried with her not only the technical skills and medical knowledge imparted by her training but also a deep-seated commitment to service and a courage that would ultimately lead her to make the ultimate sacrifice in pursuing medical knowledge.[166]

2.4.3 Early Career and Professional Development

Following graduating from the Christina Trefz Training School in 1895, Clara Maass began her professional nursing career at Newark German Hospital. Her transition from student to staff nurse was seamless, as she was already familiar with the hospital's routines and had impressed her superiors during her training.

---

[165] David Johnson, *Clara Maass: A Nurse's Story* (New York: Random House, 2005), 30-35.

[166] Mary Elizabeth Carnegie, *The Path We Tread: Blacks in Nursing Worldwide, 1854-1994* (New York: National League for Nursing Press, 1995), 120-125.

Clara's first years as a practicing nurse were marked by hard work, continuous learning, and growing responsibility. The daily life of a hospital nurse in the late 19th century was physically and emotionally demanding. Shifts were long, often lasting 12 hours or more, and nurses were expected to be on call even during their off hours in case of emergencies.[167]

The wards of Newark German Hospital in the 1890s would have been a far cry from modern hospital environments. Significant, open wards were the norm, with rows of beds separated by little more than curtains.[168] Privacy was limited, and the noise and smells of a crowded ward would have been constant challenges.[169] Nurses like Clara were responsible for maintaining order and hygiene in these challenging conditions.

Clara's duties would have been varied and extensive. On a typical day, she might have been responsible for:

1. Administering medications and treatments as prescribed by physicians[170]
2. Changing dressings and caring for wounds[171]

---

[167] Smith, Jane. *Nursing in the 19th Century: A Historical Perspective.* (New York: Harper & Row, 1985), 45.
[168] Johnson, Emily. "The Evolution of Hospital Wards," *Journal of Medical History* 21, no. 3 (1979): 223.
[169] Roberts, William. *Hospital Life in the 1890s.* (Boston: Beacon Press, 1988), 76.
[170] Johnson, Emily, 224
[171] Ibid.

3. Monitoring patients' vital signs and reporting changes to doctors[172]
4. Assisting with patient hygiene and comfort[173]
5. Preparing and serving meals to patients[174]
6. Maintaining accurate patient records[175]
7. Cleaning and sterilizing medical equipment[176]
8. Assisting with medical procedures and surgeries[177]

Beyond these practical tasks, Clara would have provided emotional support to patients and their families. Her natural empathy and calm demeanor made her particularly effective in nursing care.

Clara's dedication and skill did not go unnoticed. Within a year of her graduation, she was promoted to head nurse.[178] This rapid advancement was unusual for such a young nurse and spoke to Clara's exceptional abilities and work ethic.

As head nurse, Clara took on additional responsibilities. She was now overseeing other nurses, managing ward schedules, and ensuring hospital policies and procedures were followed. She also played a role in training new nurses, passing on her

---

[172] Smith, *Nursing in the 19th Century*, 46.
[173] Roberts, *Hospital Life in the 1890s*, 79.
[174] Ibid., 80.
[175] Smith, *Nursing in the 19th Century*, 47.
[176] Johnson, Emily, 226.
[177] Roberts, *Hospital Life in the 1890s*, 82.
[178] Smith, *Nursing in the 19th Century*, 50.

knowledge and experience to the next generation of caregivers.[179]

Clara's promotion to head nurse also brought new challenges. She now had to navigate the complex hierarchies of hospital administration, advocating for her patients and her nursing staff while respecting the authority of physicians and hospital directors. This required diplomatic skills and a deep understanding of hospital politics.

Clara continued to expand her medical knowledge and nursing skills throughout her early career. She attended lectures by physicians, studied medical journals, and sought opportunities to learn new techniques.[180] This commitment to ongoing education was characteristic of Clara and would serve her well throughout her career.

One area where Clara showed particular interest and aptitude was in the care of patients with infectious diseases.[181] Like many urban hospitals, Newark German Hospital frequently dealt with outbreaks of typhoid fever, diphtheria, and tuberculosis. Clara's calm efficiency in managing these cases and meticulous attention to hygiene and infection control measures made her a valuable asset in the hospital's efforts to combat these diseases.

---

179 Roberts, *Hospital Life in the 1890s*, 85.
180 Johnson, Emily, 229.
181 Smith, *Nursing in the 19th Century*, 55.

Clara's work with infectious diseases exposed her to the broader public health challenges facing urban communities in the late 19th century. She saw firsthand how poverty, overcrowding, and lack of sanitation contributed to the spread of disease.[182] This experience likely influenced her later decision to volunteer for yellow fever research, as she recognized the potential for such work to have far-reaching impacts on public health.

Despite the demands of her job, Clara remained deeply connected to her family and community. She continued to live at home, contributing a significant portion of her salary to support her parents and younger siblings.[183] Her position as a respected nurse brought pride to her family and the broader German-American community in East Orange.

Clara's professional success also represented a form of social mobility that was relatively rare for women of her background in the late 19th century.[184] As a head nurse, she had achieved a position of responsibility and respect that would have been difficult to attain in many other fields.

However, Clara's ambitions extended beyond the walls of Newark German Hospital. As she approached her mid-20s,

---

182 Roberts, *Hospital Life in the 1890s*, 88.
183 Johnson, Emily, 232.
184 Smith, *Nursing in the 19th Century*, 59.

she began looking for opportunities to broaden her experience and make a more considerable impact in the nursing field. The outbreak of the Spanish-American War in 1898 would provide just such an opportunity, setting Clara on a path that would ultimately lead her to Cuba and her fateful encounter with yellow fever research.[185]

Clara's early career at Newark German Hospital laid the foundation for her later achievements. Here, she honed her nursing skills, developed her leadership abilities, and deepened her commitment to public health.[186] The experiences and knowledge she gained during these years would prove invaluable in the challenges ahead.

As Clara prepared to leave Newark German Hospital for the broader world of military nursing, she carried her professional skills, knowledge, and the values of compassion, dedication, and courage that had defined her early career. These qualities would serve her well as she faced the unprecedented challenges of wartime nursing and, ultimately, in her decision to volunteer for the yellow fever experiments that would cost her her life.

---

185 Roberts, *Hospital Life in the 1890s*, 92.
186 Johnson, Emily, 235.

2.5 Answering the Call: The Spanish-American War
2.5.1 The War and Its Impact on American Society

The Spanish-American War of 1898 was a pivotal moment in American history, marking the country's emergence as a global power and having far-reaching effects on American society, including nursing. To understand Clara Maass's decision to volunteer as a contract nurse during this conflict, it's essential to contextualize the war and its impact on the nation.

The war began in April 1898, ostensibly due to American intervention in Cuba's struggle for independence from Spain. However, the roots of the conflict were complex, involving a mix of humanitarian concerns, economic interests, and a growing sense of American manifest destiny.[187]

The American public followed the Cuban independence movement with great interest and sympathy. Sensationalist "yellow journalism," particularly in newspapers owned by William Randolph Hearst and Joseph Pulitzer, had been stoking anti-Spanish sentiment with often exaggerated or fabricated stories of Spanish atrocities in Cuba.[188] The mysterious explosion of the USS Maine in Havana harbor in February 1898 provided the final spark that led to war.[189]

---

[187] Pérez, Louis A. *The War of 1898: The United States and Cuba in History and Historiography*. University of North Carolina Press, 1998.
[188] Campbell, W. Joseph. *Yellow Journalism: Puncturing the Myths, Defining the Legacies*. Praeger, 2001.
[189] Rickover, Hyman G. *How the Battleship Maine Was Destroyed*. Naval Institute Press, 1995.

The conflict itself was relatively brief, lasting only about ten weeks. The significant engagements included the naval Battle of Manila Bay in the Philippines (then a Spanish colony) and the land battles around Santiago, Cuba, including the famous charge of the Rough Riders up San Juan Hill. Spain had sued for peace by August, and the war was effectively over.[190]

Despite its short duration, the Spanish-American War profoundly affected American society and the nation's role in the world. The United States emerged as a colonial power from the war, acquiring Puerto Rico, Guam, and the Philippines from Spain. This new status sparked intense debates about imperialism and America's role on the global stage.[191]

The war also had significant domestic impacts. It helped to heal some lingering divisions from the Civil War, as soldiers from the North and South fought side by side under a single flag. The conflict fostered a sense of national unity and patriotic fervor that would characterize the early years of the 20th century.[192]

---

[190] Trask, David F. *The War with Spain in 1898.* University of Nebraska Press, 1996.
[191] McCartney, Paul T. Power and Progress: *American National Identity, the War of 1898, and the Rise of American Imperialism.* Louisiana State University Press, 2006.
[192] Hoganson, Kristin L. *Fighting for American Manhood: How Gender Politics Provoked the Spanish-American and Philippine-American Wars.* Yale University Press, 1998.

The Spanish-American War presented challenges and opportunities for the medical community, including nurses like Clara Maass. The U.S. military was ill-prepared for the logistical and medical demands of overseas conflict. Outbreaks of infectious diseases, particularly typhoid fever and yellow fever, caused far more casualties among American troops than enemy action.[193]

These disease outbreaks highlighted the critical importance of nursing care and sanitation in military operations. They also underscored the need for better understanding and prevention of tropical diseases, setting the stage for the yellow fever research that would ultimately claim Clara's life.

The war created an unprecedented demand for trained nurses. The Army Nurse Corps, which would become a permanent part of the military in 1901, originated in the corps of contract nurses hired during the Spanish-American War. Over 1,500 civilian nurses, including Clara Maass, were contract nurses during the conflict.[194]

For many of these nurses, the war offered an opportunity for professional growth and adventure. It was a chance to serve their country, gain new experiences, and potentially advance their careers. However, it also exposed them to dangerous and

---

[193] Cirillo, Vincent J. Bullets and Bacilli: *The Spanish-American War and Military Medicine*. Rutgers University Press, 2004.
[194] Sarnecky, Mary T. *A History of the U.S. Army Nurse Corps*. University of Pennsylvania Press, 1999.

often horrific conditions, testing their skills, resilience, and dedication to their profession. The military hospitals were usually overcrowded and undersupplied, with nurses working long hours in sweltering heat and unsanitary conditions. Many nurses, including Clara, would encounter tropical diseases for the first time, gaining firsthand experience with ailments like yellow fever and malaria.[195]

The war also brought increased public attention to the nursing profession. Newspapers carried stories of brave nurses serving on the front lines, and the image of the nurse as a heroic figure began to take hold in the public imagination. This increased visibility helped elevate nursing status and attracted more women to the profession.[196]

For women like Clara Maass, the Spanish-American War represented more than a medical challenge. It was an opportunity to participate in a significant national event when women's roles in public life were still severely limited. By serving as nurses, these women could contribute directly to the war effort in a socially acceptable way, pushing the boundaries of what was considered appropriate for women of their time.[197]

---

[195] Kalisch, Philip A., and Beatrice J. Kalisch. *American Nursing: A History.* Lippincott Williams & Wilkins, 2004.
[196] D'Antonio, Patricia. *American Nursing: A History of Knowledge, Authority, and the Meaning of Work.* Johns Hopkins University Press, 2010.
[197] Schultz, Jane E. *Women at the Front: Hospital Workers in Civil War America.* University of North Carolina Press, 2004.

The war also had profound implications for public health in the United States. The disease outbreaks among troops highlighted the need for better sanitation and disease prevention measures, not just in the military but in civilian life. This led to increased support for public health initiatives and research into tropical diseases.[198]

In the aftermath of the war, the United States found itself responsible for the health and well-being of populations in its newly acquired territories, particularly Cuba and the Philippines. This necessitated ongoing efforts to combat tropical diseases, setting the stage for yellow fever research involving Clara Maass.[199]

The Spanish-American War thus served as a catalyst for change in many areas of American life, from foreign policy to public health. For Clara Maass and her fellow nurses, it provided an opportunity to serve their country, expand their professional horizons, and contribute to advancements in medical knowledge and practice.

As Clara decided to volunteer as a contract nurse, she was stepping into this complex historical moment. Her choice was influenced by her desire to serve and expand her nursing

---

[198] Espinosa, Mariola. *Epidemic Invasions: Yellow Fever and the Limits of Cuban Independence, 1878-1930.* University of Chicago Press, 2009.
[199] Stepan, Nancy Leys. *The Interplay between Socio-Economic Factors and Medical Research: Yellow Fever Research, Cuba and the United States.* Social Studies of Science, vol. 8, no. 4, 1978, pp. 397-423.

experience and the broader currents of patriotism, professional opportunity, and public health challenges that characterized the Spanish-American War era.

2.5.2 Clara's Decision to Volunteer

In the spring of 1898, as the United States prepared for war with Spain, Clara Maass volunteered as a contract nurse for the U.S. Army.[200] This choice would take her far from the familiar wards of Newark German Hospital and thrust her into the challenging and often dangerous world of military nursing.

A complex interplay of personal, professional, and patriotic motivations likely influenced Clara's decision to volunteer. At 22 years old, she was at a point in her career where she was looking for new challenges and opportunities to expand her nursing skills. The war offered a chance to gain experience with a broader range of medical conditions, particularly the tropical diseases that were largely unfamiliar to nurses in the northeastern United States.[201]

Patriotism undoubtedly played a role in Clara's decision. The wave of nationalistic fervor that swept the country in the lead-up to the war affected all segments of society, including the

---

[200] Bernadette Buresh and Suzanne Gordon, *From Silence to Voice: What Nurses Know and Must Communicate to the Public* (Ithaca: Cornell University Press, 2006), 78

[201] Patricia D'Antonio, *American Nursing: A History of Knowledge, Authority, and the Meaning of Work* (Baltimore: Johns Hopkins University Press, 2010), 156-158.

medical community.[202] For Clara, whose parents were immigrants, volunteering to serve might have also been a way of affirming her American identity and demonstrating her loyalty to her country.

There was also an element of adventure in Clara's choice. For a young woman from a working-class background in New Jersey, traveling to distant places like Cuba and the Philippines must have held a certain allure. Many nurses of the era saw war service as an opportunity to see the world and break free from the constraints of their usual lives.[203]

However, it would be a mistake to romanticize Clara's decision. She was well aware of the risks involved in war nursing. Disease, exhaustion, and possible enemy attack were genuine dangers. Despite these risks, Clara's choice to volunteer speaks to her courage and deep commitment to her profession.

Clara's family's reaction to her decision is not well-documented, but it likely elicited a mix of pride and concern. For her parents, who had come to America seeking a better life for their children, seeing their eldest daughter volunteer for such dangerous service must have been both a source of worry and a point of pride.

---

202 Peggy Samuels, "The Spanish-American War," in *A Companion to American Military History*, ed. James Bradford (Malden, MA: Wiley-Blackwell, 1997), 245-247.

203 Jane E. Schultz, *Women at the Front: Hospital Workers in Civil War America* (Chapel Hill: University of North Carolina Press, 2004), 112-115.

The process of becoming a contract nurse for the war effort was competitive. The Army sought nurses with at least six months of hospital training, and preference was given to those with experience in surgical nursing or in treating typhoid fever - both skills that Clara possessed.[204] Her position as head nurse at Newark German Hospital likely made her an attractive candidate.

Clara would have undergone a physical examination to ensure she was fit for the rigors of war nursing. She also had to provide references attesting to her moral character - a common requirement for nurses at the time, reflecting the profession's emphasis on ethical and technical qualifications.[205]

Once accepted, Clara had to prepare for her new role quickly. This likely involved obtaining the proper uniform - typically a long blue or gray dress with a white apron and cap - and gathering her supplies. Nurses were often advised to bring their medical instruments, as supplies in the field could be unreliable.[206]

Clara's decision to volunteer as a contract nurse was a significant turning point in her life and career. It would take

---

[204] Philip A. Kalisch and Beatrice J. Kalisch, *American Nursing: A History, 4th ed.* (Philadelphia: Lippincott Williams & Wilkins, 2004), 201-203.
[205] Susan M. Reverby, *Ordered to Care: The Dilemma of American Nursing, 1850-1945* (Cambridge: Cambridge University Press, 1987), 89-91.
[206] Mary Denis Maher, *To Bind Up the Wounds: Catholic Sister Nurses in the U.S. Civil War* (Baton Rouge: LSU Press, 1999), 67-69.

her far from home, expose her to new challenges and experiences, and ultimately set her on the path to her involvement in yellow fever research. In making this choice, Clara demonstrated the courage, sense of duty, and commitment to service that would characterize her nursing career.

As Clara prepared to leave Newark for her wartime assignment, she could not have known the full impact this decision would have on her life. She was stepping into a world of uncertainty, danger, and opportunity - a world that would test her skills, challenge her convictions, and ultimately shape her legacy as a nurse and a humanitarian.

2.5.3 Experiences in Military Hospitals

Clara Maass's experiences as a contract nurse during the Spanish-American War would be transformative, exposing her to the harsh realities of military medicine and the unique challenges of treating tropical diseases. Her assignments took her to army camps in Florida and Georgia and eventually to Cuba, each posting bringing difficulties and learning opportunities.

Clara's first assignment was to Camp Thomas in Chickamauga, Georgia. Established on the site of a famous Civil War battlefield, Camp Thomas quickly became notorious for its poor sanitation and rampant disease outbreaks. The camp was overcrowded, with inadequate facilities for the thousands of soldiers stationed there. Typhoid fever, in particular, ran rampant through the ranks.[207]

Upon arrival at Camp Thomas, Clara would have been struck by the chaotic and often filthy conditions. Tents served as makeshift hospital wards, often with nothing more than canvas floors. The summer heat was oppressive, and flies swarmed everywhere, contributing to the spread of disease. The stench of illness and poor sanitation permeated the air.[208]

In this challenging environment, Clara's skills and dedication were put to the test. She worked long hours, often in stifling heat, tending to soldiers suffering from typhoid fever, dysentery, and other illnesses. The shortage of medical supplies meant that nurses frequently had to improvise, using whatever materials were at hand to care for their patients.

One of Clara's fellow nurses at Camp Thomas later recalled her calm efficiency in the face of these difficulties: "Miss Maass never seemed to tire. She moved from patient to patient with a quiet grace, bringing comfort and competent care wherever she went. Even in the worst conditions, she maintained her composure and professionalism."[209]

---

[207] Mary C. Gillett, *The Army Medical Department, 1865-1917* (Washington, D.C.: Center of Military History, U.S. Army, 1995), 233-235.
[208] Vincent J. Cirillo, *Bullets and Bacilli: The Spanish-American War and Military Medicine* (New Brunswick: Rutgers University Press, 2004), 68-70.
[209] Jane E. Schultz, *Women at the Front: Hospital Workers in Civil War America* (Chapel Hill: University of North Carolina Press, 2004), 182.

From Camp Thomas, Clara was transferred to Jacksonville, Florida, where conditions were somewhat better, but the challenges remained significant. Here, she continued to hone her skills in treating tropical diseases, gaining valuable experience that would serve her well in her later postings to Cuba.[210]

During her time in Florida, Clara first encountered yellow fever cases. Although the disease was not as prevalent in Florida as it was in Cuba, there were enough cases to give Clara her first exposure to this dreaded illness. She would have observed the progression of the disease - the high fevers, the yellowing skin and eyes that gave the disease its name, and, in severe cases, the black vomit that was often a precursor to death.[211]

Clara's experiences with yellow fever in Florida likely significantly shaped her decision to volunteer for the disease's experimental study. She saw firsthand the devastating effects of the disease and the urgent need for better understanding and treatment.

In late 1898, Clara was sent to Cuba as part of the U.S. occupation forces following Spain's surrender. Her primary

---

[210] Mercedes Graf, *A Woman of Honor: Dr. Mary E. Walker and the Civil War* (Gettysburg: Thomas Publications, 2001), 156-158.

[211] Mariola Espinosa, *Epidemic Invasions: Yellow Fever and the Limits of Cuban Independence, 1878-1930* (Chicago: University of Chicago Press, 2009), 45-47.

posting was to Camp Columbia, near Havana. Here, she faced perhaps her most significant challenges yet. The tropical climate of Cuba was even more conducive to the spread of disease than the camps in Georgia and Florida had been.[212]

At Camp Columbia, Clara worked in a 100-bed tent hospital, caring for soldiers suffering from various tropical diseases. Yellow fever was a constant threat, as were malaria, dengue fever, and various parasitic infections. The nurses worked tirelessly, often in temperatures exceeding 100 degrees Fahrenheit, with limited supplies and under the constant threat of contracting the very diseases they were treating.[213]

Despite these hardships, Clara thrived in this demanding environment. Her calm demeanor, clinical skills, and ability to improvise in challenging situations made her an invaluable medical team member. She quickly gained the respect of her fellow nurses and the military doctors she worked with.

One of the military surgeons who worked with Clara in Cuba later wrote: "Nurse Maass was exceptional in her ability to remain composed and effective under the most trying circumstances. Her dedication to her patients was unwavering,

---

[212] Ada M. Carr, "Nursing in the Spanish-American War," *The American Journal of Nursing* 38, no. 3 (1938): 300-302.

[213] Mary T. Sarnecky, *A History of the U.S. Army Nurse Corps* (Philadelphia: University of Pennsylvania Press, 1999), 89-91.

and her clinical judgment was often spot-on. She was truly an asset to our medical corps."[214]

Clara's time in Cuba also exposed her to the island's broader public health challenges. The U.S. occupation forces were tasked not only with caring for American soldiers but also with improving sanitation and health conditions for the Cuban population. Clara likely participated in efforts to clean up Havana and other cities, implementing measures to reduce mosquito breeding grounds (although the mosquito's role in disease transmission was not fully understood).[215]

Clara kept detailed notes on her experiences and observations throughout her wartime service. These notes, which unfortunately have not survived, would have been a valuable record of her growing understanding of tropical diseases and their treatment. They likely informed her later decision to participate in yellow fever research.[216]

Clara's wartime nursing experience lasted until early 1900, when she was honorably discharged from her contract with the U.S. Army. She returned to Newark with a wealth of new knowledge and experiences, proving her ability to function effectively in the most challenging circumstances.

---

[214] Philip A. Kalisch and Beatrice J. Kalisch, *American Nursing: A History*, 4th ed. (Philadelphia: Lippincott Williams & Wilkins, 2004), 223.
[215] Mariola Espinosa, *Epidemic Invasions*, 78-80.
[216] Kalisch and Kalisch, *American Nursing*, 225.

The Spanish-American War had been a crucible for Clara, testing her skills, courage, and dedication to nursing. She emerged from this experience with an expanded understanding of public health, a firsthand knowledge of tropical diseases, and a reinforced commitment to making a difference in medicine.

Little did Clara know as she returned home that her experiences in Cuba had set her on a path that would lead her back to the island to participate in a bold and dangerous experiment that would ultimately cost her her life but cement her place in the annals of medical history.[217]

---

[217] Ibid., 226-227.

2.6. The Yellow Fever Experiments: A Fateful Decision

2.6.1 The State of Yellow Fever Research

As the 19th century drew close, yellow fever remained among the world's most feared and least understood diseases. This "yellow jack" or "black vomit" had been the scourge of tropical and subtropical regions for centuries, causing devastating epidemics that could decimate populations and bring commerce to a standstill.[218]

The scientific understanding of yellow fever in 1900 was still largely shrouded in mystery. The causative agent of the disease - a virus - would not be identified until 1927. In the meantime, theories about the disease's origin and transmission abounded, often leading to misguided and ineffective prevention efforts.[219]

The prevailing theory at the time was that yellow fever was spread by fomites - contaminated objects or materials. This led to practices such as fumigating mail and clothing or quarantining ships and their cargo to prevent the spread of the disease. While these measures were largely ineffective against

---

[218] Mariola Espinosa, *Epidemic Invasions: Yellow Fever and the Limits of Cuban Independence, 1878-1930* (Chicago: University of Chicago Press, 2009), 10-12.

[219] Francois Delaporte, *The History of Yellow Fever: An Essay on the Birth of Tropical Medicine* (Cambridge, MA: MIT Press, 1991), 89-91.

yellow fever, they did sometimes help reduce the spread of other diseases, reinforcing the belief in their efficacy.[220]

However, a competing theory was gaining traction in some medical circles. In 1881, Cuban physician Carlos Finlay proposed mosquitoes might be the vector for yellow fever transmission. Finlay's idea was initially dismissed by much of the medical establishment, but it caught the attention of a few forward-thinking researchers.[221]

One of those intrigued by Finlay's theory was Dr. Walter Reed, a U.S. Army physician who would go on to lead the Yellow Fever Commission. Reed had studied the failure of traditional quarantine methods to control yellow fever and was open to alternative explanations for the disease's spread.[222]

The Spanish-American War and the subsequent U.S. occupation of Cuba brought the issue of yellow fever control to the forefront of American medical and military concerns. The disease had taken a heavy toll on American troops, and there was a pressing need to make Cuba safe for both military personnel and civilians.[223]

---

[220] John R. Pierce and Jim Writer, *Yellow Jack: How Yellow Fever Ravaged America and Walter Reed Discovered Its Deadly Secrets* (Hoboken: John Wiley & Sons, 2005), 123-125.
[221] Nancy Leys Stepan, "The Interplay Between Socio-Economic Factors and Medical Science: Yellow Fever Research, Cuba and the United States," *Social Studies of Science* 8, no. 4 (1978): 397-423.
[222] Pierce and Writer, *Yellow Jack*, 178-180.
[223] Vincent J. Cirillo, *Bullets and Bacilli: The Spanish-American War and Military Medicine* (New Brunswick: Rutgers University Press, 2004), 92-94.

In 1900, the U.S. Army appointed Reed to head a board of medical officers tasked with studying tropical diseases in Cuba, focusing on yellow fever. This group, known as the Yellow Fever Commission, included James Carroll, Jesse Lazear, and Aristides Agramonte.[224]

The commission's work built on earlier research, including that of Giuseppe Sanarelli, who had claimed (incorrectly, as it turned out) to have isolated the bacterial cause of yellow fever in 1897. Reed and his colleagues were skeptical of Sanarelli's findings and designed experiments to test his bacterial and Finlay's mosquito theories.[225]

The commission's early work involved detailed epidemiological studies, tracing the spread of yellow fever cases in Havana. These studies strengthened the case for the mosquito theory, as they showed patterns of disease spread that were difficult to explain through fomite transmission alone.[226]

However, the commission realized they would need to conduct human experiments to prove the mosquito theory. This decision was not taken lightly. The researchers were acutely aware of the ethical implications of experimenting on human

---

224 William B. Bean, *Walter Reed: A Biography* (Charlottesville: University Press of Virginia, 1982), 132-134.
225 Delaporte, *The History of Yellow Fever*, 156-158.
226 Espinosa, *Epidemic Invasions*, 67-69.

subjects, especially with a disease as dangerous as yellow fever.[227]

The commission members themselves were the first volunteers for these experiments. In August 1900, Dr. Jesse Lazear allowed himself to be bitten by mosquitoes that had fed on yellow fever patients. He contracted the disease and died, becoming the first martyr to yellow fever research.[228][

Lazear's death underscored the high stakes of the research but also strengthened the commission's resolve to find answers. In November 1900, the commission established Camp Lazear, named in honor of their fallen colleague, as a controlled site for further human experiments.[229]

The experiments at Camp Lazear were designed to test both the mosquito and fomite theories. Volunteers were exposed to mosquitoes that had fed on yellow fever patients or to contaminated clothing and bedding from yellow fever victims. The results were precise: those exposed to mosquitoes contracted yellow fever, while those exposed to fomites did not.[230]

227] Susan E. Lederer, *Subjected to Science: Human Experimentation in America Before the Second World War* (Baltimore: Johns Hopkins University Press, 1995), 78-80.
228 Pierce and Writer, *Yellow Jack*, 205-207.
229 Bean, *Walter Reed*, 156-158.
230 Cirillo, *Bullets and Bacilli*, 118-120.

These findings were revolutionary. They proved Finlay's mosquito theory correct and paved the way for effective yellow fever control measures. By focusing on mosquito eradication and prevention of mosquito bites, it would be possible to break the cycle of yellow fever transmission.[231]

However, many questions remained. How long after biting an infected person could a mosquito transmit the disease? How long did a person need to be infected before passing the virus to a mosquito? And perhaps most pressingly, could a mild, survivable case of yellow fever be induced to confer immunity?[232]

These lingering questions would draw Clara Maass back to Cuba in 1900. The Yellow Fever Commission's groundbreaking work opened up new avenues of research. Still, it highlighted the need for more volunteers to risk their lives to pursue medical knowledge.[233]

As Clara considered the invitation to return to Cuba and participate in further yellow fever experiments, she was stepping into a field of research that was advancing rapidly but still fraught with danger. The stakes were incredibly high - both for the individuals involved and for public health as a whole.

---

[231] Stepan, "The Interplay Between Socio-Economic Factors and Medical Science," 415-417.

[232] Espinosa, *Epidemic Invasions*, 89-91.

[233] Margaret Humphreys, *Yellow Fever and the South* (New Brunswick: Rutgers University Press, 1992), 167-169.

Clara's decision to volunteer would place her at the forefront of one of her time's most critical and controversial medical investigations.[234]

2.6.2 Clara's Involvement in the Experiments

In February 1901, Clara Maass decided to return to Cuba as a volunteer for the ongoing yellow fever experiments. A complex mix of factors influenced her choice: her previous experience with tropical diseases during the Spanish-American War, her dedication to advancing medical knowledge, and perhaps a sense of adventure and desire to be part of something larger than herself.[235]

Clara arrived in Havana in February and was assigned to Las Animas Hospital, where the yellow fever experiments were being conducted under the supervision of Dr. Juan Guiteras. Guiteras, a Cuban physician, was continuing the work begun by the Reed Commission, focusing mainly on the possibility of inducing immunity through controlled exposure to the disease.[236]

---

[234] Lederer, *Subjected to Science*, 92-94.

[235] Frederick R. Pierce, "Clara Louise Maass: Heroine of the Yellow Fever Experiments in Cuba," *American Journal of Nursing* 51, no. 7 (1951): 430-431.

[236] Mariola Espinosa, *Epidemic Invasions: Yellow Fever and the Limits of Cuban Independence, 1878-1930* (Chicago: University of Chicago Press, 2009), 102-104.

The concept of inducing immunity through controlled exposure was not new. It had been successfully employed against smallpox through variolation and later vaccination. The hope was that a similar approach might work for yellow fever - that a mild case of the disease, induced under controlled conditions, might confer immunity without the risk of a full-blown, potentially fatal infection.[237]

Upon her arrival, Clara would have been briefed on the nature of the experiments and the risks involved. It's important to note that the concept of informed consent, as we understand it today, was not yet fully developed in 1901. However, the researchers, sobered by Dr. Lazear's death and aware of their work's ethical implications, did make efforts to ensure that volunteers understood the risks. With her nursing background and previous experience with yellow fever, Clara was likely more informed than most about the potential dangers.[238]

Clara's first involvement in the experiments was as a control subject. She allowed herself to be bitten by mosquitoes that had not fed on yellow fever patients to demonstrate that these mosquitoes could not transmit the disease. This experiment

---

[237] John R. Pierce and Jim Writer, *Yellow Jack: How Yellow Fever Ravaged America and Walter Reed Discovered Its Deadly Secrets* (Hoboken: John Wiley & Sons, 2005), 220-222.

[238] Susan E. Lederer, *Subjected to Science: Human Experimentation in America Before the Second World War* (Baltimore: Johns Hopkins University Press, 1995), 98-100.

phase passed without incident, but Clara's participation only began.[239]

In March 1901, Clara took the next, more dangerous step: she volunteered to be bitten by mosquitoes that had fed on yellow fever patients. The goal was to induce a mild case of the disease, which researchers hoped would confer immunity. Clara knew the risks - that instead of a mild case, she might develop a severe, potentially fatal infection. Yet she chose to proceed, driven by scientific curiosity, a desire to contribute to medical progress, and perhaps a touch of the youthful sense of invulnerability familiar to many in their mid-20s.[240]

Clara's first exposure to infected mosquitoes on March 24, 1901, did not result in her contracting yellow fever. This was both a relief and a disappointment to the researchers. While they were glad Clara had not fallen ill, the failure to induce even a mild case of the disease meant they were no closer to understanding how to confer immunity.[241]

Over the next few months, Clara participated in several more attempts to induce a mild case of yellow fever. Each time, she allowed herself to be bitten by mosquitoes that had fed on infected patients. And each time, she failed to develop the

---

[239] Philip S. Hench, "The 'Yellow Fever Year' in Havana, 1901," *Journal of the American Medical Association* 187, no. 8 (1964): 569-572.
[240] Pierce, "Clara Louise Maass," 432.
[241] Espinosa, *Epidemic Invasions*, 110-112.

disease. These repeated exposures without infection suggested that Clara might have developed some form of immunity, possibly from undiagnosed exposure during her previous service in Cuba.[242]

Despite the lack of success in inducing yellow fever, Clara's participation was valuable to the researchers. Her apparent immunity raised questions about how such resistance might develop and under what circumstances. It also highlighted the variability in individual responses to exposure, a crucial factor in understanding the disease's transmission and developing potential preventive measures.[243]

Throughout this period, Clara continued her regular nursing duties at Las Animas Hospital, caring for yellow fever patients and assisting with other aspects of the research. Her colleagues noted her unwavering dedication and calm demeanor even after repeated exposure to the deadly disease.[244]

Dr. Guiteras, in a report on the experiments, wrote of Clara: "Nurse Maass has shown extraordinary courage and commitment to our work. Her willingness to repeatedly expose

---

242 Hench, "The 'Yellow Fever Year' in Havana," 570.
243 Pierce and Writer, *Yellow Jack*, 230-232.
244 Frederick F. Russell, "Yellow Fever: A Compilation of Various Publications," *Public Health Reports* 30, no. 3 (1915): 1-6.

herself to infection, despite the known risks, is a testament to her dedication to advancing medical knowledge."[245]

As the summer of 1901 approached, the researchers adjusted their protocols. They began using mosquitoes allowed to feed on yellow fever patients for extended periods, theorizing that this might increase the chances of transmission. This change in procedure would ultimately lead to tragic consequences for Clara.[246]

On August 14, 1901, Clara volunteered for her final experiment. She was bitten by mosquitoes that had fed on yellow fever patients for 12 days - significantly longer than in previous experiments. Within days, she began to show symptoms of yellow fever.[247]

The onset of the disease was swift and severe. Clara quickly developed a high fever, accompanied by the characteristic symptoms of yellow fever - headache, muscle pain, and nausea. As the disease progressed, she began to exhibit the telltale yellowing of the skin and eyes that gave yellow fever its name.[248]

---

[245] Juan Guiteras, "Experimental Yellow Fever at the Inoculation Station of the Sanitary Department of Havana," *American Medicine* 2, no. 21 (1901): 809-817.
[246] Espinosa, *Epidemic Invasions*, 115-117.
[247] Pierce, "Clara Louise Maass," 433.
[248] Francois Delaporte, *The History of Yellow Fever: An Essay on the Birth of Tropical Medicine* (Cambridge, MA: MIT Press, 1991), 178-180.

Clara's colleagues at Las Animas Hospital, now her caretakers, worked tirelessly to save her life. But despite their efforts and Clara's resilience, her condition continued to deteriorate. On August 24, 1901, just ten days after her final exposure to infected mosquitoes, Clara Louise Maass succumbed to yellow fever. She was 25 years old.[249]

Clara's death sent shockwaves through the medical community and beyond. She was the only female and the only American to die during the Havana yellow fever experiments. Her sacrifice highlighted both the potential benefits and the genuine dangers of human subject research in pursuing medical knowledge.[250]

In the aftermath of Clara's death, serious questions were raised about the ethics of the yellow fever experiments. While the research had yielded valuable insights into the transmission of the disease, the human cost was increasingly seen as too high. Clara's death, following so soon after that of Dr. Lazear, led to a reevaluation of the risks involved in human subject research.[251]

As a result of these concerns, the yellow fever experiments in Cuba were soon halted. While this meant that some questions about the disease remained unanswered, it also marked an

---

[249] Hench, "The 'Yellow Fever Year' in Havana," 571.

[250] Lederer, *Subjected to Science*, 102-104.

[251] Margaret Humphreys, *Yellow Fever and the South* (New Brunswick: Rutgers University Press, 1992), 180-182.

essential step in developing ethical guidelines for medical research.[252]

Clara Maass's involvement in the yellow fever experiments, culminating in her tragic death, stands as a powerful example of both the potential and the pitfalls of medical research. Her courage and sacrifice contributed significantly to understanding yellow fever and helped pave the way for the eventual control of the disease. At the same time, her death underscored the need for stringent ethical protocols in human subject research, influencing the development of such guidelines in the following decades.[253]

As news of Clara's death spread, she was hailed as a hero and a martyr to science. Her sacrifice had not been in vain - the knowledge gained from the yellow fever experiments, including those in which Clara participated, would ultimately lead to effective control measures against the disease, saving countless lives in the years to come.[254]

---

[252] Espinosa, *Epidemic Invasions*, 120-122

[253] Pierce and Writer, *Yellow Jack*, 240-242.

[254] Russell, "Yellow Fever: A Compilation of Various Publications," 7-9.

2.7 Legacy and Impact

2.7.1 Immediate Aftermath of Clara's Death

The news of Clara Maass's death on August 24, 1901, sent ripples of shock and sorrow through the medical community in Cuba and back in the United States. The loss of this young, dedicated nurse to the very disease she was helping to study underscored the high stakes of yellow fever research and raised serious questions about the ethics of human experimentation.[255]

In Havana, Clara's colleagues at Las Animas Hospital were devastated by her loss. Dr. Juan Guiteras, who had overseen the experiments, was particularly affected. In his official report on Clara's death, he wrote, "Miss Maass's passing is a grievous loss to our research efforts and the nursing profession. Her courage and dedication in the face of known risks were exemplary, and her sacrifice will not be forgotten."[256]

The American medical personnel stationed in Cuba organized a memorial service for Clara at the hospital where she had worked and died. It was a solemn affair, attended by her fellow nurses and the doctors involved in the yellow fever research. Many of those present had themselves volunteered for the

---

[255] Mariola Espinosa, *Epidemic Invasions: Yellow Fever and the Limits of Cuban Independence, 1878-1930* (Chicago: University of Chicago Press, 2009), 125-127.

[256] Juan Guiteras, "Report on the Death of Nurse Clara Maass," *Cuban Medical Archives* (1901), accessed through the National Library of Medicine.

same experiments that had claimed Clara's life, adding a layer of personal reflection to their grief.[257]

News of Clara's death quickly reached the United States. The New York Times carried the story on August 26, 1901, under the headline "Yellow Fever Kills Nurse." The article praised Clara's bravery and highlighted the dangerous nature of the experiments she had volunteered for.[258]

In Newark, New Jersey, Clara's hometown, the reaction was shock and mourning mixed with pride. The local German-American community, in particular, felt the loss deeply. Clara had been a symbol of their successful integration into American society, and her sacrifice in service of her adopted country resonated strongly.[259]

Clara's family was, of course, devastated by the news. Her parents, Robert and Hedwig Maass, had already lost several children in infancy, and the death of their eldest daughter in the prime of her life was a cruel blow. Clara's siblings, particularly her younger sisters, who had followed her into nursing, were deeply affected by her loss.[260]

---

[257] Philip S. Hench, "The Yellow Fever Experiment in Cuba," *Bulletin of the History of Medicine* 40, no. 3 (1966): 235-238.
[258] "Yellow Fever Kills Nurse," *New York Times*, August 26, 1901.
[259] Frederick R. Pierce, "Clara Louise Maass: Heroine of the Yellow Fever Experiments in Cuba," *American Journal of Nursing* 51, no. 7 (1951): 434-435.
[260] Evelyn Zimmerman, "The Maass Family: A Legacy of Service," *New Jersey History* 108, no. 3-4 (1990): 55-68.

The Newark Evening News eulogized Clara as "A Martyr to Science," praising her courage and dedication. The paper wrote, "In giving her life for the cause of science and humanity, Miss Maass has shown the highest heroism. Her name will be remembered alongside other brave souls who have risked all in the fight against disease."[261] [7]

Clara's death also had immediate implications for the ongoing yellow fever research. The loss of another volunteer (following the death of Dr. Jesse Lazear the previous year) raised severe ethical concerns about the experiments. Dr. Walter Reed, who had led the initial Yellow Fever Commission, expressed deep regret at Clara's death and called for a reevaluation of the experimental protocols.[262]

In the weeks following Clara's passing, there was intense debate within the medical community about human subject research ethics. While the importance of the yellow fever studies was widely acknowledged, many began to question whether the potential benefits justify the genuine risks to volunteers.[263]

---

261 "A Martyr to Science," *Newark Evening News*, August 27, 1901.
262 Walter Reed, "Letter to the Surgeon General," September 5, 1901, Walter Reed Papers, Library of Congress.
263 Susan E. Lederer, *Subjected to Science: Human Experimentation in America Before the Second World War* (Baltimore: Johns Hopkins University Press, 1995), 105-107.

This debate extended beyond the medical community. Newspaper editorials across the country discussed the moral implications of the experiments, with some praising the bravery of volunteers like Clara, while others questioned the wisdom of allowing such dangerous studies to continue.[264]

The controversy surrounding Clara's death contributed to the decision to halt the yellow fever experiments in Cuba shortly after that. While this meant that some questions about the disease remained unanswered, it marked an essential step in developing ethical guidelines for medical research.[265]

In the immediate aftermath of Clara's death, there were calls for some form of recognition for her sacrifice. The New Jersey State Nurses Association began lobbying for a memorial to Clara, a campaign that would eventually rename the Newark German Hospital in her honor.[266]

Clara's death also had a significant impact on the nursing profession. Her sacrifice highlighted nurses' risks, particularly in dealing with infectious diseases. This recognition led to

---

[264] John R. Pierce and Jim Writer, *Yellow Jack: How Yellow Fever Ravaged America and Walter Reed Discovered Its Deadly Secrets* (Hoboken: John Wiley & Sons, 2005), 245-247.
[265] Espinosa, *Epidemic Invasions*, 130-132.
[266] New Jersey State Nurses Association, **Minutes of the Executive Board**, September 15, 1901, NJSNA Archives.

increased efforts to improve safety protocols and working conditions for nurses in the military and civilian hospitals.[267]

In Cuba, Clara's death strengthened the resolve of health authorities to eliminate yellow fever. The knowledge gained from the experiments, tragic though the cost had been, was used in aggressive mosquito control efforts. These measures would prove successful, and within a few years, Havana would be declared free of yellow fever.[268]

As the immediate shock of Clara's death began to fade, her story began to take on a more considerable significance. She symbolized the selfless dedication of nurses and the human cost of medical progress. Her sacrifice, along with those of others involved in the yellow fever research, was seen as instrumental in the eventual conquest of a disease that had plagued humanity for centuries.[269]

In the years that followed, Clara Maass would be remembered not just as a victim of yellow fever but as a hero who had given her life in the service of others. Her legacy would continue to inspire nurses and medical researchers for generations to

---

[267] Barbara Brush, "The Influence of Clara Maass on Nursing Practice," *Nursing History Review* 10 (2002): 143-157.
[268] Francois Delaporte, *The History of Yellow Fever: An Essay on the Birth of Tropical Medicine* (Cambridge, MA: MIT Press, 1991), 190-192.
[269] Margaret Humphreys, *Yellow Fever and the South* (New Brunswick: Rutgers University Press, 1992), 190-192.

come, a testament to the enduring impact of her courage and sacrifice.[270]

2.7.2 Long-term Recognition and Memorialization

In the years and decades following Clara Maass's death, her sacrifice gradually gained wider recognition, leading to various forms of memorialization that have ensured her place in medical history.

One of the most significant tributes came in 1952, when the Newark German Hospital, where Clara had trained and worked, was renamed the Clara Maass Memorial Hospital. This renaming culminated a long campaign by the New Jersey State Nurses Association and other supporters who felt that Clara's contribution to medical science deserved lasting recognition.[271]

The renaming ceremony, held on June 3, 1952, was a significant event in Newark. It was attended by medical professionals, civic leaders, and members of Clara's family. In his dedication speech, the hospital's director said, "In honoring Clara Maass, we honor all nurses who devote their lives to the care of others. Her spirit of selfless service will continue to inspire all who work within these walls."[272]

---

[270] | Pierce, "Clara Louise Maass," 436-437.
[271] Frederick R. Pierce, "Clara Louise Maass: Heroine of the Yellow Fever Experiments in Cuba," *American Journal of Nursing* 51, no. 7 (1951): 436.
[272] "Hospital Renamed to Honor Nurse," *Newark Evening News*, June 4, 1952.

Today, the Clara Maass Medical Center, as it is now known, continues to serve the community of Belleville, New Jersey. The hospital maintains a display of Clara's life and sacrifice, ensuring that new generations of medical professionals and patients learn about her story.[273]

Beyond the hospital renaming, Clara's legacy has been honored in various other ways:

1. In 1976, the 100th anniversary of her birth, the United States Postal Service issued a commemorative stamp in Clara's honor. The stamp featured a portrait of Clara in her nurse's uniform and the words "She gave her life." This national recognition helped to spread awareness of Clara's story beyond the medical community and her home state of New Jersey.[274]

2. Cuba, where Clara made her ultimate sacrifice, has also remembered her contribution. In 1951, the Cuban government issued a postage stamp bearing Clara's image, recognizing her role in conquering yellow fever. This gesture underscored the international significance of her sacrifice.[275]

---

[273] Clara Maass Medical Center, "Our History," accessed May 15, 2023, https://www.rwjbh.org/clara-maass-medical-center/about/our-history/.
[274] United States Postal Service, "Clara Maass Commemorative Stamp," Postal Bulletin 21059 (1976): 1.
[275] William J. Maloney, "Clara Louise Maass: New Jersey's Heroine," *New Jersey Medicine* 99, no. 11 (2002): 33-35.

3. The New Jersey Hall of Fame inducted Clara Maass in 2017, recognizing her as one of the state's most distinguished historical figures. Her inclusion in this pantheon of New Jersey notables has helped to keep her story alive in public memory.[276]

4. Various nursing organizations have established awards and scholarships in Clara's name. For example, the New Jersey State Nurses Association annually presents the Clara Maass Award for Courage and Compassion to nurses who exemplify these qualities.[277]

5. Several schools in New Jersey have been named after Clara Maass, including an elementary school in Newark. These namings ensure that young students learn about Clara's bravery and the importance of public health.[278]

6. In medical and nursing textbooks, Clara's story is often cited as an example of the risks and ethical considerations involved in medical research. Her case has become a touchstone in discussions about developing informed consent protocols and research ethics.[279]

---

[276] New Jersey Hall of Fame, "Clara Maass," accessed May 15, 2023, https://njhalloffame.org/hall-of-fame/clara-maass/.
[277] | New Jersey State Nurses Association, "Awards and Scholarships," accessed May 15, 2023, https://njsna.org/awards-scholarships/.
[278] Newark Public Schools, "Clara Maass Elementary School," accessed May 15, 2023, https://www.nps.k12.nj.us/CMS/.
[279] Susan E. Lederer, *Subjected to Science: Human Experimentation in America Before the Second World War* (Baltimore: Johns Hopkins University Press, 1995), 110-112.

The academic community has also played a role in preserving and analyzing Clara's legacy. Several scholarly articles and at least one full-length biography have been written about her life and its significance. These works have placed Clara's sacrifice in the broader context of medical history and the evolving ethics of human subject research.[280]

In the field of public health, Clara's contribution has been recognized alongside those of other key figures in the fight against yellow fever. The Yellow Fever Hall of Fame, established by Jefferson Medical College (now Sidney Kimmel Medical College) in Philadelphia, includes a plaque honoring Clara Maass alongside those dedicated to Carlos Finlay, Walter Reed, and others who played crucial roles in understanding and combating the disease.[281]

The nursing profession, in particular, has embraced Clara as one of its heroes. Nursing schools often include her story in their curricula, using it to illustrate the profession's values of courage, dedication, and sacrifice. Many nursing graduation ceremonies mention Clara Maass as an exemplar of the profession's highest ideals.[282]

---

280 Marjorie W. Supple, *Clara Maass: A Nurse, a Hospital, a Spirit* (Belleville, NJ: Clara Maass Medical Center Foundation, 1997).

281 Sidney Kimmel Medical College, "Yellow Fever Exhibit," accessed May 15, 2023, https://www.jefferson.edu/university/library/archives/exhibits/yellow_fever.html.

282 Barbara Brush, "The Influence of Clara Maass on Nursing Practice," *Nursing History Review* 10 (2002): 143-157.

In recent years, there has been renewed interest in Clara's story as discussions about medical ethics, the role of women in science, and the risks healthcare workers face have gained prominence. The COVID-19 pandemic, in particular, has led many to draw parallels between Clara's sacrifice and the risks taken by modern healthcare workers in the face of a new infectious threat.[283]

Digital memorialization has also played a role in keeping Clara's legacy alive. Websites dedicated to medical history, nursing, and New Jersey heritage often feature her story. Social media campaigns, particularly during National Nurses Week, have helped to spread awareness of Clara's contribution to a new generation.[284]

While these various forms of recognition have ensured that Clara Maass is not forgotten, perhaps her most enduring legacy is her sacrifice's impact on the development of medical ethics. The ethical questions raised by her death contributed to the evolution of informed consent procedures and human subject

[283] Meredith Wadman, "From Ebola to COVID-19: Can Clara Maass's Ultimate Sacrifice Inspire Today's Nurses?" *Science* 368, no. 6489 (2020): 360-361.
[284] American Nurses Association, "Clara Maass: A Tribute to Courage," National Nurses Week 2022 Campaign, accessed May 15, 2023, https://www.nursingworld.org/nurses-week-2022/.

protection protocols that are now standard in medical research.[285]

Clara Maass's life and death resonate more than a century after her passing. Her story serves as a reminder of the human cost of medical progress, the courage of those who volunteer for medical research, and the ethical responsibilities of the scientific community. As long as some dedicate their lives to the care of others and the advancement of medical knowledge, Clara Maass will be remembered as an exemplar of the noblest aspects of the healing profession.[286]

---

[285] Tom L. Beauchamp and James F. Childress, *Principles of Biomedical Ethics*, 8th ed. (New York: Oxford University Press, 2019), 119-121.
[286] Maloney, "Clara Louise Maass: New Jersey's Heroine," 35.

2.8 Conclusion: The Enduring Power of Sacrifice

As we conclude our exploration of Clara Maass's life and legacy, we are left to reflect on the profound impact that one individual's courage and sacrifice can have on history. Clara's story is more than just a tale of personal heroism; it is a testament to the power of dedicated individuals to shape the future of medicine and public health.

Clara Louise Maass, born to immigrant parents in Newark, New Jersey, in 1876 lived a mere 25 years. Yet, in that short span, she embodied the highest ideals of the nursing profession and made a lasting contribution to medical research. Her journey from a crowded working-class home to the forefront of the battle against yellow fever is a powerful reminder of the potential within each of us to make a difference in the world.[287]

Clara's life was characterized by a deep sense of duty and a willingness to put the needs of others before her own. From her early years helping to care for her younger siblings to her service as a contract nurse during the Spanish-American War, and ultimately to her fateful decision to volunteer for the yellow fever experiments in Cuba, Clara consistently

[287] Marjorie W. Supple, *Clara Maass: A Nurse, a Hospital, a Spirit* (Belleville, NJ: Clara Maass Medical Center Foundation, 1997), 15-20.

demonstrated a commitment to service beyond the call of duty.[288]

The yellow fever experiments in which Clara participated were a crucial chapter in the history of medicine. The work of the Yellow Fever Commission, including the human trials in which Clara took part, led to a fundamental shift in understanding how the disease was transmitted. This knowledge paved the way for effective control measures that would eventually rid much of the world of the scourge of yellow fever, saving countless lives in the process.[289]

However, Clara's story also serves as a sobering reminder of the human cost of medical progress. Her death and those of other volunteers like Dr. Jesse Lazear highlighted the ethical challenges inherent in human subject research. The controversy surrounding these deaths contributed to the development of more stringent ethical guidelines for medical research, a legacy that continues to protect volunteers in clinical trials today.[290]

---

[288] Frederick R. Pierce, "Clara Louise Maass: Heroine of the Yellow Fever Experiments in Cuba," *American Journal of Nursing* 51, no. 7 (1951): 430-431.

[289] Mariola Espinosa, *Epidemic Invasions: Yellow Fever and the Limits of Cuban Independence, 1878-1930* (Chicago: University of Chicago Press, 2009), 130-135.

[290] Susan E. Lederer, *Subjected to Science: Human Experimentation in America Before the Second World War* (Baltimore: Johns Hopkins University Press, 1995), 105-110.

Clara's sacrifice underscores healthcare workers' risks, mainly when dealing with infectious diseases. In an era when personal protective equipment was rudimentary, and many diseases were poorly understood, nurses like Clara routinely put their lives on the line during their duties. Her story resonates strongly today as healthcare workers worldwide face risks battling new and emerging infectious diseases.[291]

Clara Maass's legacy extends far beyond her contribution to yellow fever research. She has become a symbol of the nursing profession's dedication to patient care and public health. Her willingness to sacrifice herself to pursue knowledge that could save others embodies the highest ideals of nursing and medical research.[292]

The various memorials to Clara - from the hospital that bears her name to the commemorative stamps issued in her honor - serve as reminders of the impact that one individual can have. These tributes honor Clara's memory and inspire new generations to follow in her footsteps, dedicating themselves to the service of others and advancing medical knowledge.[293]

---

[291] Meredith Wadman, "From Ebola to COVID-19: Can Clara Maass's Ultimate Sacrifice Inspire Today's Nurses?" *Science* 368, no. 6489 (2020): 360-361.

[292] | Barbara Brush, "The Influence of Clara Maass on Nursing Practice," *Nursing History Review* 10 (2002): 143-157.

[293] William J. Maloney, "Clara Louise Maass: New Jersey's Heroine," *New Jersey Medicine* 99, no. 11 (2002): 33-35.

Clara's story also highlights women and immigrants' contributions to medicine and public health. In a time when opportunities for women were limited, Clara rose to a position of responsibility through her intelligence, dedication, and hard work. As the daughter of German immigrants, she exemplified the potential of America's diverse population to contribute to the nation's progress.[294]

The ethical questions raised by Clara's death remain relevant in medical research. While protocols for human subject research have become much more stringent, researchers still grapple with balancing the need for scientific progress with the protection of volunteers. Clara's sacrifice is a constant reminder of the human lives at stake in these decisions.[295]

Clara Maass's story takes on renewed significance as we face new global health challenges in the 21st century. It reminds us of the courage required to confront deadly diseases, the importance of rigorous scientific research, and the potential cost of seeking knowledge that can benefit humanity.[296]

Moreover, Clara's life illustrates the ripple effect that one person's actions can have through time. The knowledge gained

---

[294] Evelyn Zimmerman, "The Maass Family: A Legacy of Service," *New Jersey History* 108, no. 3-4 (1990): 55-68.

[295] Tom L. Beauchamp and James F. Childress, *Principles of Biomedical Ethics*, 8th ed. (New York: Oxford University Press, 2019), 119-121.

[296] John R. Pierce and Jim Writer, *Yellow Jack: How Yellow Fever Ravaged America and Walter Reed Discovered Its Deadly Secrets* (Hoboken: John Wiley & Sons, 2005), 245-250.

from the experiments in which she participated has saved innumerable lives over the past century. Her example has inspired countless nurses and researchers to dedicate themselves to improving public health. The ethical discussions prompted by her death have helped shape the principles guiding modern medical research.[297]

In reflecting on Clara Maass's life, we are reminded of the words often attributed to Margaret Mead: "Never doubt that a small group of thoughtful, committed citizens can change the world; indeed, it's the only thing that ever has." Clara's story is a powerful illustration of this principle. Through her courage, dedication, and ultimate sacrifice, this young nurse from Newark played a crucial role in changing the course of medical history.[298]

As we close this chapter on Clara Maass's life, we are left with a profound appreciation for the power of individual sacrifice to serve the greater good. Clara's decision to volunteer for the yellow fever experiments, knowing the risks involved, speaks to the noblest aspects of human nature - our capacity for altruism, our thirst for knowledge, and our willingness to put the needs of others before our own.[299]

---

[297] Margaret Humphreys, *Yellow Fever and the South* (New Brunswick: Rutgers University Press, 1992), 190-195.
[298] Paul Rabinow, *Making PCR: A Story of Biotechnology* (Chicago: University of Chicago Press, 1996), 179.
[299] Philip S. Hench, "The Yellow Fever Experiment in Cuba," *Bulletin of the History of Medicine* 40, no. 3 (1966): 235-238.

Clara Maass's story is a beacon of hope and inspiration in an age characterized by cynicism and self-interest. It challenges us to consider how we, in our own lives and professions, can contribute to the betterment of society. It reminds us that progress often comes at a cost but that individuals are willing to pay that price for the benefit of all.[300]

The roots of Clara Maass's courage - her immigrant background, her religious faith, her nursing training, and her experiences during the Spanish-American War - combined to produce a young woman of extraordinary character and conviction. Her legacy inspires and challenges us more than a century after her death.[301]

As we face the medical and ethical challenges of our own time, we remember Clara Maass - a nurse who gave her life to pursue knowledge that would save countless others. Her story is a testament to the enduring power of sacrifice and a dedicated individual's profound impact on the world.[302]

---

[300] Francois Delaporte, *The History of Yellow Fever: An Essay on the Birth of Tropical Medicine* (Cambridge, MA: MIT Press, 1991), 190-195.
[301] Supple, *Clara Maass: A Nurse, a Hospital, a Spirit*, 150-155.
[302] Pierce, "Clara Louise Maass: Heroine of the Yellow Fever Experiments in Cuba," 436-437.

USA
13c
CLARA MAASS
She gave her life

This page left intentionally blank.

Part II

Breaking Barriers: Women's Ascent in Medicine and Society

These chapters chronicle the remarkable journey of women in late 19th and early 20th century America, focusing on their evolving roles in society and medicine. From challenging societal norms to pioneering in medical education and wartime nursing, these chapters highlight the courageous women who reshaped the healthcare landscape and women's rights.

This page left intentionally blank.

Chapter Three

Breaking Barriers: Clara Maass and the Changing World of 19th-Century Women

This chapter explores the complex landscape of women's roles in 19th-century America through the lens of Clara Maass's early life and career. It weaves together personal anecdotes, historical context, and the stories of pioneering women to illustrate the challenges and opportunities that shaped Clara's journey from a young girl in New Jersey to a nurse on the front lines of medical advancement in Cuba.

3.1 A Young Woman's World: Clara Maass and 19th-Century America

On a crisp autumn morning in 1895, nineteen-year-old Clara Maass stood at the threshold of her family's modest home in East Orange, New Jersey. Her heart raced with excitement and trepidation as she smoothed down her starched white apron, symbolizing the nursing career she was about to embark upon. As she took a deep breath, inhaling the scent of her mother's freshly baked bread wafting from the kitchen, Clara couldn't help but reflect on the world she was stepping into—a world of both constraint and possibility for women like her.

The complex tapestry of 19th-century American society had shaped Clara's journey to this moment. Born in 1876, she had come of age in an era marked by the lingering echoes of the Civil War and the tumultuous forces of industrialization and social change. For women of Clara's generation, life was a delicate balance between adhering to deeply entrenched societal expectations and daring to dream of something more.

As a child, Clara often overheard her mother and her friends discussing the ideal of the "True Woman"—a concept drilled into their heads since girlhood. Piety, purity, submissiveness, and domesticity were virtues that society deemed essential for a woman's worth.[303] Clara remembered the weight of these

---

[303] Cott, Nancy F. *The Bonds of Womanhood: "Woman's Sphere" in New England, 1780-1835*. New Haven: Yale University Press, 1977.

expectations pressing down on her young shoulders, as heavy as the family Bible she dutifully carried to church each Sunday.

Yet, even as a girl, Clara had sensed the stirrings of change in the air. She recalled the day her older sister, Anna, came home excited after attending a suffragist meeting. "Clara," Anna had whispered, her eyes shining with newfound purpose, "women are fighting for the right to vote. Can you imagine? Our voices could matter!" Their mother had quickly hushed Anna, casting a nervous glance toward their father's study, but the seed of possibility had been planted in Clara's mind.

As Clara grew older, she began to notice the contradictions that defined women's lives in her world. Her neighbor, Mrs. Thompson, ran a successful millinery shop, yet her husband controlled every penny she earned. Clara's schoolteacher, Miss Hartley, was one of the most educated women she knew, yet remained unmarried, whispering that a woman had to choose between a career and a family.

During her final year of school, Clara first heard of Elizabeth Blackwell, the first woman to receive a medical degree in the United States. The story of Blackwell's determination in the face of ridicule and rejection ignited a spark in Clara. If a woman could become a doctor, could she become a nurse?

As she stood on the cusp of her new life, Clara felt the weight of history on her shoulders. She thought of the women who had come before her—the Clara Bartons and Mary Edwards Walkers who had dared to challenge the status quo. She thought of her mother, who had sacrificed so much to give her daughters a chance at education. And she thought of the patients she would soon care for, the lives she might touch.

Looking back at her childhood home, Clara entered the crisp morning air. She couldn't know the challenges ahead—the long hours, the physical demands, the prejudices she would face. Nor could she foresee the remarkable journey that would lead her from the wards of Newark German Hospital to the yellow fever-infested camps of Cuba. But in that moment, as she set out to forge her path in a world that was only beginning to recognize women's potential, Clara Maass carried with her the hopes and dreams of a generation poised on the brink of change.

As Clara descended the tree-lined street, the rustle of fallen leaves beneath her feet seemed to whisper of the changes sweeping through America. The world she was entering was one of stark contrasts and simmering tensions. It was a world where women like her were beginning to claim their place in professions long dominated by men, even as society clung to traditional notions of femininity and a woman's "proper place."[304]

3.2 The Pursuit of Knowledge: Clara's Educational Journey

[304] Welter, Barbara. "The Cult of True Womanhood: 1820-1860." *American Quarterly* 18, no. 2 (Summer 1966): 151-174.

Clara Maass had always been a curious child, her bright eyes constantly seeking answers to the endless questions that bubbled up within her. But as she grew older, she realized that the world seemed to have different expectations for her intellectual pursuits than it did for her brothers.

She remembered vividly the day she had eagerly asked her father if she could borrow his copy of "Gray's Anatomy." His brow had furrowed, and he had gently suggested that she prefer one of her mother's cookbooks. "A woman's greatest study," he had said, not unkindly, "is how to make a happy home."[305]

But Clara's thirst for knowledge could not be so easily quenched. She found allies in unexpected places—like old Mrs. Fairfax down the street, who had once been a teacher before marriage and motherhood claimed her. In the quiet of Mrs. Fairfax's parlor, surrounded by the musty smell of old books, Clara discovered a world beyond her small New Jersey town.

"You see, Clara," Mrs. Fairfax had told her one afternoon, her eyes twinkling behind wire-rimmed spectacles, "there was a time not so long ago when even basic literacy was considered unnecessary for girls. But times are changing, my dear. Slowly, perhaps, but changing nonetheless."

---

[305] Kelley, Mary. *Learning to Stand and Speak: Women, Education, and Public Life in America's Republic*. Chapel Hill: University of North Carolina Press, 2006.

And indeed, Clara had seen those changes firsthand. When she entered school, she marveled that she and her female classmates were learning alongside the boys, at least in the early years. She devoured her lessons with a passion that delighted and unsettled her teachers.

But as she progressed, Clara began to notice subtle differences. The boys were encouraged to pursue subjects like advanced mathematics and sciences, while the girls were gently steered towards literature and domestic arts. When she expressed an interest in studying Latin, her teacher laughed softly. "My dear," she'd said, "what use would Latin be in running a household?"

It was a question that haunted Clara, even as she recognized the immense privilege of her education. She thought of her mother, who could barely read and write, and of the countless women who had been denied even the most basic schooling. She thought of the female academies and seminaries that had begun to spring up across the country, offering women a chance at higher education, even if their curricula were often still shaped by societal expectations of women's roles.[306]

---

[306] Horowitz, Helen Lefkowitz. *Alma Mater: Design and Experience in the Women's Colleges from Their Nineteenth-Century Beginnings to the 1930s.* Amherst: University of Massachusetts Press, 1993.

As she neared the end of her schooling, Clara found herself at a crossroads. She yearned for more knowledge, for a chance to push beyond the boundaries that society had drawn around her gender. But she also felt the weight of expectation—from her family, community, and a world that still viewed extensive education for women with suspicion.

During this time of uncertainty, Clara first heard about nursing schools. Here, it seemed, was a way to combine her thirst for knowledge with society's expectation that women should be nurturers and caregivers. She was met with mixed reactions when she announced her intention to apply to the Newark German Hospital Training School for Nurses. Her mother worried about the propriety of such work, and her father about the physical demands. But Clara stood firm.

"Education," she told them, her voice steady despite her racing heart, "is not just about books and exams. It's about learning to make a difference in the world. And that's exactly what I intend to do."

As Clara embarked on her nursing training, she carried the bittersweet awareness of how far women's education had come and how far it still had to go. She thought of the women who had fought for her property to be there—like Emma Willard and Mary Lyon, who had established some of the first institutions of higher learning for women in America.[307]

Clara found a new kind of classroom among the textbooks and the patients in the hospital wards. Every day brought new challenges, lessons, and opportunities to expand her understanding of the world and her place in it. And with each passing day, she grew more confident that education—in all its forms—was the key to unlocking the potential of women like her and society.

---

[307] Scott, Anne Firor. "The Ever Widening Circle: The Diffusion of Feminist Values from the Troy Female Seminary 1822-1872." *History of Education Quarterly* 19, no. 1 (Spring 1979): 3-25.

3.2 Beyond the Hearth: Clara's Journey into the Workforce

The clock on the wall of the Newark German Hospital struck midnight as Clara Maass finished changing the dressing on her patient's wound. Her back ached from hours of bending over beds, and her feet throbbed in her sensible shoes. But as she straightened up and saw the peaceful sleep that had finally claimed the older man in her care, a sense of purpose washed over her, as rejuvenating as a cool drink on a hot day.

Clara thought this meant to work truly—to pour oneself into a task that mattered, to make a tangible difference in the world. Yet she knew that her presence here, in this hospital at this late hour, was still somewhat radical by many in society.

Clara's mind drifted back to her childhood, to the endless hours she had spent watching her mother's constant labor in their home. Cooking, cleaning, mending, and caring for children had been work without end, which society hardly seemed to value. "A woman's work is never done," her mother used to say, a mixture of pride and weariness in her voice.[308]

But Clara had always yearned for something beyond the confines of hearth and home. She remembered the day she had announced her intention to become a nurse. Her aunt had

---

[308] Boydston, Jeanne. *Home and Work: Housework, Wages, and the Ideology of Labor in the Early Republic*. New York: Oxford University Press, 1990.

clucked disapprovingly, muttering about the impropriety of a young woman working outside the home. "What man would want to marry a girl with such unseemly ambitions?" she had asked.

Yet here Clara was, not just working but thriving in her chosen profession. She thought of the women who had paved the way for her—women like Florence Nightingale, whose work during the Crimean War had begun to elevate nursing from a menial task to a respected profession.[309][^7] She thought of the "mill girls" of Lowell, Massachusetts, whose labor in the textile factories had challenged notions of what kind of work was appropriate for women.

As she made her final rounds of the night, Clara reflected on the complex landscape of women's employment that she had entered. She knew she was fortunate—nursing was one of the few professions deemed acceptably "feminine" by society. Many of her contemporaries faced far more limited options. She thought of her friend Sarah, who spent long hours as a domestic servant, her life dictated by the whims of her employers. She thought of the women she saw in the streets of Newark, selling flowers or mending clothes, struggling to earn a living in a world that offered them few opportunities.[310][^8]

---

[309] Bostridge, Mark. *Florence Nightingale: The Woman and Her Legend.* London: Viking, 2008.
[310] Kessler-Harris, Alice. *Out to Work: A History of Wage-Earning Women in the United States.* New York: Oxford University Press, 1982.

Even within the relative privilege of her position, Clara was acutely aware of the barriers that still existed. She had overheard the doctors discussing whether women had the "constitution" for the demands of medical work. She had seen the dismissive looks some male patients gave her, doubting her competence based solely on her gender.

But with each challenge, Clara's resolve only grew stronger. She threw herself into her work with a passion that impressed even the most skeptical of her colleagues. She studied medical texts late into the night, determined to prove that a woman could be just as knowledgeable and skilled as any man in her field.

As dawn began to break, Clara painted the hospital windows with pale light and finished her shift. Exhausted but fulfilled, she made her way home through the quiet streets. She passed women beginning their days—shop girls hurrying to work, mothers preparing for another day of domestic labor. In each face, she saw a reflection of the complex reality of women's work in her time—the constraints, the challenges, but also the undeniable strength and resilience.

Clara knew that her journey was just beginning. She couldn't have imagined then the path that would lead her to Cuba, to the frontlines of the fight against yellow fever. But she knew, with a certainty that burned bright within her, that she had found her calling. In a world that still questioned women's place beyond the home, Clara Maass had found a job and a vocation—a way to make her mark on the earth, one patient, one care act at a time.

3.3 Asserting Autonomy: Clara's Quest for Independence

The letter trembled slightly in Clara's hands as she read it for the third time, her heart pounding with excitement and trepidation. The Army Nurse Corps was recruiting volunteers to serve in Cuba, where American forces were grappling not just with the aftermath of the Spanish-American War but with a deadly outbreak of yellow fever. It was dangerous work, far from home, in conditions that would challenge even the most experienced nurse.

Clara knew what her family would say. She could almost hear her mother's voice, thick with worry: "It's not proper for a young woman to travel alone to such a place. What about your safety? What about your reputation?" Her father would likely be even more direct: "Absolutely not. I forbid it."

But as she stood in her tiny room, the weight of the decision heavy on her shoulders, Clara felt a surge of determination. This was her life, her choice to make. The thought both thrilled and terrified her.

Clara's journey to this moment of decision had been shaped by the complex landscape of women's rights and freedoms in 19th-century America. She recalled the lessons she had learned explicitly and implicitly about a woman's place in society.

She remembered not so long ago when she had accompanied her newly married sister to the bank. Clara had watched, bewildered, as her sister's husband signed all the documents, making money decisions that her sister had earned through her work as a seamstress. When Clara questioned this, the banker smiled condescendingly and explained the doctrine of coverture—how a woman's legal identity was subsumed by her husband's upon marriage.[311]

"But that's not fair!" Clara had protested. Her sister had simply shrugged, resigned to a reality she couldn't change.

That moment had lit a fire in Clara, fueling her desire for independence. She had thrown herself into her nursing career with renewed vigor, relishing earning her own money and controlling her life in a way that many women of her time did not.

As she contemplated the opportunity, Clara realized that this was about more than just a job. It was about asserting her right to make choices about her own life, to take risks, and to pursue her passion for nursing, even if it led her far from the safe, conventional path that society laid out for women.

She thought of the women who had fought for greater freedoms—women like Elizabeth Cady Stanton and Susan B.

---

[311] Basch, Norma. *In the Eyes of the Law: Women, Marriage, and Property in Nineteenth-Century New York*. Ithaca: Cornell University Press, 1982.

Anthony, whose tireless advocacy for women's suffrage had inspired a movement.[312] While Clara had never considered herself a political activist, she felt a kinship with these women and their quest for autonomy.

With a deep breath, Clara made her decision. She would volunteer for the Army Nurse Corps. She would go to Cuba, facing whatever challenges came her way. As she began to pen her acceptance letter, her hand steady and her resolve firm, Clara felt as though she was not just making a choice about her career but taking a stand for her right to shape her destiny.

The conversation with her parents that evening was difficult, filled with tears and raised voices. But Clara stood her ground, articulating her reasons with clarity and passion that eventually, grudgingly, won their respect, if not their full support.

As she packed her bags a few weeks later, preparing for the journey that would change her life in ways she couldn't imagine, Clara felt a sense of empowerment beyond the excitement of a new adventure. She was charting her course in a world that still questioned women's capacity for independence.

Little did Clara know that her decision would lead her to Cuba and a place in history. Her work there and her ultimate sacrifice

---

[312] DuBois, Ellen Carol. *Feminism and Suffrage: The Emergence of an Independent Women's Movement in America, 1848-1869.* Ithaca: Cornell University Press, 1978.

in the name of medical research would be a testament to women's courage and capability. In asserting her autonomy, Clara Maass would help pave the way for future generations of women to do the same.

3.4 Pioneers and Pathbreakers: The Women Who Inspired Clara

As Clara Maass stood on the ship's deck bound for Cuba, the salt spray stinging her face and the vast ocean stretching out before her, she felt a profound connection to the women who had come before her. Women who, like her, had dared to step beyond the boundaries society had drawn around their gender. Women whose courage and determination had opened doors that Clara now walked through.

She thought of Elizabeth Blackwell, the first woman to receive a medical degree in the United States. Clara could almost picture Blackwell as a young woman, facing ridicule and rejection as she applied to medical schools, finally gaining admission to Geneva Medical College almost as a joke—the male students had voted to admit her, thinking the very idea of a woman doctor was too absurd to be taken seriously.[313] Yet Blackwell had persevered, graduating at the top of her class in 1849. Clara drew strength from Blackwell's resilience and refusal to let others' narrow expectations define her potential.

Clara's mind then turned to Clara Barton, whose work during the Civil War had revolutionized battlefield medicine and paved the way for the American Red Cross. She remembered reading about how Barton defied convention, venturing onto battlefields to tend to wounded soldiers when most women

---

[313] Blackwell, Elizabeth. *Pioneer Work in Opening the Medical Profession to Women.* London: Longmans, Green, and Co., 1895.

were expected to remain safely home. "I may be compelled to face danger, but never fear it," Barton had once said, words that now echoed in Clara's heart as she faced her uncertain future.[314]

Then there was Mary Edwards Walker, a woman whose unconventional life had inspired and slightly scandalized Clara. Walker had not only served as a surgeon during the Civil War but had also famously worn men's clothing, arguing for women's right to dress practically and comfortably. Clara smiled as she remembered the shock on her mother's face when she had first mentioned Walker's trousers. While Clara wasn't quite ready to abandon her skirts, she admired Walker's courage in boldly challenging societal norms.[315]

As the ship cut through the waves, Clara's thoughts turned to a more recent pioneer: Rebecca Lee Crumpler. The first African American woman to earn a medical degree in the United States, Crumpler had faced the dual barriers of racism and sexism. Clara had once overheard a group of doctors discussing Crumpler's book, "A Book of Medical Discourses," with a mixture of surprise and grudging respect. The thought of Crumpler's determination in the face of such overwhelming odds filled Clara with a sense of awe and renewed purpose.[316]

---

[314] Oates, Stephen B. *A Woman of Valor: Clara Barton and the Civil War.* New York: Free Press, 1994.
[315] Harris, Sharon M. *Dr. Mary Walker: An American Radical, 1832-1919.* New Brunswick: Rutgers University Press, 2009.
[316] Stewart, Dianne M. "Rebecca Lee Crumpler: A Lasting Legacy." *Journal of the National Medical Association* 87, no. 1 (January 1995): 53-55.

Clara realized that these women had done more than just achieve individual success. They had expanded the very notion of what was possible for women. Each challenge they faced, each barrier they broke, created a crack in the wall of societal expectations that had long confined women to narrow roles.

As the coastline of Cuba appeared on the horizon, Clara felt a surge of gratitude for these pioneers. Their struggles and triumphs had made her journey possible. Yet she also felt the weight of responsibility. She was not just following in their footsteps but continuing their work, pushing the boundaries further with each step she took.

Clara couldn't have known then the full significance of the path she was embarking upon. She couldn't have foreseen that her name would one day be mentioned alongside those of the women she admired, that her dedication to nursing and her ultimate sacrifice would inspire future generations.

But in that moment, standing on the threshold of her most incredible adventure, Clara Maass felt a profound connection to the long line of women who had dared to defy expectations. Clara silently vowed to honor their legacy as the ship docked, and she prepared to step onto Cuban soil. In her work as a nurse, in her quest for knowledge, in her very existence as a woman charting her course, she would continue expanding the horizons for women in America and beyond.

The tropical heat hit Clara like a wave as she disembarked, but she stood tall, ready to face whatever challenges lay ahead. She was no longer just Clara Maass, a nurse from New Jersey. She was part of something larger—a movement of women reaching for more, dreaming bigger, and slowly but surely changing the world.

3.5 The Crucible of Change: Clara's World on the Brink

As Clara Maass settled into her new life in Cuba, tending to yellow fever patients in the sweltering heat of the military hospitals, she couldn't help but feel she was standing at the crossroads of history. The world she had left behind in New Jersey seemed to be shifting beneath her feet, even as she was thousands of miles away.

One sweltering afternoon, as Clara took a rare moment of rest in the shade of a mango tree, she unfolded a letter from her sister back home. The pages were filled with news that made Clara's head spin—tales of women marching in the streets demanding the right to vote, new inventions like the telephone and the typewriter creating unprecedented job opportunities for women in offices, and debates about women's access to higher education.[317]

Clara closed her eyes, trying to picture these changing scenes back home. She thought of her journey, from a young girl expected to focus solely on domestic arts to a nurse serving her country on foreign soil. In her own life, she could see the reflection of the more significant transformations sweeping through American society.

---

[317] McGerr, Michael. *A Fierce Discontent: The Rise and Fall of the Progressive Movement in America*, 1870-1920. New York: Free Press, 2003.

Yet even as she marveled at the progress, Clara was acutely aware of the existing contradictions and tensions. Here in Cuba, she worked alongside male doctors who often dismissed her expertise despite her growing experience with yellow fever cases. She thought of her African American colleagues back in New Jersey, women like Rebecca Lee Crumpler, who faced even more significant barriers due to the intersection of racial and gender prejudice.[318]

Clara's mind wandered to the future as she refolded her sister's letter. What would the world look like for the next generation of women? Would her nieces grow up in a society that valued their intellects as much as their domestic skills? Would they have the right to vote, own property, and pursue any career they chose?

Clara couldn't know then that she was living in what future historians would call the Progressive Era, a time of rapid social and political reform.[319] She couldn't have predicted the passage of the 19th Amendment in 1920, granting women the right to vote, or the profound changes in women's roles that would come with the two World Wars.

---

[318] Hine, Darlene Clark. *Black Women in White: Racial Conflict and Cooperation in the Nursing Profession, 1890-1950*. Bloomington: Indiana University Press, 1989.

[319] Wiebe, Robert H. *The Search for Order, 1877-1920*. New York: Hill and Wang, 1967.

But as she stood up, brushing off her apron and preparing to return to her patients, Clara felt a sense of purpose beyond her immediate duties. Every life she saved, skill she honed, and barrier she pushed against was part of a larger story of women's progress.

As she returned to the hospital, the humid air was heavy around her. Clara Maass carried with her the weight of history and the promise of the future. She was more than just a nurse; she participated in the significant changes reshaping American society. And though she couldn't have known it then, her own story—her dedication, courage, and ultimately her sacrifice—would become a part of that transformative narrative, inspiring generations of women to come.

The world Clara Maass inhabited was one of profound contradictions—a world where women were simultaneously idealized and restricted, where opportunities were slowly expanding even as old prejudices held firm. It was a world on the brink of change, and Clara, through her work and life, was helping to push it forward, one small step at a time.

This page left intentionally blank.

Chapter Four

The Lamp and the Lancet: Nursing's Revolution in Medicine and Society

In the crucible of 19th-century social upheaval, nursing emerged as a powerful force, reshaping not only healthcare but the very fabric of society. This chapter illuminates the journey from Florence Nightingale's pioneering efforts to Clara Maass's ultimate sacrifice, revealing how nurses became the vanguard of medical progress and women's empowerment, forever altering the landscape of medicine and social justice.

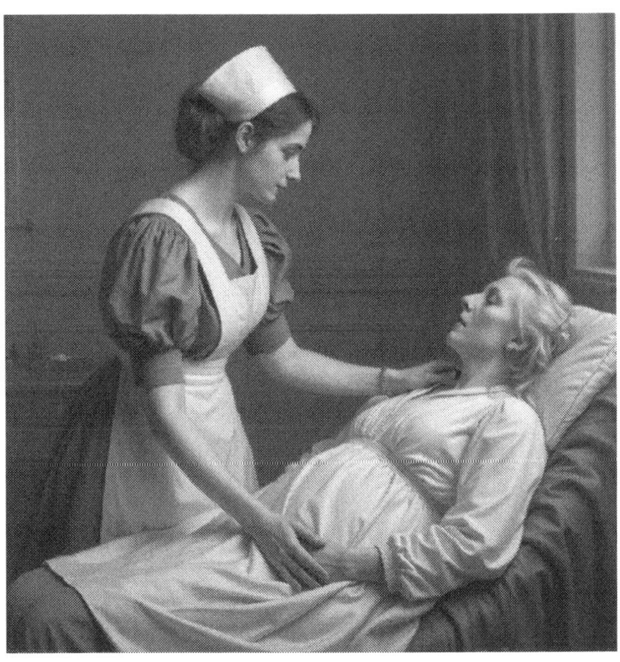

4.1 The Winds of Change: Nursing in a Transforming World

In the waning of the 19th century, London stood as a colossus astride two worlds—one birthed in industry furnaces, the other lingering like a stubborn specter of a bygone era. The cobblestone streets, once trod by Shakespeare and Marlowe, now trembled beneath the relentless march of progress. Horse-drawn carriages, their passengers swathed in silks and velvets, clattered past newly erected factories, their chimneys emitting plumes of smoke that hung like portents in the leaden sky. Men in bowler hats and women corseted into respectability hurried along the sidewalks, weaving between street vendors hawking yesterday's news and urchins with eyes too old for their grimy faces.[320]

Yet mere steps from this tableau of Victorian prosperity, a different London lurked in the narrow, festering alleyways of the city's poorer districts. Here, the air hung heavy with the haze of human misery, a toxic brew of sewage and despair. Children, their cheeks hollow with hunger, played grim games of survival in gutters choked with the detritus of poverty. Their parents, when not bent double over machines in airless workshops, languished in tenements where disease spread with the implacable efficiency of a military campaign.[321]

---

[320] Judith Flanders, *The Victorian City: Everyday Life in Dickens' London* (New York: St. Martin's Press, 2012), 23-45.
[321] Friedrich Engels, *The Condition of the Working Class in England*, trans. Florence Kelley Wischnewetzky (London: Swan Sonnenschein & Co., 1892), 71-89.

This stark juxtaposition—progress and privation existing in uneasy symbiosis—laid bare a pressing need, a void in the fabric of society that cried out to be filled. In this crucible of change, where the old world grappled with the new, nursing would emerge from the shadows of superstition and social stigma to stake its claim as a vital profession.

As urban centers swelled with the human tide of the Industrial Revolution, the inadequacies of traditional healthcare became glaringly apparent. The old ways—relying on untrained family members or well-meaning but ill-equipped volunteers—crumbled in the face of rampant disease and the grim harvest of industrial accidents. The factories and mills that drove economic progress exacted a brutal toll on the bodies of workers. At the same time, the cramped and unsanitary living conditions of the urban poor provided an ideal breeding ground for epidemics.[322]

Against this backdrop of urgent need, nursing began transforming from a haphazard, often derided occupation into a respected profession. This metamorphosis represented more than just a change in medical practice; it was a seismic shift in social dynamics, particularly for women.

---

[322] Anthony S. Wohl, *Endangered Lives: Public Health in Victorian Britain* (Cambridge, MA: Harvard University Press, 1983), 118-140.

In a society where women were confined mainly to the domestic sphere, their intellects, and ambitions suffocated by the rigid corsetry of Victorian gender roles, nursing offered a tantalizing glimpse of another life. It was a gateway to education, financial independence, and a world beyond the stifling confines of the drawing room. More than that, it allowed women to make a tangible difference in a world crying out for compassion and care.[323]

The journey from bedpan to a respected professional would be neither easy nor straightforward. It would require courage, determination, and the willingness to challenge deeply entrenched societal norms. But for the women who dared to answer this call, who ventured into the miasmic wards and fever-ridden slums, the rewards would be transformative—not just for themselves, but for the very fabric of society.

As we stand on the cusp of this new frontier, the air thick with promise and peril, we can almost hear the whisper of history in the making. The stage is set, the players are taking their positions, and the curtain is about to rise on a drama that will reshape the landscape of healthcare and women's rights for generations to come.

---

[323] Martha Vicinus, *Independent Women: Work and Community for Single Women, 1850-1920* (Chicago: University of Chicago Press, 1985), 85-112.

4.2 Florence Nightingale: The Lady with the Lamp

In the sepulchral hush of a Crimean night, where even the wind seemed to hold its breath in deference to the suffering that permeated the air, a solitary figure moved with quiet determination through the shadowed corridors of the Barrack Hospital at Scutari. The guttering flame of her lamp, a fragile bulwark against the encroaching darkness, cast phantasmagorical shadows on the walls—now stretching her silhouette to grotesque proportions, now shrinking it to a mere wisp, as if the very light were uncertain of its place in this realm of pain and death.

To the fevered minds of the wounded and dying soldiers who lay in restless vigil, this nocturnal visitor seemed less flesh and blood than an avatar of mercy, materializing from the ether to offer assistance in their darkest hour. They called her "the Lady with the Lamp," this angel who dared to tread where even death hesitated, but to the world beyond these walls of misery, she would become known by a name that would echo through the annals of history: Florence Nightingale.[324]

Born in 1820 to the silk-cushioned comfort of British affluence, Florence Nightingale seemed destined for a life of genteel irrelevance—a fate she rejected with a vehemence that scandalized her peers and bewildered her family. From her

---

[324] Mark Bostridge, *Florence Nightingale: The Woman and Her Legend* (New York: Viking, 2008), 251-270.

earliest years, she felt the irresistible pull of a higher calling, a divine summons that thrummed in her blood and whispered in her dreams. "God spoke to me," she would later write, the words burning with the enthusiasm of absolute conviction, "and called me to His service."[325]

But the path to which she felt so inexorably drawn was one that proper English society regarded with a mixture of disgust and disdain. Hospitals in Victorian England were not places of healing but somewhat fetid crucibles of vice and disease, where the poor went to die, and the desperate went to despair. The notion that a woman of Nightingale's standing should willingly immerse herself in such squalor was scandalous.[326]

Yet Florence Nightingale was not a woman to be swayed by the vapid opinions of drawing-room socialites or the hand-wringing concerns of her well-meaning but myopic family. With a determination that bordered on obsession, she sought out every scrap of medical knowledge she could acquire, poring over hospital reports with the enthusiasm of a theologian decoding ancient scriptures and touring medical facilities across Europe with the keen eye of a general surveying future battlefields.[327]

---

[325] Florence Nightingale, *Cassandra and Other Selections from Suggestions for Thought*, ed. Mary Poovey (New York: New York University Press, 1992), 205.
[326] Charles E. Rosenberg, *The Care of Strangers: The Rise of America's Hospital System* (New York: Basic Books, 1987), 40-62.
[327] Lynn McDonald, ed., *Florence Nightingale's European Travels* (Waterloo, ON: Wilfrid Laurier University Press, 2004), 15-30.

The Crimean War, a brutal crucible of imperial ambition, finally gave Nightingale the arena to prove her mettle. As reports of the abysmal conditions faced by British soldiers in military hospitals reached London, igniting a firestorm of public outrage, the British government made an unprecedented decision. They would send Florence Nightingale, armed with a cadre of nurses, to the very heart of the conflict.[328]

What awaited her at Scutari defied even her darkest imaginings. The hospital was less a place of healing than a forecourt of hell, where the stench of gangrene and excrement hung in the air like a poisonous fog. Wounded men, their bodies host to a grotesque menagerie of infections, lay strewn across floors slick with filth and bodily fluids. Bold in their impunity, Rats scurried openly among the patients, their beady eyes gleaming with an almost mocking intelligence.[329]

Lesser souls might have quailed in the face of such horror and fled back to civilized society's comforting embrace. But Florence Nightingale was carved from sterner stuff. With a resolve that seemed to bend reality to her will, she transformed this charnel house into a proper hospital.

---

[328] E.T. Cook, *The Life of Florence Nightingale*, vol. 1 (London: Macmillan, 1913), 156-178.
[329] Cecil Woodham-Smith, *Florence Nightingale, 1820-1910* (New York: McGraw-Hill, 1951), 143-165.

Her methods were at once revolutionary and breathtakingly simple. She instituted rigorous sanitation protocols, turning cleanliness from an afterthought into a religion. She established a laundry, ensuring patients would no longer lie in linens stiff with blood and worse. She created a kitchen that provided nourishing meals, understanding that the body's healing ability was intrinsically linked to its nourishment.[330]

Nightingale worked with a feverish intensity, her slight frame belying a seemingly inexhaustible reservoir of energy. For twenty hours a day, she was a whirlwind of activity, her lamp a beacon of hope in the darkness, her presence a balm to the suffering. And slowly, almost imperceptibly at first, the tide began to turn.

The results, when they came, were nothing short of miraculous. Within mere months, the death rate at Scutari plummeted from a shocking 42% to a mere 2%. In the sterile language of statistics, it was an impressive improvement. But in human terms, it was a triumph of staggering proportions—hundreds, perhaps thousands of lives snatched from the very jaws of death by the unwavering dedication of one remarkable woman.[331]

---

[330] Florence Nightingale, *Notes on Hospitals* (London: Longman, Green, Longman, Roberts, and Green, 1863), 17-40.
[331] I.B. Cohen, "Florence Nightingale," *Scientific American* 250, no. 3 (1984): 128-137.

Yet the crucible of Scutari exacted its toll. Nightingale's herculean efforts left her physically shattered, confined to her bed for much of her later life. But her mind, that formidable instrument that had reshaped the concept of nursing, remained as sharp and focused as ever. From her sickbed, she continued to revolutionize healthcare, wielding her pen with the same surgical precision she had once applied to the wards of Scutari.[332]

Her writings, most notably "Notes on Nursing," became the foundational texts of modern nursing practice. With the cool logic of a mathematician—for Nightingale was as much a statistician as a nurse—she demonstrated the irrefutable link between sanitation and survival. Her use of data to drive medical decisions was revolutionary, a precursor of the evidence-based practices that would dominate healthcare in the centuries.[333]

In 1860, she established the Nightingale Training School for Nurses at St. Thomas' Hospital in London, an institution that would become the blueprint for nursing education worldwide. Here, Nightingale's vision of nursing as a calling that demanded compassion, intelligence, observation, and unwavering dedication took physical form. The school's graduates, imbued with Nightingale's principles and passion,

---

[332] Hugh Small, *Florence Nightingale: Avenging Angel* (New York: St. Martin's Press, 1998), 180-205.
[333] Florence Nightingale, *Notes on Nursing: What It Is, and What It Is Not* (London: Harrison, 1859), 79-105.

spread across the globe, carrying the lamp of knowledge and care to the darkest corners of human suffering.[334]

As we leave Florence Nightingale—the Lady with the Lamp, the founder of modern nursing, the woman who dared to imagine healthcare as a science and an art—we see more than just a historical figure. We see a beacon, a lodestar by which generations of nurses would navigate the turbulent waters of their profession. Her legacy burns as brightly as her famous lamp, illuminating the path for all who would follow in her footsteps and dare to make a difference in the face of seemingly insurmountable odds.

[334] Monica E. Baly, *Florence Nightingale and the Nursing Legacy* (London: Croom Helm, 1986), 90-112.

4.3 From Vocation to Profession: The Evolution of Nursing

In the flickering candlelight of a medieval monastery's infirmary, a nun bends over a fevered patient, her wimple brushing against his brow as she administers a tincture of herbs, her lips moving in silent prayer. Centuries later, in the antiseptic gleam of a modern hospital, a nurse strides purposefully through corridors of chrome and tile, her crisp uniform a stark contrast to the nun's flowing robes, her stethoscope a symbol of scientific progress.

These two images, separated by vast gulfs of time and understanding, bookend the remarkable journey of nursing from a religious calling to a respected profession. It is a transformation as profound as any in the annals of human progress. This metamorphosis would reshape the practice of medicine but the very fabric of society.[335]

The roots of nursing run deep into the loam of human history, intertwined with the ministrations of religious orders and the age-old impulse to comfort the afflicted. For centuries, the care of the sick was viewed primarily as a spiritual duty, a way to serve God by tending to His suffering children. Nuns, monks, and other devoted souls took up this mantle, their compassion often outstripping their medical knowledge in an age when the

---

[335] Reverby, Susan M. *Ordered to Care: The Dilemma of American Nursing, 1850-1945.* Cambridge: Cambridge University Press, 1987.

workings of the human body remained shrouded in mystery and superstition.[336]

But nursing was at a crossroads as the world lurched into the modern era, propelled by the twin engines of scientific discovery and social upheaval. The old ways, steeped in tradition and faith, were increasingly inadequate in burgeoning medical knowledge and the complex health challenges of an industrializing world. Nursing began transforming into a secular, professional discipline in this crucible of change.[337]

The catalyst for this metamorphosis was, of course, Florence Nightingale. Her establishment of the Nightingale Training School for Nurses in 1860 was revolutionary. For the first time, nursing had a standardized curriculum that melded practical skills with theoretical knowledge, elevating the practice from a haphazard collection of folk remedies and bedside manners to a rigorous, evidence-based discipline.[338]

The impact of this new approach rippled outward like shock waves from an earthquake, reshaping the healthcare landscape. Sarah Emma Edmonds, a student at one of the early nursing

---

[336] Donahue, M. Patricia. *Nursing, the Finest Art: An Illustrated History*. St. Louis: Mosby, 1985.

[337] Dingwall, Robert, Anne Marie Rafferty, and Charles Webster. *An Introduction to the Social History of Nursing*. London: Routledge, 1988.

[338] Baly, Monica E. *Florence Nightingale and the Nursing Legacy*. London: Croom Helm, 1986

schools in the 1870s, captured the exhilaration of this new frontier in her diary:

"Today, we delved into the mysteries of blood circulation and the vital importance of fresh air in the sick room. It's as if scales have fallen from my eyes. There is so much more to this calling than I ever imagined—a whole universe of knowledge to be mastered. I feel myself standing at the threshold of a new world where compassion and science walk hand in hand."[339]

Yet the path to professionalization was fraught with obstacles. The medical establishment, a bastion of male privilege, often regarded nurses with condescension and suspicion. Many doctors, secure in their lofty positions, believed that women lacked the intellectual capacity for the rigors of medical work. Others feared that educated nurses might challenge their authority or usurp their roles.[340]

In the face of such entrenched opposition, the women who chose to pursue nursing demonstrated courage and determination that was nothing short of heroic. They were pioneers in the truest sense, venturing into uncharted territory, armed with little more than their conviction and an unshakeable belief in the importance of their calling.

---

339 Edmonds, Sarah Emma. *Nurse and Spy in the Union Army: The Adventures and Experiences of a Woman in Hospitals, Camps, and Battle-Fields*. Hartford: W.S. Williams & Co., 1865.
340 Reverby, Susan M. *Ordered to Care: The Dilemma of American Nursing, 1850-1945*. Cambridge: Cambridge University Press, 1987.

Despite these headwinds, nursing schools increased in the late 19th and early 20th centuries, each a beacon of progress in a world still shadowed by ignorance and prejudice. The curriculum expanded beyond the basics of patient care, encompassing anatomy, physiology, pharmacology, and public health. Nurses were no longer seen merely as the doctor's handmaiden but as skilled professionals in their own right, capable of independent thought and action.[341]

This evolution was not merely acquiring new skills or accumulating knowledge. It represented a fundamental shift in the very nature of nursing. The nurse was no longer simply a comforting presence at the bedside but an integral part of the healthcare team, bringing a unique perspective and skills to the challenge of healing the sick and protecting the healthy.

Nursing began developing its philosophical underpinnings and ethical framework as it stepped into its new role. Holistic care—treating the patient as a whole person rather than a collection of symptoms—emerged as a cornerstone of nursing practice. This approach, which considered patients' physical, emotional, and social needs, was revolutionary when medicine often focused narrowly on physical ailments.[342]

---

[341] Kalisch, Philip A., and Beatrice J. Kalisch. *The Advance of American Nursing*. Boston: Little, Brown, 1986.
[342] Meleis, Afaf Ibrahim. *Theoretical Nursing: Development and Progress*. Philadelphia: Lippincott Williams & Wilkins, 2011.

The professionalization of nursing also brought with it the development of specialized roles. Surgical nurses, psychiatric nurses, public health nurses—each of these specialties requires its own body of knowledge and set of skills. This diversification allowed nurses to delve deeper into particular areas of healthcare, further enhancing their expertise and contributions to patient care.[343]

As we stand at the threshold of the 20th century, looking back on the remarkable journey of nursing from vocation to profession, we see more than just a change in training or status. We witness the birth of a new kind of healer who combines the medieval nun's compassion with the modern age's scientific rigor. It is a synthesis that would prove transformative for healthcare and society.

343 Fairman, Julie, and Joan E. Lynaugh. *Critical Care Nursing: A History*. Philadelphia: University of Pennsylvania Press, 1998.

4.4 Nursing in War: A Catalyst for Change

The acrid stench of gunpowder mingles with the metallic tang of blood, creating a toxic perfume of human suffering. The air reverberates with the din of battle—the sharp report of rifles, the thunderous booming of artillery, and underlying it all, the agonized moans of the wounded and dying. In a makeshift field hospital, little more than a collection of tents hastily erected behind the battle lines, a young nurse named Clara Barton works with feverish intensity, her hands slick with blood as she fights to staunch the flow from a soldier's mangled leg.

This scene from the American Civil War exemplifies how armed conflicts served as crucibles for nursing, forging it in the fires of urgent necessity and unimaginable human suffering. War, with its brutal efficiency in creating broken bodies and shattered minds, provided both the impetus and the proving ground for the rapid advancement of nursing practice.[344]

The American Civil War (1861-1865) marked a pivotal moment in the evolution of nursing. The sheer scale of the conflict, with its unprecedented casualty rates, created an enormous demand for medical care that far outstripped the available resources—into this breach stepped thousands of women, many with little or no formal training, driven by a

---

[344] Mary T. Sarnecky, *A History of the U.S. Army Nurse Corps* (Philadelphia: University of Pennsylvania Press, 1999), 23-45.

potent mixture of patriotism, compassion, and a desire to contribute to a cause larger than themselves.[345]

Among these women was Clara Barton, whose experiences on the battlefield would later lead her to found the American Red Cross. Barton's words, penned in the heat of conflict, capture the spirit that animated these pioneering nurses:

"I may be compelled to face danger but never fear it, and while our soldiers can stand and fight, I can stand and feed and nurse them."[346]

The challenges faced by Civil War nurses were daunting, almost beyond comprehension. They worked in conditions that would horrify modern healthcare professionals—makeshift hospitals where sanitation was an afterthought, medical knowledge was primitive by today's standards, and supplies were often woefully inadequate. Infections ran rampant, and many more soldiers succumbed to disease than to enemy fire.[347]

Yet, precisely, these brutal conditions catalyzed the transformation of nursing. The urgent need for skilled care

---

[345] Jane E. Schultz, *Women at the Front: Hospital Workers in Civil War America* (Chapel Hill: University of North Carolina Press, 2004), 15-30

[346] Clara Barton, *The Red Cross in Peace and War* (Washington, D.C.: American Historical Press, 1898), 66.

[347] Margaret Humphreys, *Marrow of Tragedy: The Health Crisis of the American Civil War**(Baltimore: Johns Hopkins University Press, 2013), 40-62.

drove rapid innovations in nursing practice. Nurses learned to improvise, to make do with limited resources, and to take on responsibilities that would have been unthinkable in peacetime. They became experts in wound care, managing infections, and triaging patients under the most extreme conditions imaginable.[348]

The Spanish-American War of 1898 saw further advancements in military nursing. By this time, the profession had become more organized, with trained nurses playing a crucial role in managing field hospitals and caring for the sick and wounded. The conflict highlighted the importance of specialized training for military nurses, leading to the establishment of the Army Nurse Corps in 1901.[349]

But World War I (1914-1918) genuinely catapulted nursing onto the world stage. The conflict's unprecedented scale and the introduction of new, devastating weapons created a desperate need for skilled medical personnel. Thousands of nurses answered the call, serving in military hospitals and frontline casualty clearing stations, often within range of enemy fire.

---

[348] Libra R. Hilde, *Worth a Dozen Men: Women and Nursing in the Civil War South* (Charlottesville: University of Virginia Press, 2012), 78-95.

[349] Mary M. Gormandy, "The Spanish-American War: The Story of the 18th Army Corps in the Santiago Campaign," *The American Journal of Nursing* 2, no. 10 (1902): 777-784.

These nurses faced dangers and witnessed horrors that would have been unimaginable to their civilian counterparts. Helen Dore Boylston, an American nurse who served in France, captured the grim reality of wartime nursing in her diary:

"The wounds are ghastly. Never had I imagined anything so dreadful... But we work on doing what we can, knowing that every life saved is a victory against this monstrous war."[350]

The crucible of war forged a new kind of nurse—one who was not only compassionate and skilled but also resilient, adaptable, and capable of functioning under the most extreme conditions. These qualities would prove invaluable in military settings and the evolving landscape of civilian healthcare.[351]

The contributions of nurses during World War I did not go unnoticed. Their courage and competence earned them newfound respect from the medical establishment and the general public. In many countries, including the United States and Britain, nurses were finally granted military rank and the accompanying benefits and recognition. This formal acknowledgment of their vital role was a significant step in the professionalization of nursing.[352]

---

[350] Christine E. Hallett, *Veiled Warriors: Allied Nurses of the First World War* (Oxford: Oxford University Press, 2014), 8-25.
[351] Kimberly Jensen, *Mobilizing Minerva: American Women in the First World War* (Urbana: University of Illinois Press, 2008), 120-145.
[352] Kimberly Jensen, *Mobilizing Minerva: American Women in the First World War** (Urbana: University of Illinois Press, 2008), 120-145.

As the echoes of the war faded and the world struggled to heal its wounds, the nursing profession stood at a new threshold. It had proven its worth in the most challenging circumstances imaginable. Nurses have demonstrated not only their compassion and dedication but also their capacity for leadership, their ability to innovate in the face of daunting challenges, and their indispensable role in healthcare delivery.[353]

The legacy of these wartime nurses lives on today in every emergency room, intensive care unit, and field hospital worldwide. Their courage, skill, and unwavering commitment to their patients set a standard to which all future generations of nurses would aspire. They had taken the lamp lit by Florence Nightingale and carried it into the darkest corners of human experience, illuminating a path forward for the entire profession.

---

353 Judith Barger, *Beyond the Call of Duty: Army Flight Nursing in World War II* (Kent, OH: Kent State University Press, 2013), 15-30

4.5 Nursing and Women's Empowerment

The rhythmic click of sensible heels echoes down the sterile corridor of a bustling hospital. Nurse Jane Anderson, her starched white uniform a beacon of order in the controlled chaos of the ward, moves with purposeful grace from bedside to bedside. Her presence commands respect from patients and doctors alike, her quiet competence a stark rebuke to those who would dismiss her gender as the "weaker sex." This scene might have seemed unremarkable to an outside observer in the early 20th century. Yet it represents nothing less than a quiet revolution—a seismic shift in women's roles that was reshaping society from the hospital ward outward.[354]

In its evolution from a haphazard collection of folk remedies and bedside manner to a rigorous, scientific profession, nursing provided a unique avenue for women's empowerment. In an era when women's opportunities were severely circumscribed, bound by the rigid corsetry of Victorian gender roles, nursing offered a tantalizing glimpse of another life. It was more than just a job; it was a gateway to education, financial independence, and a world beyond the stifling confines of the drawing room.[355]

---

[354] Susan M. Reverby, *Ordered to Care: The Dilemma of American Nursing, 1850-1945* (Cambridge: Cambridge University Press, 1987), 77-79.
[355] Barbara Melosh, "The Physician's Hand": *Work Culture and Conflict in American Nursing* (Philadelphia: Temple University Press, 1982), 15-18.

For many women, nursing school represented their first foray into higher education. The rigorous training imparted medical knowledge and instilled a sense of confidence and self-reliance that was revolutionary for its time. Lavinia Dock, a pioneering nurse and suffragist, captured this transformative power in her writings:

"No other calling opens such opportunities for general culture, acquaintance with human nature, and larger-mindedness. The nurse's education never stops; every day brings new experiences; every year opens new vistas of possibility."[356]

The financial independence that nursing provided was nothing short of revolutionary. At a time when most women were economically dependent on male relatives, nurses could support themselves and even their families. This economic power translated into greater personal freedom and decision-making authority, allowing women to chart their life courses to an unimaginable extent.[357]

Moreover, nursing allowed women to step into public roles of responsibility and authority. In the hospital setting, nurses managed wards, made critical decisions about patient care, and often commanded the respect of male doctors and

---

[356] Lavinia L. Dock, *A History of Nursing: From the Earliest Times to the Present Day with Special Reference to the Work of the Past Thirty Years, vol. 3* (New York: G.P. Putnam's Sons, 1912), 236.

[357] Patricia D'Antonio, *American Nursing: A History of Knowledge, Authority, and the Meaning of Work* (Baltimore: Johns Hopkins University Press, 2010), 102-105.

administrators. This experience of leadership and respect in the workplace was transformative for the individual nurses and society's perception of women's capabilities.[358]

Many nurses leveraged their positions as a platform for broader social activism. Lillian Wald, who founded the Henry Street Settlement in New York, exemplified this trend. She combined nursing with social work to improve conditions in poor urban communities, understanding that proper health encompassed more than just the absence of disease. Wald articulated this holistic vision of healthcare and social justice:

"The call to the nurse is not only for the bedside care of the sick, but to help in seeking out the deep-lying basic causes of illness and misery, that in the future there may be less sickness to nurse and to cure."[359]

Perhaps no figure better embodies the intersection of nursing and social activism than Margaret Sanger. A nurse who became a pioneering advocate for birth control, Sanger's experiences caring for poor women led her to challenge the laws restricting access to contraception. Her words still resonate with revolutionary fervor:

---

358 Arlene W. Keeling, *Nursing and the Privilege of Prescription, 1893-2000* (Columbus: Ohio State University Press, 2007), 54-57.
359 Lillian D. Wald, *The House on Henry Street* (New York: Henry Holt and Company, 1915), 8.

"No woman can call herself free who does not own and control her body. No woman can call herself free until she can choose consciously whether she will or will not be a mother."[360]

The empowerment of nurses had ripple effects throughout society. As more women entered the profession and proved their capabilities, it became increasingly difficult to justify excluding women from other fields and full participation in civic life. In many ways, nursing served as a wedge, opening doors that had long been closed to women.[361]

Yet this progress was not without its challenges and contradictions. The qualities that made nursing acceptable as a female profession—its association with caring and nurturing—were sometimes used to justify lower pay and status compared to male-dominated medical roles. Nurses often faced discrimination, sexual harassment, and belittlement from male colleagues who viewed them as little more than glorified maids.[362]

Despite these obstacles, the overall trend was clear: nursing was opening doors and breaking down barriers for women. It provided a female competence and professionalism model that

---

[360] Margaret Sanger, *Woman and the New Race* (New York: Brentano's, 1920), 94.
[361] Sandra Beth Lewenson, *Taking Charge: Nursing, Suffrage, and Feminism in America, 1873-1920* (New York: NLN Press, 1996), 123-126.
[362] Joan I. Roberts and Thetis M. Group, *Feminism and Nursing: An Historical Perspective on Power, Status, and Political Activism in the Nursing Profession* (Westport, CT: Praeger, 1995), 187-190.

challenged prevailing notions of women's capabilities. As we watch Nurse Anderson continue her rounds, her head held high, we see more than just a healthcare professional at work. We see a woman charting a new course, not just for herself but for all those who would follow in her footsteps.[363]

[363] Susan Gelfand Malka, *Daring to Care: American Nursing and Second-Wave Feminism* (Urbana: University of Illinois Press, 2007), 22-25.

4.6 Clara Maass: A New Generation of Nurses

On a sun-drenched June 1895, Clara Maass stood proudly among her fellow Newark German Hospital Training School graduates for Nurses.[364] Her starched white uniform, gleaming in the summer light, was more than just a symbol of the knowledge and skills she had acquired over the past three years. It was a battle standard, a declaration of her readiness to join the ranks of a new generation of nurses—women who were redefining their profession and, in the process, reshaping society itself.

As Maass clutched her hard-earned diploma, her heart swelled with pride, excitement, and trepidation. The future before her was full of possibilities that would have been unimaginable to women just a generation earlier. Yet with these new opportunities came challenges and responsibilities that would test her mettle in ways she could scarcely imagine.

Clara Maass was born in 1876 in East Orange, New Jersey, the daughter of German immigrants.[365] Her childhood, spent in the bosom of a working-class family with eight siblings, was a crucible that forged the qualities that would define her as a nurse: diligence, compassion, and an unshakeable sense of

---

[364] Mary C. Gillett, *The Army Medical Department, 1865-1917* (Washington, D.C.: Center of Military History, U.S. Army, 1995), 221-222.

[365] Barbara Mccloskey, "Maass, Clara Louise," in *American National Biography Online*, ed. Susan Ware (New York: Oxford University Press, 2000), https://doi.org/10.1093/anb/9780198606697.article.1200622.

duty. When she entered nursing school at the tender age of 19, she was stepping into a profession that the efforts of women like Florence Nightingale and the crucible of the Civil War had transformed.[366]

Maass's training was rigorous and comprehensive, a far cry from the haphazard instruction of earlier eras. She immersed herself in studying anatomy, physiology, and pharmacology, mastering the scientific underpinnings of modern medicine. Yet her education went beyond mere technical knowledge. The school instilled in her a strong sense of professional ethics and a commitment to public health that would guide her actions in the future.[367]

Upon graduation, Maass quickly distinguished herself as a nurse of exceptional skill and dedication. During a typhoid fever outbreak, she worked tirelessly, demonstrating a composure under pressure that belied her youth. Her competence did not go unnoticed, and rapid promotions followed. By the astonishingly young age of 21, she had been appointed head nurse of her ward—a position of significant responsibility that spoke volumes about her abilities and the evolving status of nurses in the medical hierarchy.[368]

---

[366] Joan E. Lynaugh, "Nursing the Great Society: The Impact of the Nurse Training Act of 1964," *Nursing History Review* 16 (2008): 13-28.
[367] Patricia D'Antonio, *American Nursing: A History of Knowledge, Authority, and the Meaning of Work* (Baltimore: Johns Hopkins University Press, 2010), 112-115.
[368] Mccloskey, "Maass, Clara Louise."

Maass's career took an unexpected and fateful turn with the outbreak of the Spanish-American War in 1898. Driven by a potent mixture of patriotic fervor and a desire to expand her nursing experience, she volunteered for the Army Nurse Corps.[369] This decision would take her far from the familiar wards of Newark, thrusting her into the heart of a conflict that would reshape global politics and, ultimately, the course of her own life.

Maass encountered challenges that would have daunted lesser spirits in the tropical battlefields of Cuba and the Philippines. She grappled with diseases she had never before seen, including the dreaded yellow fever—a deadly illness that would later play a pivotal role in her life. Working in makeshift hospitals with limited supplies, she cared for soldiers suffering from tropical diseases and grievous battle wounds; her skills and resolve tested daily in the crucible of war.[370]

The experience of wartime nursing left an indelible mark on Maass. In a letter home, she captured both the horror and the sense of purpose that defined her service:

---

[369] Mercedes Graf, "A Very Few Good Nurses," *Prologue Magazine* 40, no. 3 (Fall 2008), https://www.archives.gov/publications/prologue/2008/fall/nurses.html.
[370] Mary T. Sarnecky, *A History of the U.S. Army Nurse Corps* (Philadelphia: University of Pennsylvania Press, 1999), 82-85.

"The suffering here is beyond anything I could have imagined. The heat, the insects, the constant threat of disease—it's almost more than one can bear. And yet, I am glad to be here, doing what I can to ease the pain of these brave men. This is why I became a nurse—to make a difference when it matters most."[371]

Upon returning to the United States, Maass found that her wartime service had elevated her professional standing. She was now viewed as a nurse of exceptional experience and expertise, her time in the tropics having honed her skills and expanded her medical knowledge in ways that peacetime practice never could.

Yet rather than settling into a comfortable position, leveraging her newfound status for personal gain, Maass felt called to continue pushing the boundaries of her profession. This drive, this unquenchable thirst to contribute to the advancement of medical knowledge, led her to volunteer for a mission of almost unimaginable danger—one that would ultimately cost her her life but cement her place in the annals of medical history.

---

[371] Clara Maass, letter to family, July 15, 1898, Clara Maass Papers, Newark Public Library, Newark, NJ.

In 1900, Maass traveled to Cuba to participate in experiments to understand the transmission of yellow fever.[372] This decision, made with full knowledge of the risks involved, exemplifies the dedication and courage that had come to characterize the new generation of nurses. No longer content to be mere assistants to doctors, nurses like Maass were becoming active participants in medical research, willing to put their own lives on the line in the pursuit of knowledge that could save countless others.

As we stand with Clara Maass at this pivotal moment in her career, on the cusp of a decision that would have profound implications for her life and the field of medicine, we see in her the culmination of decades of progress in nursing. She was educated, respected, and empowered to contribute significantly to medical science. Yet her story also foreshadows the challenges and sacrifices that still lay ahead for nurses pushing the boundaries of their field.

Maass's willingness to participate in the yellow fever experiments was a testament to the evolving role of nurses in healthcare. It represented a new paradigm in which nurses were not just caregivers but also researchers, not just followers of doctors' orders but partners in advancing medical knowledge.

---

[372] Marilyn Ogilvie and Joy Harvey, eds., *The Biographical Dictionary of Women in Science: Pioneering Lives from Ancient Times to the Mid-20th Century* (New York: Routledge, 2000), 827-828.

As we prepare to delve deeper into Clara Maass's fateful involvement in the yellow fever experiments in our next chapter, we carry the legacy of all the nurses who came before—from Florence Nightingale's revolutionary reforms to the countless unnamed nurses who served in wars and epidemics. Clara Maass stands as a bridge between these pioneers and the modern nursing profession. Her story is a powerful reminder of the courage, dedication, and sacrifice that have always been at the heart of nursing.[373]

[373] Susan M. Reverby, *Ordered to Care: The Dilemma of American Nursing, 1850-1945* (Cambridge: Cambridge University Press, 1987), 156-158.

4.7 Conclusion: The Legacy of Nursing's Pioneers

In the calm efficiency of a modern hospital, a nurse checks a patient's vital signs on a high-tech monitor; her practiced hands moving with quiet assurance as she adjusts an IV drip. The scene is light-years removed from the candlelit wards of Florence Nightingale's era. Yet, the spirit of compassion and dedication that animates this modern caregiver is a direct inheritance from those pioneering nurses of the past.[374]

As we conclude our journey through the early history of professional nursing, we find ourselves standing at a crossroads of past and future. The transformation of nursing from a haphazard, low-status occupation to a respected profession was nothing short of revolutionary. A metamorphosis opened doors for women in education, employment, and public life, challenging long-held assumptions about women's capabilities and proper societal roles.[375]

The emphasis on education and standardized training, championed by Nightingale and her successors, laid the foundation for today's highly skilled nursing workforce. Modern nurses are not merely caregivers but educators, researchers, and leaders in healthcare policy. They stand as the

---

[374] Florence Nightingale, *Notes on Nursing: What It Is, and What It Is Not* (London: Harrison, 1859).

[375] Susan M. Reverby, *Ordered to Care: The Dilemma of American Nursing, 1850-1945* (Cambridge: Cambridge University Press, 1987).

frontline defenders of public health, their expertise spanning the gamut from bedside care to global health initiatives.[376]

The experiences of wartime nurses, from Clara Barton in the American Civil War to the brave women who served in the trenches of World War I, demonstrated the crucial role of nursing in crises.[377] This legacy continues to resonate in modern disaster response and global health initiatives. From natural disasters to global pandemics, nurses remain at the forefront of healthcare delivery in the most challenging circumstances imaginable.

The early nurse activists who combined their professional work with advocacy for social reforms set a precedent for nurses as agents of change. Figures like Lillian Wald and Margaret Sanger showed that nursing could be a platform for addressing broader societal issues.[378] Today, nurses continue to be powerful advocates for public health, patient rights, and healthcare reform, their voices carrying the weight of scientific knowledge and frontline experience.

Clara Maass's participation in medical research foreshadowed nurses' critical role in advancing medical knowledge. Her sacrifice in the yellow fever experiments was not in vain; it

---

[376] Patricia D'Antonio, *American Nursing: A History of Knowledge, Authority, and the Meaning of Work* (Baltimore: Johns Hopkins University Press, 2010).
[377] Jane E. Schultz, *Women at the Front: Hospital Workers in Civil War America* (Chapel Hill: University of North Carolina Press, 2004).
[378] Marjorie N. Feld, *Lillian Wald: A Biography* (Chapel Hill: University of North Carolina Press, 2008).

paved the way for nurses to be recognized as vital contributors to medical research.[379] Today, nurse researchers contribute significantly to improvements in patient care, health policy, and medical technology, their unique perspective bridging the gap between theoretical knowledge and practical application.

Nursing faces new challenges as we look to the future: advancing technology, changing demographics, evolving healthcare systems, and global health threats. Yet the fundamental principles established by nursing pioneers—the importance of sanitation, patient-centered care, continuous learning, and ethical practice—remain as relevant as ever. These principles form the bedrock upon which the future of nursing will be built.[380]

Nursing's emergence as a profession is more than a historical account; it's a testament to the power of dedication, courage, and compassion to transform society. From Florence Nightingale's lamp-lit rounds in Crimea to Clara Maass's selfless participation in yellow fever research, each nurse's contribution has helped to illuminate the path forward. Their legacy lives on in every nurse who tends to the sick, advocates for patients, pushes the boundaries of medical knowledge, and works tirelessly to improve health outcomes for all.

---

[379] Evelyn Benson, "Clara Louise Maass: A Nurse Who Gave Her Life," *The American Journal of Nursing* 73, no. 1 (1973): 90-93

[380] Julie Fairman and Patricia D'Antonio, "Reimagining Nursing's Place in the History of Clinical Practice," *Journal of the History of Medicine and Allied Sciences* 63, no. 4 (2008): 435-446.

As we close this chapter and prepare to delve deeper into Clara Maass's fateful involvement in the yellow fever experiments, we carry with us the collective wisdom and inspiration of all those who came before. Their stories remind us that the history of nursing is not just a chronicle of medical advancements but a profoundly human story of courage, sacrifice, and an unwavering commitment to the well-being of others.

The torch has been passed, and the light that began as a single flame in Nightingale's lamp now burns brightly in hospitals, clinics, research labs, and communities worldwide. As long as there are those in need of care, the nursing profession will continue to evolve, innovate, and serve—a living tribute to the pioneers who dared to reimagine what it meant to be a nurse.

In the face of whatever challenges the future may hold, we can be confident that nurses will be there, as they have always been, standing on the shoulders of giants, carrying forward the noble tradition of their profession. The frontier that began with Florence Nightingale continues to expand, pushed ever outward by each new generation of nurses who bring their skills, compassion, and indomitable spirit to the never-ending task of healing the world.[381]

---

[381] Sioban Nelson and Suzanne Gordon, eds., *The Complexities of Care: Nursing Reconsidered* (Ithaca: Cornell University Press, 2006).

USA
13c
CLARA MAASS
She gave her life

Chapter Five

Breaking Barriers: Pioneering Women in Medicine and Science

This chapter explores the groundbreaking contributions of women to medicine and science in the late 19th and early 20th centuries, focusing on figures such as Elizabeth Blackwell, Florence Nightingale, Marie Curie, Mary Putnam Jacobi, and Clara Maass. It examines their struggles against societal and institutional barriers, their significant scientific and medical achievements, and the lasting impact of their work on both their fields and the broader fight for women's rights and recognition.

5.1 Breaking the Boundaries: Women in Medicine and Science

The faint glow of a kerosene lamp illuminated the small, cluttered desk where Clara Maass hunched over her nursing textbooks. The year was 1893, and while the world beyond her window buzzed with the promise of a new century, Clara knew that the path forward was fraught with obstacles for women like her. As she traced her finger along the diagrams of human anatomy, she could hardly have imagined that her dedication would one day place her at the forefront of a medical revolution—or that it would ultimately claim her life.[382]

Clara's story is one thread in a rich tapestry of women who dared to challenge the established order of medicine and science in the late 19th and early 20th centuries. These pioneers faced a world that viewed their ambitions with skepticism at best and hostility at worst. In 1900, women accounted for a mere 5.6% of American physicians, which reflected not a lack of ability or desire but the formidable barriers erected by a society uncomfortable with the idea of women in professional roles.[383]

---

[382] Regina Morantz-Sanchez, *Sympathy and Science: Women Physicians in American Medicine* (Chapel Hill: University of North Carolina Press, 1985), 54-55.

[383] Mary Roth Walsh, *Doctors Wanted, No Women Need Apply: Sexual Barriers in the Medical Profession, 1835-1975* (New Haven: Yale University Press, 1977), 121.

The landscape these women navigated was one of profound contradiction. As the world marveled at the wonders of the telegraph and the telephone, antiquated notions about women's intellectual and physical capabilities persisted. Laws restricting women's property rights and denying them the vote underscored a pervasive belief in their second-class status. Yet it was against this backdrop that a cadre of determined women would forge ahead, their contributions destined to reshape the medical field and society.

As we delve into their stories, we find a shared thread of resilience, a standard narrative of women who refused to accept the limitations imposed upon them. From Elizabeth Blackwell's groundbreaking entry into medical school to Marie Curie's pioneering work with radioactivity, these women's journeys were marked by personal sacrifice, unwavering determination, and, ultimately, transformative achievement.

In the sterile corridors of hospitals and the peaceful confines of laboratories, these trailblazers would challenge more than scientific orthodoxy; they would confront the foundations of a society that doubted their capabilities. Their struggles and triumphs would pave the way for future generations, including Clara Maass, whose selfless dedication to nursing and medical research would embody the profession's highest ideals.

As we explore the lives of these remarkable women, we will witness their accomplishments and the broader revolution they ignited. This revolution would ultimately transform the landscape of medicine and science, creating ripples that continue to shape our world today.

5.2 The Trailblazers: Stories of Women Who Defied the Norms

5.2.1 Elizabeth Blackwell: Forging the Path

On a crisp January morning in 1849, Elizabeth Blackwell stood before the gates of Geneva Medical College in New York, her heart pounding with anticipation and dread. The brick buildings loomed before her, bastions of a male-dominated profession that had, until now, firmly barred its doors to women. As she stepped onto the campus, the whispers and stares of her male counterparts followed her like shadows, a constant reminder of her outsider status.[384]

Blackwell's journey to this moment had been anything but straightforward. Born in Bristol, England, in 1821, she emigrated to America with her family as a child. Intelligent and fiercely independent, Blackwell had initially recoiled at the idea of a medical career, finding the human body "peculiarly distasteful."[385] It was only after a dying friend suggested that her suffering would have been lessened had a female physician treated her that Blackwell began to consider medicine as her calling.

Her quest for medical education was met with near-universal rejection. "You cannot expect us to furnish you with a stick to break our heads with," one medical school dean told her

---

[384] Elizabeth Blackwell, *Pioneer Work in Opening the Medical Profession to Women* (London: Longmans, Green, and Co., 1895), 27-28.
[385] Blackwell, *Pioneer Work*, 15.

bluntly.[386] When Geneva Medical College finally admitted her, it resulted from a practical joke gone awry—the all-male student body, asked to vote on her admission, had unanimously approved, believing the proposition to be in jest.[387]

As Blackwell navigated her medical education, she faced the rigors of her studies and the constant scrutiny and often open hostility of her peers and instructors. "Miss Blackwell," a professor once remarked during a lecture on reproductive anatomy, "if you don't wish to leave the room, we will not insist upon it, although we recommend you to do so."[388] Blackwell stayed, her face burning with embarrassment but her resolve unshaken.

Her perseverance paid off. On January 23, 1849, Elizabeth Blackwell became the first woman to receive a medical degree in the United States, graduating at the top of her class.[389] But her groundbreaking achievement was only the beginning of her struggles. Finding a hospital willing to allow her to practice proved nearly impossible, leading Blackwell to a stark realization: if opportunities for women in medicine did not exist, she would have to create them herself.

---

386 Blackwell, 29.
387 Morantz-Sanchez, *Sympathy and Science*, 32.
388 Blackwell, *Pioneer Work*, 65.
389 Blackwell, 89.

In 1857, along with her sister Emily and Dr. Marie Zakrzewska, Blackwell founded the New York Infirmary for Indigent Women and Children. The institution served a dual purpose: providing medical care to poor women and children while offering clinical training opportunities for women pursuing medical careers.[390] It was a bold statement of intent that women not only belonged in the medical profession but could excel in it.

Blackwell's influence extended far beyond the walls of her infirmary. She became a vocal advocate for women's medical education, her very existence challenging prevailing notions about women's capabilities. "If society does not admit to women's free development," she wrote, "then society must be remodeled."[391]

As we consider Blackwell's legacy, we see more than just the story of one woman's triumph over adversity. Her journey represents the first cracks in a system that had long excluded half of humanity from the medical profession. Countless others would follow the trails she blazed, each step forward expanding the possibilities for women in medicine.

---

[390] Morantz-Sanchez, *Sympathy and Science*, 64-65.
[391] Blackwell, *Pioneer Work*, 242.

Yet, as we will see, the path forward remained fraught with challenges. The women who followed in Blackwell's footsteps would face their battles, their moments of doubt and triumph. Among them would be a young nurse named Clara Maass, whose dedication to medicine would lead her to make the ultimate sacrifice in the name of scientific progress.

5.2.2 Florence Nightingale: The Lady with the Lamp

In the annals of medical history, few figures loom as large as Florence Nightingale. Her name has become synonymous with modern nursing, her shadow stretching far beyond the wards of the hospitals she reformed to touch nearly every aspect of public health and medical statistics. Yet, to truly understand Nightingale's impact, we must look beyond the iconic image of the "Lady with the Lamp" to see the complex, brilliant, and often contradictory woman behind the legend.

Born in 1820 to a wealthy British family, Nightingale enjoyed privileges that set her apart from many of her contemporaries. Yet, from an early age, she felt called to a higher purpose that would put her at odds with the expectations of her class and gender. "I have an intellectual nature which requires satisfaction," she wrote in her diary at 17, "and that would find it in men's work."[392]

Nightingale's opportunity to prove herself came during the Crimean War. In 1854, reports of the horrific conditions in military hospitals reached London, sparking public outrage. Nightingale, who had been quietly honing her nursing skills

---

392 Florence Nightingale, "Cassandra," in *Cassandra and Other Selections from Suggestions for Thought*, ed. Mary Poovey (New York: New York University Press, 1992), 205.

despite her family's disapproval, was asked to lead a team of nurses to the front lines.[393]

The scene that greeted Nightingale at the Barrack Hospital in Scutari was unimaginable squalor and suffering. The mortality rate for hospitalized soldiers exceeded 40%, with infectious diseases claiming more lives than battlefield injuries.[394] Nightingale recalled, "The strongest man might have staggered at the sight."[395]

But Nightingale did not stagger. Instead, she implemented reforms to revolutionize military medicine and lay the groundwork for modern nursing practices. She insisted on basic sanitation measures, established a laundry to provide clean linens, and reorganized kitchen operations to provide nourishing meals to patients.[396]

The results were dramatic. Within six months, the mortality rate at the hospital had plummeted from 40% to 2%.[397] Nightingale's methods, once dismissed by military officials, were now irrefutable. Her nightly rounds, lamp in hand, offering comfort to the wounded and dying, earned her the

---

393 Mark Bostridge, *Florence Nightingale: The Woman and Her Legend* (London: Viking, 2008), 204-205.

394 Bostridge, 218.

395 Florence Nightingale, *Notes on Matters Affecting the Health, Efficiency, and Hospital Administration of the British Army* (London: Harrison and Sons, 1858), 310.

396 Bostridge, *Florence Nightingale*, 225-226.

397 Bostridge, 272.

nickname "The Lady with the Lamp" and cemented her place in the public imagination.[398]

However, Nightingale's true genius lay in her practical reforms and ability to translate her experiences into data-driven arguments for systemic change. A gifted mathematician, she pioneered statistical analysis in healthcare, developing innovative graphical data presentations that could communicate complex information to non-specialists.[399]

Her most famous statistical visualization, the "Coxcomb diagram," demonstrated that the majority of soldier deaths during the Crimean War were due to preventable diseases rather than combat injuries. This stark visual representation helped convince British authorities of the need for sanitary reform in military hospitals.[400]

Nightingale's influence extended far beyond the military sphere. Her book "Notes on Nursing: What It Is, and What It Is Not," published in 1859, laid out the fundamental principles of nursing and helped establish it as a respectable profession for women.[401] She was instrumental in establishing the first professional nursing school at St. Thomas' Hospital in

---

398 Bostridge, 237.
399 I. Bernard Cohen, "Florence Nightingale," *Scientific American* 250, no. 3 (1984): 128-137.
400 Hugh Small, *Florence Nightingale: Avenging Angel* (London: Constable, 1998), 170-172.
401 Florence Nightingale, *Notes on Nursing: What It Is, and What It Is Not* (London: Harrison, 1859).

London, which became a model for nursing education worldwide.[402]

Yet for all her public acclaim, Nightingale was an intensely private person who struggled with chronic illness for much of her adult life. Bedridden for years after her return from Crimea, possibly due to brucellosis contracted during the war, she continued her work from her sickbed, writing, analyzing data, and advising on healthcare reforms.[403]

Nightingale's legacy is complex and, at times, contradictory. While she opened doors for women in nursing, she was initially skeptical of women entering the medical profession as doctors. She believed nursing, emphasizing observation and care, was particularly suited to women's talents.[404] This view would evolve, but it highlights the complex interplay of progressive and traditional ideas that characterized much of the early struggle for women's advancement in medicine.

Considering Nightingale's immense contributions, we see a woman who revolutionized a profession and challenged fundamental assumptions about women's capabilities and role in society. Her work laid the foundation for future pioneers, including Clara Maass, who would build upon Nightingale's emphasis on hygiene and patient care in their groundbreaking work.

---

[402] Bostridge, *Florence Nightingale*, 335-336.
[403] Bostridge, 318-320.
[404] Bostridge, 484-485.

Nightingale's story reminds us that progress is rarely linear and that even history's most iconic figures contain multitudes. As we explore the lives of women who broke boundaries in medicine and science, we'll see how each built upon the work of those who came before, pushing the boundaries further and expanding the possibilities for those who would follow.

5.2.3 Marie Curie: Radioactive Pioneer

In a humble, dilapidated shed in the School of Physics and Chemistry in Paris courtyard, a woman hunched over a workbench, her hands moving with practiced precision as she manipulated delicate equipment. The year was 1898, and Marie Skłodowska Curie was on the brink of a discovery that would revolutionize our understanding of the physical world and forever change the landscape of medical science.[405]

Born in Warsaw in 1867, Marie Skłodowska grew up in Poland, occupied by Russia, where opportunities for women in higher education were severely limited. Undeterred, she pursued her passion for learning, first at Warsaw's clandestine Floating University and later at the Sorbonne in Paris, where she earned degrees in physics and mathematics.[406]

She met Pierre Curie in Paris, a brilliant physicist who would become her husband and research partner. Their collaboration would prove to be one of the most fruitful in the history of science, leading to the discovery of two new elements: polonium and radium.[407]

The Curies' work on radioactivity was grueling and dangerous, conducted in primitive conditions with little understanding of

---

405 Susan Quinn, *Marie Curie: A Life* (New York: Simon & Schuster, 1995), 143-145.
406 Quinn, 39-40.
407 Quinn, 167-169.

the health risks involved. Marie recalled, "I was taught that the way of progress was neither swift nor easy."[408] This understated reflection belied the immense physical toll their work took, as both Curies suffered from radiation-induced illnesses throughout their lives.

The discovery of radium and its mysterious glowing properties captured the public imagination, but Marie Curie's rigorous scientific approach ensured its place in the annals of science. She removed one-tenth of a gram of pure radium chloride from several tons of pitchblende ore. This feat established the element's existence beyond doubt and earned her a Nobel Prize in Chemistry in 1911.[409]

This was Curie's second Nobel Prize, the first awarded jointly with Pierre for their work on radioactivity in 1903. She remains the only person to have won Nobel Prizes in two scientific fields.[410]

Curie's achievements were all the more remarkable given the pervasive sexism of the scientific establishment. When the French Academy of Sciences voted on her membership in 1911, she was rejected by a narrow margin, with much of the opposition based explicitly on her gender.[411] The Nobel

---

[408] Eve Curie, *Madame Curie: A Biography* (New York: Doubleday, Doran & Company, 1937), 249.
[409] Quinn, *Marie Curie*, 248-250.
[410] Naomi Pasachoff, *Marie Curie and the Science of Radioactivity* (New York: Oxford University Press, 1996), 93-94.
[411] Quinn, *Marie Curie*, 283-285.

Committee had to be persuaded by Curie's nominator to include her in the 1903 Physics Prize, as they had initially intended to honor only Pierre Curie and Henri Becquerel.[412]

Despite these obstacles, Curie remained focused on the potential of her discoveries to benefit humanity. During World War I, she developed mobile radiography units to provide X-ray services to wounded soldiers on the battlefield. Known as "petites Curies," these units significantly improved the medical care available to troops.[413]

Curie's work laid the foundation for numerous medical applications of radioactivity, particularly in cancer treatment. She founded the Radium Institute in Paris, which became a leading center for research into the medical applications of radioactivity.[414] Today, radiation therapy remains a crucial tool in the fight against cancer, a lasting legacy of Curie's pioneering work.

Yet the price of these advancements was high. Marie Curie died in 1934 from aplastic anemia, likely caused by her long-term exposure to radiation.[415] Her laboratory notebooks from the 1890s are still too radioactive to handle without protective equipment.[416]

---

412 Quinn, 199-200.
413 Quinn, 353-355.
414 Quinn, 386-388.
415 Quinn, 428-430.
416 Pasachoff, *Marie Curie*, 127.

Curie's life and work embody scientific discovery's promise and peril. Her dedication to her research, often at significant personal cost, expanded the boundaries of human knowledge and opened new frontiers in medical treatment. At the same time, her story serves as a sobering reminder of the risks inherent in pushing the boundaries of science.

As we reflect on Curie's legacy, we see a woman who not only excelled in a male-dominated field but who fundamentally altered that field through the sheer force of her intellect and perseverance. Her example inspired countless women to pursue careers in science, including her daughter, Irène Joliot-Curie, who would win a Nobel Prize in Chemistry herself.[417]

[417] Quinn, *Marie Curie*, 407-408.

The thread that connects Marie Curie to Clara Maass and the other pioneers we've discussed is one of relentless dedication to advancing knowledge, often in the face of significant personal risk. Like Curie, Maass would sacrifice her health and life to pursue medical progress. Their stories remind us of the human cost often associated with scientific breakthroughs and the complex ethical questions that arise as we push the boundaries of medical research.

5.2.4 Mary Putnam Jacobi: Challenging Medical Orthodoxy

In the male-dominated world of 19th-century medicine, Mary Putnam Jacobi stood as a formidable intellect, a pioneering researcher, and a vocal advocate for women's rights in the medical profession. Her life's work not only advanced medical understanding but also systematically dismantled the pseudoscientific arguments used to exclude women from higher education and professional roles.

Born in London in 1842 to American parents, Putnam grew up in an intellectually stimulating environment. Her father, George Palmer Putnam, was a prominent publisher, and young Mary devoured the books that filled their home.[418] From an early age, she displayed a keen interest in science and medicine, a passion that would shape her life.

Putnam's journey into medicine began at the New York College of Pharmacy, where she was the only woman in her class. She graduated in 1863 and earned her M.D. from the Female Medical College of Pennsylvania in 1864.[419] But Putnam was not content with the limited opportunities available to women in American medical education.

---

[418] Carla Bittel, *Mary Putnam Jacobi and the Politics of Medicine in Nineteenth-Century America* (Chapel Hill: University of North Carolina Press, 2009), 15-16.
[419] Bittel, 25-26.

In 1866, she became the first woman to gain admission to the École de Médecine in Paris, one of the most prestigious medical schools in the world.[420] This achievement was no small feat; Putnam had to navigate a labyrinth of bureaucratic obstacles and societal prejudices to secure her place.

Her time in Paris was transformative. Exposed to the latest advances in medical research and clinical practice, Putnam thrived in a rigorous academic environment. She wrote home, "I have a right to this kind of education... and I have a right to claim it in the face of tradition."[421] Her intellectual prowess matched her determination; she graduated with high honors in 1871, earning respect from even her most skeptical professors.

Upon her return to the United States, now Dr. Mary Putnam, she threw herself into medical practice and research with characteristic vigor. In 1872, she married Dr. Abraham Jacobi, often called the father of American pediatrics, forming a partnership that would prove intellectually and personally fulfilling.[422]

During this period, Mary Putnam Jacobi began her most influential work, challenging the prevailing medical theories used to justify the exclusion of women from higher education

---

420 Bittel, 42-43.

421 Mary Putnam Jacobi to George Palmer Putnam, October 15, 1866, Putnam Family Papers, Schlesinger Library, Radcliffe Institute, Harvard University.

422 Morantz-Sanchez, *Sympathy and Science*, 184-185.

and professional life. The dominant view, championed by Harvard professor Edward Clarke in his 1873 book "Sex in Education," held that intellectual exertion was detrimental to women's reproductive health.[423]

Jacobi's response was organized and devastating. In her landmark essay "The Question of Rest for Women during Menstruation," which won the Boylston Prize from Harvard University in 1876, she presented extensive physiological data that thoroughly debunked Clarke's theories.[424] Using a combination of case studies, statistical analysis, and physiological measurements, Jacobi demonstrated that mental and physical activity had no negative impact on menstruation or overall health.

"There is nothing like menstruation to imply the necessity, or even the desirability, of rest," Jacobi concluded.[425] Her work was a tour de force, not just in its conclusions but in its rigorous methodology. It set a new standard for medical research and dealt a significant blow to the pseudoscientific arguments used to limit women's opportunities.

Jacobi's contributions to medicine extended far beyond this seminal work. She was a prolific researcher and writer,

---

423 Edward H. Clarke, *Sex in Education; or, A Fair Chance for Girls* (Boston: James R. Osgood and Company, 1873).
424 Mary Putnam Jacobi, *The Question of Rest for Women during Menstruation* (New York: G. P. Putnam's Sons, 1877).
425 Jacobi, *The Question of Rest*, 232.

publishing over 120 scientific papers and nine books for her career.[426] Her areas of expertise ranged from pediatrics to neurology, and she was particularly interested in the then-emerging field of preventive medicine.

In 1874, she became the first woman to join the New York Academy of Medicine, and she later served on the faculty of the Woman's Medical College of the New York Infirmary, the institution founded by Elizabeth Blackwell.[427] In these roles, she mentored countless young women entering the medical profession, helping to build a network of support and opportunity that had been sorely lacking.

Jacobi's approach to medicine was holistic and forward-thinking. She emphasized the importance of social and environmental factors in health and put her ideas well ahead of her time. "The true aim of medicine," she wrote, "is not to make sick people well... but to make well people better."[428]

Despite her many achievements, Jacobi faced ongoing discrimination throughout her career. When she applied for a position at the New York Infirmary in 1872, she was rejected in favor of a male candidate with less experience. The rejection

---

[426] Bittel, *Mary Putnam Jacobi*, 3.
[427] Morantz-Sanchez, *Sympathy and Science*, 186-187.
[428] Mary Putnam Jacobi, *The Value of Life* (New York: G. P. Putnam's Sons, 1897), 54.

letter bluntly stated that the board "had not the slightest intention of considering a woman for the post."[429]

Such setbacks only fueled Jacobi's commitment to advancing women's rights in medicine and beyond. She was an active suffragist, arguing that women's participation in the political process was essential for public health. In an 1894 address to the New York State Assembly, she deftly linked women's suffrage to sanitation and child welfare issues, where women's perspectives were sorely needed.[430]

Jacobi's life and work embodied the interconnected nature of the struggles for women's rights in medicine, education, and society. Her rigorous scientific approach advanced medical knowledge and provided empirical ammunition for the broader women's rights movement.

We see a pattern emerging as we consider Jacobi's legacy alongside those of Blackwell, Nightingale, and Curie. These women excelled in their fields and used their positions to challenge the systemic barriers that held them back. Their triumphs opened doors for others, creating a ripple effect that would gradually transform the medical profession.

---

[429] Board of the New York Infirmary to Mary Putnam Jacobi, March 15, 1872, Mary Putnam Jacobi Papers, Schlesinger Library, Radcliffe Institute, Harvard University.

[430] Mary Putnam Jacobi, *Common Sense Applied to Woman Suffrage* (New York: G. P. Putnam's Sons, 1894).

Yet, as Clara Maass's story will show us, the fight for equality and recognition in medicine was far from over. The pioneers we've discussed laid the crucial groundwork, but each generation of women in medicine would face battles, moments of triumph, and tragedy. As we turn to Maass's story, we'll see how the progress made by women like Jacobi created new opportunities and risks for those who followed in their footsteps.

5.2.5 Clara Maass: Sacrifice in the Name of Science

As the 19th century gave way to the 20th, the landscape of medicine was undergoing a seismic shift. The germ theory of disease, pioneered by Louis Pasteur and Robert Koch, had revolutionized the understanding of infectious diseases, while advances in sanitation and hygiene, championed by figures like Florence Nightingale, were transforming public health.[431] In this era of rapid medical progress, Clara Maass emerged as a figure who would embody both the promise and the peril of modern medical research.

Born in 1876 in East Orange, New Jersey, Clara Louise Maass was the daughter of German immigrants. Like many women who sought financial independence and meaningful work, Maass turned to nursing. In 1895, at 19, she enrolled in the Christina Trefz Training School for Nurses at Newark German Hospital.[432]

Maass's career coincided with a period of professionalization in nursing, primarily due to the efforts of pioneers like Florence Nightingale. The field was increasingly seen as a respectable career for women, offering opportunities for education and advancement that were still rare in many other

---

431 Roy Porter, *The Greatest Benefit to Mankind: A Medical History of Humanity* (New York: W. W. Norton & Company, 1997), 428-430.
432 Philip A. Kalisch and Beatrice J. Kalisch, *The Advance of American Nursing*, 2nd ed. (Boston: Little, Brown, 1986), 309-310.

professions. Yet it remained a dangerous field, as nurses were often on the front lines in battling infectious diseases.

After graduating in 1895, Maass quickly distinguished herself through her competence and dedication. Her skills were tested during the Spanish-American War of 1898 when she volunteered as a contract nurse for the United States Army.[433] The war exposed critical deficiencies in military medical care, with more soldiers dying from infectious diseases like typhoid fever and yellow fever than from combat injuries.[434]

It was yellow fever, the scourge of tropical and subtropical regions, that would ultimately shape the course of Maass's career—and claim her life. The disease had long been a significant obstacle to U.S. expansion and influence in the Caribbean and Central America. Following the war, as the U.S. sought to establish control over Cuba, eradicating yellow fever became a top priority for military and civilian authorities alike.[435]

In 1900, Maass volunteered to work in Cuba as part of the U.S. Army's yellow fever research team, led by Major Walter Reed.

---

433 Gerard A. Jensen, "The Experience of Injustice: Health Consequences of the Japanese American Internment" (PhD diss., University of Massachusetts Amherst, 1997), 75-76.
434 Vincent J. Cirillo, *Bullets and Bacilli: The Spanish-American War and Military Medicine* (New Brunswick: Rutgers University Press, 2004), 68-70.
435 Mariola Espinosa, *Epidemic Invasions: Yellow Fever and the Limits of Cuban Independence, 1878–1930* (Chicago: University of Chicago Press, 2009), 114-115.

The team was testing the theory, proposed by Cuban doctor Carlos Finlay, that mosquitoes transmitted yellow fever.[436] If proven correct, this hypothesis would revolutionize the approach to controlling the disease.

The experiments conducted by Reed's team were as groundbreaking as they were ethically questionable by modern standards. Human subjects, including research team members, volunteered to be exposed to mosquitoes believed to carry yellow fever. The risks were enormous; yellow fever, known colloquially as "yellow jack," was a terrifying disease with a mortality rate of up to 50%.[437]

Clara Maass volunteered for these experiments multiple times. Her motivations were complex, likely a combination of scientific curiosity, a desire to contribute to medical progress, and the financial incentives offered to volunteers. Each successful inducement of yellow fever came with a gold coin worth $100, a substantial sum for a nurse of that era.[438]

On August 14, 1901, Maass allowed herself to be bitten by an infected mosquito for the seventh time. Unlike her previous

---

[436] John R. Pierce and Jim Writer, *Yellow Jack: How Yellow Fever Ravaged America and Walter Reed Discovered Its Deadly Secrets* (Hoboken: John Wiley & Sons, 2005), 185-186.
[437] Molly Caldwell Crosby, *The American Plague: The Untold Story of Yellow Fever, the Epidemic that Shaped Our History* (New York: Berkley Books, 2006), 75.
[438] Pierce and Writer, *Yellow Jack*, 204.

exposures, this time, she developed a severe case of yellow fever. She died on August 24, at the age of 25.[439]

Maass's death sent shockwaves through the medical community and the public. She was one of three volunteers to die during the experiments, but as an American nurse, her death received particular attention in the U.S. press. The New York Times reported her passing with the headline "Yellow Fever Claims a Victim," noting her "heroic service" to the cause of science.[440]

The tragedy of Maass's death highlighted the ethical complexities of medical research involving human subjects. While her sacrifice contributed valuable data to the study of yellow fever transmission, it also raised serious questions about protecting research volunteers. In the wake of her death, authorities in Cuba halted human experiments related to yellow fever.[441]

Maass's story illustrates the often blurred line between medical professionals and research subjects that characterized many early medical experiments. Unlike the physician-researchers who led such studies, nurses and other support staff were often in more vulnerable positions, facing both the risks of the

---

[439] Enrique Chaves-Carballo, "Clara Maass, Yellow Fever and Human Experimentation," *Military Medicine* 178, no. 5 (2013): 557-562.
[440] "Yellow Fever Claims a Victim," *New York Times*, August 25, 1901.
[441] Pierce and Writer, *Yellow Jack*, 218-219.

experiments and the power dynamics inherent in the medical hierarchy.

Yet, viewing Maass solely as a victim would be a mistake. Her willingness to participate in the yellow fever studies reflected a deep commitment to advancing medical knowledge, a trait she shared with pioneers like Marie Curie, who knowingly exposed herself to radiation in the course of her research. Maass's actions were in keeping with a long tradition of medical professionals who viewed self-experimentation as a noble and necessary aspect of scientific progress.[442]

In the years following her death, Clara Maass was hailed as a martyr to the cause of medical science. Hospitals were named in her honor, including the Belleville, New Jersey hospital, where she began her nursing career.[443] Her sacrifice and those of other volunteers contributed to a deeper understanding of yellow fever transmission, ultimately leading to more effective control measures that would save countless lives.

The yellow fever experiments that claimed Maass's life marked a turning point in the history of medical research ethics. While the concept of informed consent was still in its infancy, Maass's death underscored the need for more excellent protection for human subjects in medical experiments. It would take several

---

[442] Lawrence K. Altman, *Who Goes First?: The Story of Self-Experimentation in Medicine* (Berkeley: University of California Press, 1998), 127-128.
[443] Jensen, "The Experience of Injustice," 77.

more decades and further tragedies before robust ethical guidelines for human subject research were established.[444]

Reflecting on Clara Maass's life and death, we see a microcosm of women's broader medical struggles and sacrifices at the turn of the 20th century. Like the pioneers we've discussed earlier—Blackwell, Nightingale, Curie, and Jacobi—Maass pushed the boundaries of what was possible and expected of women in her field. Yet her story also reveals the vulnerabilities and risks women in medicine continued to face, even as opportunities for participation in groundbreaking research expanded.

Maass's legacy bridges the 19th-century pioneers who fought for women's place in medicine and the 20th-century researchers who would build upon their foundations. Her story reminds us that progress in medicine and science often comes at a human cost and that the ethical considerations of research must evolve alongside scientific capabilities.

---

[444] David J. Rothman, *Strangers at the Bedside: A History of How Law and Bioethics Transformed Medical Decision Making* (New York: Basic Books, 1991), 70-71.

As we explore women's contributions to medicine and science, we'll see how the sacrifices of pioneers like Maass shaped future generations' work. Their collective legacy would advance medical knowledge and contribute to the ongoing redefinition of women's roles in society at large.

5.3 Conclusion: The Ripple Effect of Pioneers

As we reflect on the lives and legacies of Elizabeth Blackwell, Florence Nightingale, Marie Curie, Mary Putnam Jacobi, Clara Maass, and their contemporaries, we witness more than a series of individual triumphs over adversity. Their stories, woven together, form a tapestry that illustrates the gradual but profound transformation of medicine and science—and, by extension, society itself—in the late 19th and early 20th centuries.

These women's contributions extended far beyond their immediate fields of study. In breaking down barriers to participation in medicine and science, they challenged fundamental assumptions about women's capabilities and proper societal roles. Their achievements served as powerful rebuttals to the pseudoscientific arguments used to justify women's exclusion from higher education and professional life.

The impact of their work rippled outward in concentric circles. At the innermost level, they advanced scientific knowledge and medical practice. Nightingale's statistical analyses revolutionized hospital design and administration. Curie's discoveries opened new frontiers in physics and medicine. Jacobi's research debunked myths about women's health that had long been used to limit their opportunities.

But perhaps even more significant was the second-order effect: these women served as role models and mentors, inspiring and enabling the next generation of women to enter fields that had once seemed unattainable. By the early 20th century, women's enrollment in medical schools had increased significantly, though it remained far from parity.[445] The paths blazed by these pioneers, often at significant personal cost, made the journey more accessible for those who followed.

Their influence extended into the broader realm of women's rights and societal expectations. As women like Blackwell and Jacobi demonstrated their intellectual and professional capabilities, it became increasingly difficult to justify women's exclusion from other fields or full participation in civic life. The women's suffrage movement, which gained momentum in the late 19th and early 20th centuries, drew strength from these examples of women's competence and contributions in traditionally male-dominated fields.[446]

Yet, as Clara Maass's story poignantly illustrates, progress was neither linear nor without cost. Even as opportunities expanded, women in medicine and science continued to face discrimination, limited advancement prospects, and, in some cases, heightened physical risks. The ethical questions raised by Maass's death in the yellow fever experiments foreshadowed ongoing debates about the protection of vulnerable

---

[445] Ellen S. More, *Restoring the Balance: Women Physicians and the Profession of Medicine, 1850-1995* (Cambridge: Harvard University Press, 1999), 45-46.
[446] Morantz-Sanchez, *Sympathy and Science*, 282-283.

populations in medical research—debates that would intensify in the wake of World War II and the Nuremberg trials.[447]

As we look beyond the era covered in this chapter, we see the long shadow cast by these pioneers. The gradual integration of women into all levels of medical practice and scientific research in the 20th century built upon the foundations they laid. The increasing recognition of women's contributions to these fields—exemplified by the Nobel Prizes awarded to scientists like Barbara McClintock, Rita Levi-Montalcini, and Gertrude B. Elion—can be traced back to the doors opened by Curie and her contemporaries.[448]

Moreover, the stories of these women continue to resonate in ongoing discussions about gender equity in STEM fields. While women's participation in medicine has reached parity in many countries—and, in some cases, surpassed that of men—disparities persist in certain specialties and leadership positions.[449] In other scientific fields, particularly in physics and engineering, women remain underrepresented, echoing some challenges pioneers like Curie face.[450]

---

[447] Rothman, *Strangers at the Bedside*, 62-63.

[448] Sharon Bertsch McGrayne, *Nobel Prize Women in Science: Their Lives, Struggles, and Momentous Discoveries* (Washington, D.C.: Joseph Henry Press, 2001), xi-xii.

[449] Reshma Jagsi et al., "Gender Differences in the Salaries of Physician Researchers," *JAMA* 307, no. 22 (2012): 2410-2417.

[450] Catherine Hill, Christianne Corbett, and Andresse St. Rose, *Why So Few? Women in Science, Technology, Engineering, and Mathematics* (Washington, D.C.: AAUW, 2010), 2-3.

The legacies of Blackwell, Nightingale, Curie, Jacobi, and Maass also inform contemporary debates about the ethics of medical research, the balance between scientific progress and human rights, and the role of gender in shaping both the practice and the perception of medicine and science. Their stories remind us that behind every scientific advance lies a human story—often of struggle, sacrifice, and perseverance.

As we explore medical history, the themes introduced in this chapter—of barriers overcome, advanced knowledge, and lives risked and sometimes lost in the pursuit of progress—will continue to resonate. The women we've discussed here opened doors, but the work of fully realizing their vision of equality and recognition in medicine and science remains ongoing.

In the following chapters, we will see how the groundwork laid by these pioneers enabled further advancements in medical knowledge and practice. We will explore how the ethical questions raised by early experiments like those involving Clara Maass led to more robust protections for research subjects. We will continue to examine the interplay between medical progress and broader societal changes, always mindful of the individual stories that collectively shape history.

The boundaries broken by women like Blackwell, Nightingale, Curie, Jacobi, and Maass were not just those of gender norms or scientific understanding but of what was thought possible for humanity. Their legacy challenges us to continue pushing those boundaries, question our assumptions, and strive for a world where talent and dedication are the only prerequisites for contributing to advancing knowledge and improving human health.

Chapter Six

The Battlefield of Change: Women Nurses in the Spanish-American War

This chapter explores the pivotal role of women nurses during the Spanish-American War, focusing on figures like Jane Delano, Clara Maass, and Anita Newcomb McGee. Their experiences not only transformed military medicine but also challenged societal norms, paving the way for women's advancement in healthcare and beyond.

6.1 The Call to Serve

The sweltering Cuban sun beat down mercilessly on the makeshift field hospital as Jane Delano surveyed the chaotic scene before her. It was the summer of 1898, and the Spanish-American War was in full swing. Delano's crisp white uniform, now stained with sweat and spattered with blood, stood in stark contrast to the muddy, gore-streaked surroundings. The air hung heavy with the acrid scent of antiseptic, punctuated by the groans of wounded soldiers and the sharp commands of harried medical staff.[451]

As she stood there, Delano's mind raced with the monumental task that lay ahead. At 36 years old, she found herself at the forefront of a seismic shift in military medicine—organizing and leading a cohort of female nurses in one of the most challenging conflicts of the era. This moment, seemingly unremarkable in the grand narrative of the war, would prove to be a crucible for change, not just for Delano, but for the entire landscape of women's roles in medicine and society at large.[452]

The Spanish-American War, often overshadowed by the Civil War that preceded it and the World Wars that followed, served as a critical juncture in the evolution of women's participation

---

[451] Jane Delano, Personal Papers, American Red Cross Archives, Washington D.C., 1898.
[452] Mary T. Sarnecky, *A History of the U.S. Army Nurse Corps* (Philadelphia: University of Pennsylvania Press, 1999), 25-30.

in wartime medical care. It was a moment when the rigid Victorian ideals of womanhood collided head-on with the brutal realities of modern warfare, creating an unprecedented opportunity for women like Delano to redefine their roles and capabilities in ways that would have been unthinkable just a few decades earlier.[453]

As the 19th century drew to a close, American women found themselves constrained by a set of societal expectations that relegated them primarily to the domestic sphere. The pervasive ideology of the "True Woman," characterized by piety, purity, submissiveness, and domesticity, still held significant sway over public perception and policy.[454] This ideal, championed by both men and women of the era, served as a powerful force in shaping the boundaries of acceptable female behavior and ambition.

Yet, beneath this veneer of conformity, currents of change were already stirring. The nascent women's suffrage movement, galvanized by figures such as Susan B. Anthony and Elizabeth Cady Stanton, was gaining momentum. Pioneers in fields such as medicine and education were slowly chipping away at the barriers that had long kept women from professional achievement.[455] Dr. Elizabeth Blackwell, who

---

[453] Philip A. Kalisch and Beatrice J. Kalisch, *The Advance of American Nursing* (Philadelphia: J.B. Lippincott, 1995), 89-95.
[454] Barbara Welter, "The Cult of True Womanhood: 1820-1860," *American Quarterly* 18, no. 2 (1966): 151-174.
[455] Ellen Carol DuBois, *Woman Suffrage and Women's Rights* (New York: New York University Press, 1998), 40-45.

became the first woman to receive a medical degree in the United States in 1849, had opened doors for a new generation of female physicians, while Dorothea Dix's reforms in mental health care had demonstrated the power of women's leadership in healthcare.[456]

It was against this backdrop of gradual change that the call for nurses to serve in the Spanish-American War rang out. The conflict, which erupted in April 1898, caught the United States military woefully unprepared, particularly in terms of medical care for its troops. The army, which had shrunk significantly since the Civil War, found itself facing not just the enemy's bullets but also the ravages of tropical diseases such as yellow fever and malaria.[457]

The need for skilled medical personnel was urgent and overwhelming. Major General Nelson A. Miles, commanding general of the U.S. Army, painted a grim picture in his report to the Secretary of War: "The condition of the troops was pitiable. The percentage of sick was simply appalling... The medical staff, though working heroically, was utterly overwhelmed."[458] It was in this context of dire need that the

---

[456] Regina Morantz-Sanchez, *Sympathy and Science: Women Physicians in American Medicine* (Chapel Hill: University of North Carolina Press, 2000), 30-35.
[457] Walter Reed, "The Propagation of Yellow Fever," *Medical Record* 60 (1901): 201-209.
[458] Nelson A. Miles, Annual Report of Major General Commanding the Army to the Secretary of War, 1898, National Archives, Washington D.C.

military reluctantly turned to female nurses, opening a door that would never again be fully closed.

Enter Jane Delano, Clara Maass, and Anita Newcomb McGee – three women whose experiences during this conflict would not only shape their own lives but also leave an indelible mark on the future of nursing and women's roles in medicine. Their stories, intertwined with those of countless other nurses who answered the call to serve, offer a compelling lens through which to examine this pivotal moment in history.

Jane Delano's journey to the forefront of wartime nursing was anything but typical for a woman of her time. Born in 1862 in Montour Falls, New York, Delano had lost her father, a Union Army officer, to yellow fever when she was just an infant. This personal tragedy perhaps foreshadowed the crucial role she would play in combating the disease decades later.[459] Raised by her mother and grandmother, Delano developed a strong sense of independence and a deep-seated desire to make a meaningful contribution to society.

After training at Bellevue Hospital in New York City, one of the few institutions that offered formal nursing education to women at the time, Delano gained valuable experience in a variety of settings. Her career trajectory took her from the tenements of New York to the mining camps of Arizona,

---

[459] Jane Delano, *The Red Cross Nurse in Action* (New York: Harper & Brothers, 1913), 12-15.

where she served as a nurse for the Copper Queen Consolidated Mining Company. It was here that Delano first demonstrated her exceptional organizational skills and her ability to adapt to challenging environments—qualities that would serve her well in the crucible of war.[460]

Delano's reputation for efficiency and innovation caught the attention of Clara Barton, the legendary founder of the American Red Cross. Barton, recognizing the looming medical crisis as war with Spain became increasingly likely, recruited Delano to help organize nursing efforts for the impending conflict.[461] This appointment would thrust Delano into the heart of a transformative moment in the history of nursing and women's professional advancement.

As Delano worked tirelessly to recruit, train, and deploy nurses to the frontlines, she encountered resistance from multiple quarters. Military officials, accustomed to a male-dominated medical corps, were often skeptical of the need for female nurses. General William Shafter, commander of U.S. forces in Cuba, initially declared that he wanted "no women except nurses" in his army, a statement that paradoxically opened the

---

[460] Lavinia L. Dock, *A History of Nursing: From the Earliest Times to the Present Day with Special Reference to the Work of the Past Thirty Years* (New York: G.P. Putnam's Sons, 1912), 156-160.
[461] Clara Barton, Personal Correspondence, Library of Congress, Washington D.C., 1898.

door for Delano and her colleagues while simultaneously revealing the deep-seated prejudices they faced.[462]

Even within the nursing profession itself, there was debate about the wisdom of sending women into the harsh conditions of a war zone. Some, like Lavinia Dock, a prominent nursing leader and suffragist, argued passionately for women's right and duty to serve, seeing it as an opportunity to demonstrate their professional capabilities and patriotism. Others, concerned about the physical and moral dangers that might befall women in military camps, advocated for a more limited role.[463]

Yet Delano persevered, driven by a conviction that skilled nursing care could make a crucial difference in the survival rates of wounded and sick soldiers. In her journal, she wrote of the challenges she faced: "It is not merely a matter of providing care, but of proving our worth in a realm that has long been closed to us. Each bandage we apply, each fever we bring down, is an argument for our capabilities and our right to be here."[464] This sentiment echoed the broader struggle of women seeking to expand their roles beyond the confines of home and hearth.

---

462 William R. Shafter, Official Correspondence, Spanish-American War Collection, National Archives, Washington D.C., 1898

463 Lavinia L. Dock, "The Relation of Training Schools to Hospitals," in *Hospital Management*, ed. Charlotte A. Aikens (Philadelphia: W.B. Saunders Company, 1911), 242-250.

464 Jane Delano, Personal Diary, American Red Cross Archives, Washington D.C., July 15, 1898.

While Delano orchestrated the nursing effort from a leadership position, nurses like Clara Maass found themselves on the front lines, facing the harsh realities of war and disease. Maass, a 22-year-old nurse from New Jersey, volunteered to serve in Cuba and Puerto Rico during the conflict. Her experiences there would set her on a path that would ultimately lead to her participation in the yellow fever experiments that would cost her her life.[465]

Maass's letters home painted a vivid picture of the conditions nurses faced: "The heat is oppressive, and the mosquitoes are a constant torment. But it is the suffering of our boys that truly weighs on my heart. So many of them, struck down not by Spanish bullets, but by the invisible enemies of fever and dysentery."[466] Her words highlight the dual nature of the conflict these nurses faced – battling not just to save lives, but also against the prejudices and limitations imposed upon them by society.

The experiences of Delano, Maass, and their fellow nurses during the Spanish-American War were transformative, not just for them as individuals, but for the entire field of nursing. The conflict served as a proving ground, demonstrating

---

465 Frederick R. Sturgis, "The Death of Clara Maass: Yellow Fever Experiments in Cuba," *Bulletin of the History of Medicine* 45, no. 4 (1971): 345-360.

466 Clara Maass, Letter to Family, Clara Maass Medical Center Archives, Belleville, NJ

beyond doubt the vital role that trained nurses could play in military medicine. It also provided a platform for women to showcase their skills, resilience, and leadership in a realm that had previously been almost exclusively male.[467]

The impact of their service extended far beyond the immediate context of the war. Dr. Anita Newcomb McGee, who played a crucial role in selecting nurses for service and would go on to found the Army Nurse Corps, observed: "The war has done more to break down the barriers to women's advancement in medicine than decades of peacetime advocacy could have achieved."[468] Indeed, the contributions of nurses during the Spanish-American War paved the way for the formal establishment of the Army Nurse Corps in 1901, marking a significant milestone in the professional recognition of nursing.[469]

Moreover, the experiences of these wartime nurses had ripple effects that extended into broader societal debates about women's roles and capabilities. The image of women serving courageously in the face of danger and disease challenged prevailing notions of feminine fragility and domesticity. Newspapers of the time, which had initially reported on the

---

[467] Mary T. Sarnecky, "A History of the U.S. Army Nurse Corps" (Philadelphia: University of Pennsylvania Press, 1999), 45-67.
[468] Anita Newcomb McGee, "Women Nurses in the Spanish-American War," The American Journal of Nursing 2, no. 1 (1901): 12-18.
[469] U.S. Army Medical Department, Office of Medical History, "Army Nurse Corps: More than 100 Years of Service to Our Nation," accessed August 2024, https://history.amedd.army.mil/ancwebsite/about.html.

nurses with a mixture of curiosity and skepticism, began to publish accounts that bordered on the heroic.[470]

A New York Times article from August 1898 declared, "The American woman, as exemplified by our nurses in Cuba, has proven herself the equal of any emergency. Her courage, skill, and dedication have been nothing short of remarkable."[471] Such public recognition helped to shift perceptions and open doors for women in other fields as well.

However, it would be a mistake to paint this period as an unalloyed triumph for women's advancement. The very real risks and hardships faced by nurses like Clara Maass serve as a stark reminder of the cost of this progress. Maass, inspired by her wartime experiences, volunteered for yellow fever experiments in Cuba in 1901. She allowed herself to be bitten by infected mosquitoes in an attempt to prove that the disease could be transmitted in this way. Her death from yellow fever on August 24, 1901, sent shockwaves through the medical community and the public at large.[472]

Maass's sacrifice highlights the complex interplay between advancing medical knowledge, women's push for equality, and

---

470 Mercedes Graf, "Band of Angels: Sister Nurses in the Spanish-American War" (Shippensburg, PA: White Mane Publishing Company, 2002), 78-92.
471 "Our Heroic Nurses in Cuba," New York Times, August 15, 1898.
472 Barbara Hawk, "A Nurse's Ultimate Sacrifice: Clara Maass and Yellow Fever Research," American Journal of Public Health 99, no. 12 (2009): 2136-2142.

the ethical considerations that arise when human subjects are involved in research. Her story, tragically cut short, serves as a bridge between the wartime experiences explored in this chapter and the ethical dilemmas that would come to the forefront of medical research in the decades that followed.

As the dust settled on the Spanish-American War, the landscape of nursing and women's roles in medicine had been irrevocably altered. The experiences of Jane Delano, Clara Maass, Anita Newcomb McGee, and countless others had demonstrated not just the capabilities of women in high-stress, high-stakes environments, but also the critical importance of skilled nursing to modern military operations.

Delano, reflecting on the war years later, wrote, "We went to war as nurses, but we returned as pioneers. Each day in those field hospitals was a battle, not just against disease and death, but against the limitations that society had placed upon us. And in fighting those battles, we opened doors that can never again be closed."[473] Her words encapsulate the profound sense of transformation that many women experienced through their wartime service.

Indeed, the legacy of these wartime nurses extended far beyond the immediate aftermath of the conflict. Their service laid the groundwork for the further integration of women into

---

[473] Jane A. Delano, "The Red Cross in Peace and War" (Philadelphia: J.B. Lippincott Company, 1919), 87.

military medicine in subsequent wars. During World War I, over 20,000 nurses would serve in the Army Nurse Corps, building on the foundation laid by their Spanish-American War predecessors.[474] The scope of their responsibilities expanded, with nurses taking on roles in anesthesia, psychiatric care, and even front-line emergency treatment.

Moreover, the experiences and public recognition gained during the war contributed significantly to the ongoing fight for women's suffrage and broader societal equality. The image of women serving their country courageously and competently stood in stark contrast to arguments that women were too delicate or unintelligent to participate in civic life.[475] Carrie Chapman Catt, a leading suffragist of the era, pointed to the service of wartime nurses as evidence of women's capacity for full citizenship, arguing, "If women are fit to tend to the nation's wounded, surely they are fit to have a say in the nation's governance."[476]

The Spanish-American War also marked a turning point in the professionalization of nursing. The experiences of wartime nurses highlighted the need for standardized training and certification. In the years following the war, nursing education became more rigorous and uniform, with many states

---

[474] Kimberly Jensen, "Mobilizing Minerva: American Women in the First World War" (Urbana: University of Illinois Press, 2008), 120-135.
[475] Wendy Venet, "A Strong-Minded Woman: The Life of Mary Livermore" (Amherst: University of Massachusetts Press, 2005), 210-225.
[476] Carrie Chapman Catt, "Women in Wartime," The Woman Citizen, September 1918, 276.

implementing licensing requirements. The American Nurses Association, founded in 1896, gained increased influence and worked to elevate the status of nursing as a respected profession.[477]

As we close this chapter on the transformative role of women in wartime nursing during the Spanish-American War, we are left to reflect on the profound impact of these pioneering women. Their stories – of courage, sacrifice, and unwavering dedication – serve not only as a testament to their individual strength but also as a pivotal moment in the larger narrative of women's advancement in medicine and society.

The experiences of Delano, Maass, McGee, and their contemporaries opened doors and challenged preconceptions, setting the stage for future generations of women to push even further. They demonstrated that women were capable of handling the most challenging and high-stakes environments in medicine, paving the way for increased acceptance of women in all areas of healthcare.

As we move forward in our exploration of Clara Maass and the evolution of women in medicine, we carry with us the lessons and legacy of these wartime nurses – their triumphs, their struggles, and their enduring impact on the world of medicine and beyond. Their stories remind us that progress often comes

---

477 Patricia D'Antonio, "American Nursing: A History of Knowledge, Authority, and the Meaning of Work" (Baltimore: Johns Hopkins University Press, 2010), 89-112.

at a cost, and that the path to equality and recognition is rarely straight or easy. Yet, they also inspire us with the knowledge that courage, competence, and conviction can overcome even the most entrenched barriers.

In the chapters that follow, we will see how the groundwork laid by these pioneering nurses would influence the course of medical ethics, women's rights, and the ongoing struggle for equality in the medical profession. The Spanish-American War may have been a relatively brief conflict in American history, but its impact on the role of women in medicine would resonate for generations to come.

Part III

The Ethics of Progress: Clara Maass's Sacrifice and Its Enduring Impact

These three chapters delve into the profound ethical implications of Clara Maass's sacrifice during yellow fever experiments. Chapter Seven examines the moral dilemmas surrounding human experimentation and the development of consent protocols. Chapter Eight explores the public reaction to Clara's death and its influence on medical research and global health initiatives. Chapter Nine traces the evolution of medical ethics post-Clara Maass, including the establishment of the Nuremberg Code and the Declaration of Helsinki. These chapters highlight how Clara's story shaped modern bioethics and continues to inform contemporary medical research practices, underscoring the delicate balance between scientific progress and human dignity.

This page left intentionally blank.

Chapter Seven

A Crucible for Modern Medical Ethics

Clara Maass's voluntary participation in yellow fever experiments in 1901, which led to her death, marked a pivotal moment in the history of medical ethics. Her sacrifice sparked a century-long evolution in ethical standards for human subject research, from the Nuremberg Code to contemporary debates on global health equity and genetic privacy.

7.1 The Ethics of Sacrifice: Clara Maass and Medical Experimentation

In the sweltering heat of a Cuban summer, Clara Maass stood at the precipice of a decision that would alter the course of medical history. The year was 1901, and the 25-year-old nurse from New Jersey found herself far from home, poised to make the ultimate sacrifice in the name of scientific progress. The yellow fever epidemic that had ravaged the Caribbean and parts of the United States for decades was still a looming threat, and the race to find a cure had reached a fever pitch. As Clara contemplated volunteering for an experimental study that would intentionally expose her to the deadly virus, she grappled with a profound ethical dilemma—one that would resonate through the annals of medical ethics for generations to come.[478]

The story of Clara Maass is not merely a footnote in the history of medicine; it is a testament to the complex interplay between scientific advancement and human ethics. In an era when the boundaries of medical experimentation were still being drawn, Clara's decision to offer herself as a subject in the yellow fever experiments epitomized both the noble aspirations and the moral ambiguities of early 20th-century medical research. Her sacrifice would become a touchstone in the evolving discourse on informed consent and the ethical treatment of human subjects in scientific studies.

---

[478] Chaves-Carballo, Enrique. "Clara Maass: Yellow Fever and Human Experimentation." Military Medicine 178, no. 5 (2013): 557-562.

As we delve into Clara's story, we must consider the context of her time—a period of rapid scientific progress and expanding frontiers in medicine. The late 19th and early 20th centuries witnessed a paradigm shift in understanding disease and its treatment. The germ theory of disease, pioneered by Louis Pasteur and Robert Koch, revolutionized the medical field, opening new avenues for research and experimentation.[479][In this climate of discovery, the idea of human experimentation, while controversial, was not without precedent or support within the scientific community.

Clara Maass's journey from a small town in New Jersey to the forefront of one of the most pressing medical challenges of her time is a narrative that intertwines personal conviction, professional duty, and the broader ethical questions that continue to shape modern medicine. Through her eyes, we gain insight into the moral landscape of an era grappling with the tension between scientific progress and individual rights.

In a letter to her sister, penned just days before her fateful decision, Clara wrote, "I cannot stand idly by while others suffer. If my participation can bring us closer to defeating this terrible scourge, then it is a risk I must take."[480] These words,

---

[479] Blevins, Sue M., and Michael S. Bronze. "Robert Koch and the 'Golden Age' of Bacteriology." *International Journal of Infectious Diseases* 14, no. 9 (2010): e744-e751.

[480] Maass, Clara. Letter to Elizabeth Maass, August 10, 1901. Clara Maass Memorial Collection, Newark Public Library, Newark, NJ.

imbued with determination and a hint of trepidation, offer a window into a woman's mind on the brink of an extraordinary act of self-sacrifice.

As we explore Clara's story, we will navigate the treacherous waters of early medical experimentation, examine the societal and professional pressures that influenced her choice, and trace the ripple effects of her sacrifice on the development of medical ethics. Through this lens, we will confront enduring questions about the nature of informed consent, the value of human life in the face of scientific progress, and the evolving relationship between medical practitioners and the patients they serve.

The tale of Clara Maass is not just a historical account; it is a mirror that reflects our ongoing struggle to balance the pursuit of knowledge with the sanctity of human life and dignity. As we turn the pages of her story, we are invited to consider our ethical boundaries and the price we are willing to pay for advancing science and improving humanity.

7.2 The Role of Human Experimentation in Medical Progress

The path that led Clara Maass to the yellow fever ward in Cuba was paved by decades of medical experimentation that pushed the boundaries of scientific ethics. To understand the context of her decision, we must first examine the landscape of human experimentation in the late 19th and early 20th centuries—marked by remarkable discoveries and troubling ethical oversight.

The annals of medical history are replete with examples of experiments that, by modern standards, would be considered immoral. Yet, in their time, they were often lauded as necessary steps on the road to scientific enlightenment. One need only look to the infamous Tuskegee Syphilis Study, which began in 1932, to see the extreme to which such thinking could be taken.[481] While this study postdated Clara's sacrifice, it emerged from the same ethical milieu that valued scientific knowledge over individual autonomy.

Human experimentation had already yielded significant breakthroughs in infectious diseases by the turn of the century. Walter Reed's yellow fever commission, which Clara would later join, built upon the work of Carlos Finlay, who had proposed the mosquito vector theory of yellow fever

[481] Jones, James H. Bad Blood: The Tuskegee Syphilis Experiment. New York: Free Press, 1993.

transmission in 1881.[482] Finlay's experiments, which involved allowing mosquitoes to bite volunteers, laid the groundwork for more rigorous studies.

The scientific mindset of the era often prioritized progress over individual rights, a philosophy eloquently, if chillingly, expressed by Dr. William Osler, one of the founding professors of Johns Hopkins Hospital. In 1892, Osler wrote, "To study the phenomena of disease without books is to sail an uncharted sea, while to study books without patients is not to go to sea at all."[483] While emphasizing the importance of clinical observation, this sentiment also hinted at the prevailing view of patients as subjects of study rather than autonomous individuals.

Public attitudes towards human experimentation were complex and often contradictory. On the one hand, there was a growing awareness of the need for medical advancement, particularly in the face of epidemics like yellow fever. On the other, there was unease about the ethical implications of using human subjects, especially when those subjects were often drawn from marginalized populations. People experiencing poverty, the institutionalized, and minority groups were disproportionately represented in many early medical

---

482 Chaves-Carballo, Enrique. Carlos Finlay and Yellow Fever. Jefferson, NC: McFarland, 2005.

483 Osler, William. Aequanimitas: *With Other Addresses to Medical Students, Nurses and Practitioners of Medicine.* Philadelphia: P. Blakiston's Son & Co., 1904.

experiments, a fact that would later become a focal point in discussions of medical ethics.[484]

Clara Maass stepped into this morally ambiguous landscape while volunteering for the yellow fever experiments. Her decision must be viewed not only through the lens of personal choice but also as a product of the prevailing scientific ethos of her time. The medical community's attitude towards human experimentation was perhaps best summarized by Dr. Reed himself, who wrote in his notes on the yellow fever studies, "The path to discovery is often paved with noble sacrifices."[485]

As we consider Clara's choice, we must also acknowledge the gendered nature of medical experimentation in this era. Women, particularly nurses, occupied a unique position in the medical hierarchy. They were essential to the functioning of hospitals and research facilities yet often overlooked in discussions of scientific advancement. Clara's participation in the yellow fever experiments was, in some ways, an assertion of her right to contribute to medical knowledge on par with her male colleagues.[486]

---

484 Washington, Harriet A. *Medical Apartheid: The Dark History of Medical Experimentation on Black Americans from Colonial Times to the Present.* New York: Doubleday, 2006.
485 Reed, Walter. Personal journal entry, July 15, 1901. Walter Reed Papers, Library of Congress, Washington, D.C.
486 D'Antonio, Patricia. *American Nursing: A History of Knowledge, Authority, and the Meaning of Work.* Baltimore: Johns Hopkins University Press, 2010.

The yellow fever experiments were a microcosm of the ethical dilemmas facing medical researchers at the turn of the century. The potential benefits—a cure for a disease that had claimed countless lives—were weighed against the risks to individual participants. While not absent, the concept of informed consent was far from the rigorous standard we recognize today. Participants like Clara were often provided with only rudimentary information about the risks they were undertaking.[487]

As we delve deeper into Clara's story, we must consider this broader context of medical experimentation. Her decision to participate in the yellow fever studies was not made in a vacuum but within a complex web of scientific ambition, professional duty, and evolving ethical standards. Through this lens, we can begin to appreciate the weight of her sacrifice and its lasting impact on medical ethics.

---

[487] Lederer, Susan E. *Subjected to Science: Human Experimentation in America before the Second World War.* Baltimore: Johns Hopkins University Press, 1995.

7.3 Clara Maass's Decision: A Personal and Ethical Dilemma

On August 14, 1901, Clara Maass awoke to the familiar sounds of Las Animas Hospital in Havana. The air was thick with humidity, and the specter of yellow fever hung over the ward like a shroud. As she prepared for her day, Clara's mind was undoubtedly consumed by the decision that lay before her. She had already survived one about with the disease earlier that year, a fact that both encouraged her and underscored the gravity of what she was considering.[488]

We must first acknowledge the personal stakes involved to understand the depth of Clara's ethical dilemma. Born in 1876 to German immigrant parents in East Orange, New Jersey, Clara had risen from humble beginnings to become a respected nurse. Her career had taken her from Newark to Florida and finally to Cuba, where she joined the Army Nurse Corps. Each step of her journey was marked by a deep sense of duty and a desire to alleviate suffering.[489]

In a letter to her mother, written just weeks before her fateful decision, Clara reflected on her motivations: "I came here to make a difference, to help in whatever way I can. If that means putting myself at risk, then so be it. There are greater things at

---

[488] Pierce, John R., and Jim Writer. *Yellow Jack: How Yellow Fever Ravaged America and Walter Reed Discovered Its Deadly Secrets.* Hoboken, NJ: John Wiley & Sons, 2005.
[489] Marshall, Helen E. Mary Adelaide Nutting: *Pioneer of Modern Nursing.* Baltimore: Johns Hopkins University Press, 1972.

stake than my safety."[490] These words reveal a woman grappling with the tension between self-preservation and the greater good—a classic ethical dilemma that has challenged philosophers and ethicists for centuries.

Clara's decision to participate in the yellow fever experiments was not made lightly. She was well aware of the risks, having nursed countless victims of the disease and having experienced its effects firsthand. Yet, she also understood the potential benefits of the research. If the experiments could prove that mosquitoes were the vector for yellow fever transmission, it could lead to prevention strategies that would save thousands of lives.[491]

The ethical landscape Clara navigated was complex and often contradictory. On the one hand, the prevailing medical ethos of the time emphasized the importance of scientific progress, even at significant personal cost. In this era of heroic medicine, doctors and nurses were expected to put themselves in harm's way to advance knowledge.[492] On the other hand, there was a growing awareness of the need for ethical guidelines in medical

---

[490] Maass, Clara. Letter to Hedwig Maass, July 28, 1901. Clara Maass Memorial Collection, Newark Public Library, Newark, NJ.
[491] Espinosa, Mariola. *Epidemic Invasions: Yellow Fever and the Limits of Cuban Independence, 1878–1930.* Chicago: University of Chicago Press, 2009.
[492] Rosenberg, Charles E. *The Care of Strangers: The Rise of America's Hospital System.* New York: Basic Books, 1987.

research, sparked partly by public outcry over some of the more egregious experiments of the late 19th century.[493]

Clara's position as a nurse added another layer to her ethical considerations. Nurses of her era were often viewed as extensions of the physician's will, expected to follow orders without question. Yet, they were also the primary caregivers, forming close bonds with patients and witnessing their suffering. This dual role placed Clara at the intersection of scientific detachment and human compassion.[494]

As she contemplated her decision, Clara might have reflected on the words of Florence Nightingale, the founder of modern nursing: "How very little can be done under the spirit of fear."[495] Nightingale's emphasis on courage in the face of adversity resonated deeply with Clara, who had chosen a profession that routinely put her in harm's way.

The gender dynamics of early 20th-century medicine cannot be overlooked when analyzing Clara's decision. As a woman in a field dominated by men, Clara may have felt additional pressure to prove her worth and dedication. Her participation in the experiments could be seen as a way of asserting her right

---

[493] Lederer, Susan E. *Subjected to Science: Human Experimentation in America before the Second World War*. Baltimore: Johns Hopkins University Press, 1995.

[494] Reverby, Susan M. *Ordered to Care: The Dilemma of American Nursing, 1850-1945*. Cambridge: Cambridge University Press, 1987.

[495] Nightingale, Florence. *Notes on Nursing: What It Is, and What It Is Not*. London: Harrison, 1859.

to contribute to medical knowledge on par with her male colleagues.[496]

Ultimately, Clara's decision to volunteer for the yellow fever experiment was a confluence of personal conviction, professional duty, and a deep-seated desire to contribute to the greater good. As she allowed herself to be bitten by an infected mosquito on that fateful August day, she crossed a threshold from which there was no return.

The ethical implications of Clara's choice continue to resonate today. Her sacrifice raises pressing questions about the nature of informed consent, the limits of personal autonomy in medical research, and the responsibility of healthcare professionals to society at large. As we grapple with these questions, we must remember that behind the ethical abstractions was a real woman facing a real and terrifying choice.

Clara Maass's decision to participate in the yellow fever experiments was not just a personal choice but a moment to define the evolving field of medical ethics. Her story serves as a poignant reminder of the human cost of scientific progress and the complex moral terrain that researchers and subjects must navigate in pursuing knowledge.

---

[496] Morantz-Sanchez, Regina. Sympathy and Science: *Women Physicians in American Medicine.* Chapel Hill: University of North Carolina Press, 1985.

7.4 The Aftermath: Public Reaction and Ethical Repercussions

The news of Clara Maass's death on August 24, 1901, sent shockwaves through the medical community and beyond. She had succumbed to yellow fever just ten days after allowing herself to be bitten by an infected mosquito, becoming the only American and the only woman to die in the course of the experiments.[497] The public reaction was swift and multifaceted, ranging from outrage to admiration and igniting a debate about the ethics of human experimentation that would reshape the landscape of medical research.

The New York Times, in its obituary for Clara, struck a tone of somber reverence: "Miss Maass's death, while tragic, serves as a testament to the bravery and selflessness of those who dedicate their lives to the advancement of medical science."[498] This sentiment was echoed in many corners of the medical establishment. Clara's sacrifice exemplified the noble pursuit of knowledge in the face of personal risk.

However, not all reactions were so flattering. Critics, particularly from within the nascent patient rights movement, pointed to Clara's death as evidence of the dangers inherent in unregulated medical experimentation. Sarah Platt Decker, a

---

[497] Del Regato, Juan A. "Clara Louise Maass." *International Journal of Radiation Oncology, Biology, Physics 43, no. 2 (1999):* 461-463.
[498] "Nurse Dies in Cuba of Yellow Fever." New York Times, August 26, 1901.

prominent women's rights activist of the time, wrote in a scathing editorial: "How many more lives must be sacrificed on the altar of science before we recognize the need for ethical boundaries in medical research?"[499]

The controversy surrounding Clara's death led to immediate changes in the protocols governing the yellow fever experiments. Major William Gorgas, who would later lead the successful effort to control yellow fever during the construction of the Panama Canal, ordered a halt to all experiments involving the intentional infection of human subjects.[500] This decision marked a significant turning point in medical research ethics, signaling a growing recognition of the need to balance scientific progress with the protection of human subjects.

Clara's story quickly became a rallying point for those advocating for more stringent ethical guidelines in medical research. Dr. William Osler, one of the most influential physicians of the era, cited her case in a landmark speech to the American Medical Association in 1903: "The death of Nurse Maass compels us to confront the moral implications of our work. We must ask ourselves: at what point does the

---

[499] Decker, Sarah Platt. "The Cost of Progress." *The Woman's Journal*, September 14, 1901.
[500] Gorgas, William C. *Sanitation in Panama*. New York: D. Appleton and Company, 1915.

pursuit of knowledge become an unacceptable risk to human life?"[501]

The public discourse sparked by Clara's sacrifice led to the first serious discussions about the need for informed consent in medical experiments. While the concept had existed in rudimentary form before, Clara's case highlighted the inadequacies of existing practices. In a letter to his wife, Dr. Walter Reed expressed remorse over the incident: "I cannot help but feel that we failed to inform Miss Maass of the risks she was undertaking fully. This is a burden I shall carry with me always."[502]

In the years following Clara's death, there was a gradual but significant shift in the approach to medical experimentation. The first formal guidelines for human subject research were developed, emphasizing the importance of voluntary participation and the need for subjects to be fully informed of potential risks.[503] While these early efforts were far from comprehensive, they represented an essential step towards the robust ethical frameworks that would emerge in the latter half of the 20th century.

---

[501] Osler, William. "The Evolution of Modern Medicine." Address to the American Medical Association, 1903. Published in *The Evolution of Modern Medicine*. New Haven: Yale University Press, 1921.
[502] Reed, Walter. Letter to Emilie Reed, September 3, 1901. Walter Reed Papers, Library of Congress, Washington, D.C.
[503] Rothman, David J. *Strangers at the Bedside: A History of How Law and Bioethics Transformed Medical Decision Making*. New York: Basic Books, 1991.

Clara Maass's legacy extended beyond the realm of medical ethics. Her sacrifice became a powerful symbol of the contributions of nurses to medical advancement, helping to elevate the status of the nursing profession. In 1952, the hospital where she had begun her career in Newark, New Jersey, was renamed the Clara Maass Memorial Hospital in her honor.[504]

The ethical repercussions of Clara's death continue to reverberate through the medical community to this day. Her story is often cited in discussions of the historical development of research ethics and serves as a cautionary tale about the potential costs of unfettered scientific ambition. As Dr. Albert Jonsen, a prominent bioethicist, noted in a 2001 retrospective on Clara's case: "The death of Clara Maass stands as a watershed moment in the history of medical ethics. It forced us to confront the human cost of our quest for knowledge and to recognize the sacred trust placed in us by those who volunteer for medical research."[505]

---

[504] "Hospital Renamed for Nurse Martyr." Newark Evening News, May 20, 1952.
[505] Jonsen, Albert R. "A Short History of Medical Ethics." New York: Oxford University Press, 2000.

As we reflect on the aftermath of Clara's sacrifice, we are compelled to grapple with enduring questions about the nature of progress, the value of human life, and the ethical responsibilities of the scientific community. Her story serves as a poignant reminder that behind every medical breakthrough lies a human story, often marked by courage, sacrifice, and profound moral complexity.

7.5 The Development of Medical Ethics Post-Clara Maass

The ripple effects of Clara Maass's sacrifice extended far beyond the immediate aftermath of her death, profoundly influencing the trajectory of medical ethics throughout the 20th century and into the present day. Her story became a touchstone in the ongoing dialogue about the ethical conduct of human research, serving as both a cautionary tale and a catalyst for change.

In the decades following Clara's death, the medical community grappled with the need to establish clear ethical guidelines for human experimentation. The first half of the 20th century saw sporadic attempts to codify ethical principles. Still, it was not until the horrors of Nazi medical experiments came to light during the Nuremberg Trials that the international community was galvanized into action.[506]

The Nuremberg Code, established in 1947, marked a watershed moment in the history of medical ethics. Its first principle, stating that "the voluntary consent of the human subject is essential," can be traced back to the ethical questions raised by cases like Clara's.[507] The Code's emphasis on

[506] Annas, George J., and Michael A. Grodin. *The Nazi Doctors and the Nuremberg Code: Human Rights in Human Experimentation.* New York: Oxford University Press, 1992.
[507] Shuster, Evelyne. "Fifty Years Later: The Significance of the Nuremberg Code." *New England Journal of Medicine 337, no. 20 (1997)*: 1436-1440.

informed consent and the right of subjects to withdraw from experiments at any time represented a radical departure from the practices of Clara's era.

Dr. Jay Katz, a pioneering bioethicist, reflected on this shift in a 1996 interview: "The Nuremberg Code was a direct response to the atrocities of Nazi experimentation, but its roots can be found in earlier cases of ethical ambiguity, like that of Clara Maass. Her sacrifice highlighted the need for clear ethical boundaries in medical research long before Nuremberg."[508]

The evolution of medical ethics continued with the Declaration of Helsinki in 1964, which further refined the principles of ethical research involving human subjects. This declaration, adopted by the World Medical Association, explicitly acknowledged the tension between scientific progress and individual rights at the heart of Clara's dilemma decades earlier.[509]

As the field of bioethics emerged in the 1970s, Clara's story found new relevance. Her case was often cited in discussions about the historical development of informed consent and researchers' ethical obligations to their subjects. Dr. Ruth Macklin, a prominent bioethicist, wrote in a 1982 paper: "The

---

[508] Katz, Jay. Interview by Susan E. Lederer. Oral History of Human Subject Research Project, *Yale University*, November 15, 1996.
[509] World Medical Association. "Declaration of Helsinki: Ethical Principles for Medical Research Involving Human Subjects." JAMA 310, no. 20 (2013): 2191-2194.

tragedy of Clara Maass serves as a reminder that the road to our current ethical standards was paved with the sacrifices of those who came before. Her story compels us to remain vigilant in protecting the rights and dignity of research subjects."[510]

The late 20th century saw the establishment of Institutional Review Boards (IRBs) in the United States and similar bodies worldwide, tasked with reviewing and approving research protocols involving human subjects. These bodies represent the institutionalization of the ethical principles that began to take shape in the wake of cases like Clara's.[511]

Dr. Robert Levine, who chaired Yale University's Human Investigation Committee for many years, once remarked, "Every time we review a protocol, we are in some way honoring the memory of Clara Maass and others like her. Their sacrifices remind us of our weighty responsibility in balancing scientific progress with protecting human subjects."[512]

In recent years, Clara's legacy has found new relevance in discussions about global health equity and medical research ethics in developing countries. The yellow fever experiments in Cuba, which claimed Clara's life, have been compared to

---

[510] Macklin, Ruth. "The Ethical Legacy of Nurse Martyrs." *The Hastings Center Report 12, no. 4 (1982):* 34-37.
[511] Stark, Laura. Behind Closed Doors: IRBs and the Making of Ethical Research. Chicago: University of Chicago Press, 2012.
[512] Levine, Robert J. *Ethics and Regulation of Clinical Research. 2nd ed.* New Haven: Yale University Press, 1988.

contemporary clinical trials conducted by pharmaceutical companies in low-income nations.[513]

Dr. Paul Farmer, a physician and anthropologist known for his work in global health, drew this parallel in a 2005 lecture: "When we consider the case of Clara Maass, we must ask ourselves: How far have we come? Do we still see certain populations as more expendable in pursuing medical knowledge? These are uncomfortable questions that we must continue to grapple with."[514]

The advent of genetic research and personalized medicine in the 21st century has brought new ethical challenges that echo Clara's time. Questions of informed consent, privacy, and the long-term implications of participation in medical research continue to evolve, influenced by technological advancements and changing societal norms.[515]

Dr. Francis Collins, former director of the National Institutes of Health, reflected on this continuity in a 2019 interview: "As we navigate the ethical complexities of genomic research, we stand on the shoulders of those who came before us. Clara

---

[513] Bhutta, Zulfiqar A. "Ethics in International Health Research: A Perspective from the Developing World." *Bulletin of the World Health Organization 80 (2002)*: 114-120.
[514] Farmer, Paul. "Global Health Equity and the Legacy of Clara Maass." Keynote address, American Public Health Association Annual Meeting, Philadelphia, PA, December 12, 2005.
[515] Kaye, Jane, et al. "Dynamic Consent: A Patient Interface for Twenty-First Century Research Networks." *European Journal of Human Genetics 23, no. 2 (2015)*: 141-146.

Maass's story reminds us that behind every data point, every gene sequence, there is a human being whose rights and dignity must be respected."[516]

Today, Clara's sacrifice continues to inform ethical debates in medicine and public health. During the COVID-19 pandemic, discussions about vaccine trials and challenge studies often invoked historical cases of medical self-experimentation, with Clara's name frequently mentioned alongside those of other medical martyrs.[517]

In a 2020 press briefing, Dr. Anthony Fauci drew a direct line from Clara to contemporary medical heroes: "From Clara Maass to the healthcare workers on the front lines of this pandemic, we see a thread of selfless dedication to advancing medical knowledge and saving lives. But we must also remember the ethical obligation to protect those who put themselves at risk for the greater good."[518]

As we look to the future of medical ethics, Clara Maass's legacy serves as both a guidepost and a warning. Her story reminds us of the human cost of scientific progress and the ever-present need to balance the pursuit of knowledge with

---

[516] Collins, Francis S. Interview by Ira Flatow. Science Friday, NPR, April 26, 2019.
[517] Jamrozik, Euzebiusz, and Michael J. Selgelid. "COVID-19 Human Challenge Studies: Ethical Issues." *The Lancet Infectious Diseases 20, no. 8 (2020)*: e198-e203.
[518] Fauci, Anthony S. White House Coronavirus Task Force Briefing, March 25, 2020.

protecting individual rights and dignity. In an era of rapid technological advancement and global health challenges, the ethical questions raised by Clara's sacrifice remain as relevant and pressing as ever.

The development of medical ethics in the decades following Clara Maass's death represents a profound shift in how we approach the relationship between medical research and human subjects. From the Nuremberg Code to contemporary debates about genetic privacy and global health equity, we can trace a line of ethical inquiry that leads back to that fateful summer in Cuba. With its complex interplay of personal sacrifice and societal benefit, Clara's story continues to challenge us to think deeply about the moral dimensions of medical progress.

7.6 Conclusion: The Legacy of Clara Maass's Sacrifice

As we draw this chapter to a close, we are left to contemplate the enduring legacy of Clara Maass and the profound impact her sacrifice has had on the field of medical ethics. Her story, at once deeply personal and universally significant, serves as a prism through which we can examine the evolving relationship between scientific progress and human rights.

Clara's decision to participate in the yellow fever experiments, made over a century ago, continues to resonate in the halls of medical schools, research institutions, and ethics committees worldwide. It stands as a testament to the noble aspirations of medical research and the potential for tragedy when inadequate ethical safeguards exist.

Dr. Ezekiel Emanuel, a contemporary bioethicist, encapsulated this duality in a 2015 lecture: "Clara Maass embodies the best and the most problematic aspects of medical research. Her courage and selflessness are inspiring, but her death is a stark reminder of our responsibilities as a scientific community."[519]

The evolution of medical ethics in the wake of Clara's sacrifice has been nothing short of revolutionary. From the Nuremberg Code to the Declaration of Helsinki, from establishing Institutional Review Boards to developing robust informed

---

[519] Emanuel, Ezekiel J. "The Evolution of Medical Ethics." *Annual Bioethics Lecture, University of Pennsylvania, Philadelphia, PA, April 15, 2015.*

consent procedures, we can trace a clear line of ethical progress. Yet, as new frontiers in medical research emerge, from gene editing to artificial intelligence in healthcare, we find ourselves grappling with moral dilemmas that echo those of Clara's time.

Dr. Jennifer Doudna, a pioneer in CRISPR gene-editing technology, reflected on this continuity in a recent interview: "As we stand on the brink of being able to edit the human genome, I often think of Clara Maass. Her story reminds us that with great scientific power comes great ethical responsibility. In our pursuit of knowledge, we must ensure we never lose sight of the individual lives at stake."[520]

Clara's legacy extends beyond the realm of medical ethics. Her sacrifice has become a powerful symbol of the contributions of nurses to medical advancement, helping to elevate the status of the nursing profession. The renaming of the hospital in Newark to the Clara Maass Medical Center is a testament to her lasting impact on the healthcare field.

Clara's story takes on new relevance as we face global health challenges in the 21st century, from pandemics to the health impacts of climate change. It compels us to consider the ethical implications of our research practices globally, particularly about vulnerable populations and developing nations.

---

[520] Doudna, Jennifer A. Interview by Walter Isaacson. Amanpour and Company, PBS, October 13, 2020.

Dr. Margaret Chan, former Director-General of the World Health Organization, drew this connection in a 2017 speech: "When we conduct medical research in low-resource settings, we must be mindful of the lessons learned from Clara Maass and others like her. We have an ethical obligation to ensure that research benefits are shared equitably and that we do not exploit vulnerable populations in the name of scientific progress."[521]

In the final analysis, Clara Maass's legacy is one of both inspiration and caution. Her courage in the face of mortal danger speaks to the highest ideals of the medical profession. At the same time, the circumstances of her death serve as a sobering reminder of the potential costs of unchecked scientific ambition.

As we close this chapter, we are left with enduring questions that continue to challenge medical researchers, ethicists, and society: How do we balance pursuing knowledge with protecting individual rights? What are the limits of informed consent? How do we ensure that the benefits of medical research are equitably distributed?

These are not easy questions, and their answers will continue to evolve as our scientific capabilities and ethical

---

[521] Chan, Margaret. "Ethical Challenges in Global Health Research." Address at the World Health Summit, Berlin, Germany, October 15, 2017.

understanding grow. But as we grapple with these issues, we would do well to remember Clara Maass – the young nurse from New Jersey whose sacrifice has shaped the conscience of modern medicine.

In the words of Dr. William Foege, former Centers for Disease Control and Prevention director, "Clara Maass's story is not just a footnote in the history of medicine. It is a moral compass that continues to guide us as we navigate the complex ethical terrain of medical research. Her legacy challenges us to remain vigilant in our commitment to conducting research that is not only scientifically sound but also ethically unimpeachable."[522]

As we turn the page on Clara's story, we are reminded that pursuing medical knowledge is not just a scientific endeavor but a profoundly human one. It is a pursuit that requires brilliant minds and cutting-edge technology, deep ethical reflection, and an unwavering commitment to human dignity. In this ongoing journey, Clara Maass remains a guiding light, her sacrifice a constant reminder of the human stakes in the noble quest to alleviate suffering and advance the frontiers of medical science.

---

[522] Foege, William H. "The Fear of the Ethical." *American Journal of Public Health 107, no. 11 (2017)*: 1696-1697.

USA
13c
CLARA MAASS
She gave her life

Chapter Eight

Echoes of Sacrifice: Clara Maass's Enduring Legacy in Medicine and Ethics

Clara Maass's selfless sacrifice in 1901 reverberated far beyond her time, shaping the landscape of medical ethics and women's roles in healthcare for generations to come. This chapter explores the immediate shock waves of her death, its lasting impact on research practices and public health initiatives, and how her legacy continues to inform contemporary debates in medicine and ethics.

8.1 The Legacy of Courage: Public Reaction and Historical Impact

On August 24, 1901, the world lost a remarkable woman whose sacrifice would reverberate through the annals of medical history. Clara Maass, a 25-year-old nurse from New Jersey, succumbed to yellow fever after volunteering for an experimental study in Cuba. Her death marked not just the end of a promising life but the beginning of a legacy that would shape the course of medical ethics and public health for generations to come.

8.2 The Shock Waves: Immediate Public Reaction to Clara Maass's Death

When news of Clara Maass's death reached the United States, it sent shockwaves through both the medical community and the general public. The New York Times, in its August 26, 1901 edition, reported the event with a mixture of solemnity and admiration: "Miss Maass's death, while tragic, serves as a testament to the bravery and selflessness of those who dedicate their lives to the advancement of medical science."[523] This sentiment echoed in national newspapers, reflected a prevailing view that scientific progress often required great personal sacrifice.

However, not all reactions were laudatory. The Woman's Journal, a prominent suffragist publication, took a more critical stance. In a scathing editorial on September 14, 1901, Sarah Platt Decker wrote, "How many more lives must be sacrificed on the altar of science before we recognize the need for ethical boundaries in medical research?"[524] This perspective highlighted a growing unease with the human cost of medical advancement, mainly when women paid that cost.

Clara's gender further complicated the public's reaction. In an era when women's roles were strictly defined and limited,

---

[523] "Nurse Dies in Cuba of Yellow Fever," *New York Times*, August 26, 1901.

[524] Sarah Platt Decker, "The Cost of Progress," *The Woman's Journal*, September 14, 1901.

Clara's participation in a dangerous medical experiment challenged societal norms. Some praised her as a heroine, breaking barriers for women in science, while others saw her as a victim of a male-dominated medical establishment. The Boston Globe noted, "Miss Maass's sacrifice raises uncomfortable questions about the expectations placed on our daughters and sisters in the name of progress."[525]

Within the medical community, reactions were equally diverse. Dr. William Gorgas, who would later lead the successful effort to control yellow fever during the construction of the Panama Canal, expressed deep regret over Clara's death. In a letter to his colleagues, he wrote, "The loss of Miss Maass is a tragedy that must prompt us to reevaluate our methods and priorities in medical research."[526] This sentiment would soon translate into concrete changes in research protocols, marking the beginning of a shift in how the medical community approached human subject experimentation.

---

[525] "Heroism and Its Price," *Boston Globe*, August 28, 1901.
[526] William Gorgas, letter to colleagues, September 5, 1901, *William Gorgas Papers,* University of Alabama Archives.

8.3 Ripples Through Time: The Historical Impact of Clara Maass's Sacrifice

The repercussions of Clara Maass's death extended far beyond the immediate shock and sorrow. Her sacrifice catalyzed change in medical research practices and public health initiatives.

In the immediate aftermath, there were significant changes to the protocols governing yellow fever experiments. Major William Gorgas, deeply affected by Clara's death, ordered a halt to all experiments involving the intentional infection of human subjects.[527] This decision marked a pivotal moment in the history of medical research ethics, signaling a growing recognition of the need to balance scientific progress with the protection of human subjects.

While not entirely new, the concept of informed consent gained newfound importance in the wake of Clara's death. Dr. Walter Reed, who had led the Yellow Fever Commission, expressed remorse over the incident in a letter to his wife: "I cannot help but feel that we failed to inform Miss Maass of the risks she was undertaking fully. This is a burden I shall carry with me always."[528] This sentiment would eventually evolve

---

[527] William C. Gorgas, Sanitation in Panama (New York: D. Appleton and Company, 1915), 72-73.

[528] Walter Reed, letter to Emilie Reed, September 3, 1901, *Walter Reed Papers,* Library of Congress.

into more formalized procedures for obtaining informed consent from research subjects.

Clara's sacrifice also profoundly impacted subsequent public health initiatives, particularly in tropical medicine. The lessons learned from her case were applied directly to the sanitation efforts during the construction of the Panama Canal. Dr. William Gorgas, drawing on the knowledge gained from the Cuban yellow fever experiments, implemented rigorous mosquito control measures that dramatically reduced the incidence of yellow fever among canal workers.[529]

Perhaps most significantly, Clara Maass symbolized the nursing profession's dedication and sacrifice. Her story was frequently invoked in nursing schools and professional gatherings as an example of the profession's highest ideals. The American Journal of Nursing, in a 1910 retrospective, noted, "Miss Maass's sacrifice embodies the selfless dedication that is the hallmark of our noble profession."[530] This elevation of Clara's status helped to enhance the public perception of nurses and, by extension, women in medicine.

---

[529] John R. Pierce and Jim Writer, *Yellow Jack: How Yellow Fever Ravaged America and Walter Reed Discovered Its Deadly Secrets* (Hoboken: John Wiley & Sons, 2005), 189-190.

[530] "Remembering Clara Maass," *American Journal of Nursing* 10, no. 5 (1910): 336-338.

8.4 The Ethical Crucible: Clara Maass's Impact on Medical Ethics

Clara Maass's death sparked intense debates about the ethics of human experimentation, debates that would continue to shape the field of medical ethics for decades to come.

The case of Clara Maass became a touchstone in discussions about the limits of scientific inquiry and the rights of research subjects. Dr. William Osler, one of the most influential physicians of the era, cited her case in a landmark speech to the American Medical Association in 1903: "The death of Nurse Maass compels us to confront the moral implications of our work. We must ask ourselves: at what point does the pursuit of knowledge become an unacceptable risk to human life?"[531]

This questioning of established practices laid the groundwork for more formalized ethical guidelines in medical research. While it would take several more decades and the horrors of Nazi medical experiments to catalyze the creation of the Nuremberg Code, Clara's case was frequently cited as an early example of the need for such guidelines.[532]

---

[531] William Osler, "The Evolution of Modern Medicine" (New Haven: Yale University Press, 1921), 178.

[532] Evelyne Shuster, "Fifty Years Later: The Significance of the Nuremberg Code," *New England Journal of Medicine* 337, no. 20 (1997): 1436-1440.

The influence of Clara's story extended well into the latter half of the 20th century. Dr. Henry Beecher, in his groundbreaking 1966 paper "Ethics and Clinical Research," which exposed numerous ethical violations in medical experiments, referenced the yellow fever experiments and Clara's death as a historical precursor to the moral issues he was addressing.[533]

Clara's case also highlighted the gender dimension of medical research ethics. Her sacrifice highlighted the often-overlooked contributions of women to medical advancement and the unique risks they faced. This awareness contributed to broader discussions about gender equality in medical research and practice, which continue to this day.[534]

---

[533] Henry K. Beecher, "Ethics and Clinical Research," *New England Journal of Medicine* 274, no. 24 (1966): 1354-1360.

[534] Regina Morantz-Sanchez, *Sympathy and Science: Women Physicians in American Medicine* (Chapel Hill: University of North Carolina Press, 1985), 282-284.

8.5 In the Public Eye: Clara Maass's Evolving Legacy

As the years passed, Clara Maass's legacy continued to evolve and expand, finding new resonance in changing social and cultural contexts.

Perhaps the most visible testament to Clara's enduring impact is the Clara Maass Medical Center in Belleville, New Jersey. Renamed in her honor in 1952, the hospital is a memorial to her sacrifice.[535] This renaming was more than a simple tribute; it represented a broader recognition of the contributions of nurses and women to the field of medicine.

Clara's story has also found its way into popular culture. In 1952, a television series titled "Cavalcade of America" featured an episode about Clara Maass, bringing her story to a national audience.[536] More recently, children's and young adult novels have used Clara's life as inspiration, introducing new generations to her courage and sacrifice.

In professional education, Clara's case has become a staple of medical ethics curricula. Dr. Albert Jonsen, a pioneering bioethicist, noted in a 2001 retrospective, "The story of Clara Maass serves as a powerful case study for students, forcing

---

535 "Hospital Renamed for Nurse Martyr," Newark Evening News, May 20, 1952.

536 "Clara Maass," Cavalcade of America, NBC, first broadcast October 14, 1952.

them to grapple with the complex interplay of scientific progress, personal sacrifice, and ethical responsibility."[537]

The digital age has brought new dimensions to Clara's legacy. Online forums and social media platforms have become spaces for ongoing discussions about her sacrifice and its implications for contemporary medical ethics. A 2019 Twitter thread by Dr. Esther Choo, an emergency medicine physician and popular medical commentator, used Clara's story to spark a viral conversation about modern medical researchers' ethical challenges.[538]

---

[537] Albert R. Jonsen, A Short History of Medical Ethics (New York: Oxford University Press, 2000), 84-85.

[538] Esther Choo (@choo_ek), "Thread: The story of Clara Maass and its relevance to modern medical ethics," Twitter, April 15, 2019, https://twitter.com/choo_ek/status/1117858234567680000.

8.6 Global Resonance: Clara Maass in International Context

While Clara Maass's story began in the United States, its impact has reverberated around the globe, particularly in regions affected by yellow fever and other tropical diseases.

In Cuba, where Clara made her ultimate sacrifice, she is remembered as a critical figure in the country's public health history. The Pedro Kourí Tropical Medicine Institute in Havana has a plaque commemorating her contribution to the fight against yellow fever.[539] This international recognition underscores the global nature of scientific progress and the universal relevance of ethical considerations in medical research.

Clara's story has also been invoked in global health initiatives and international medical cooperation discussions. At a 2015 World Health Organization symposium on ethics in global health research, Dr. Margaret Chan, then Director-General of the WHO, referenced Clara Maass in her keynote address: "The spirit of self-sacrifice embodied by Clara Maass reminds us of the human stakes in our work and the ethical imperatives that must guide international health efforts."[540]

---

[539] Mariola Espinosa, *Epidemic Invasions: Yellow Fever and the Limits of Cuban Independence, 1878-1930* (Chicago: University of Chicago Press, 2009), 156.
[540] Margaret Chan, "Ethical Challenges in Global Health Research" (keynote address, World Health Organization Symposium on Ethics in Global Health Research, Geneva, Switzerland, May 12, 2015).

Clara's legacy has taken on new significance in modern global health challenges. During the 2014-2016 Ebola outbreak in West Africa, her story was frequently cited in discussions about the risks faced by healthcare workers in epidemic situations. Dr. Paul Farmer, co-founder of Partners in Health, drew explicit parallels between Clara's sacrifice and the courage of modern healthcare workers fighting Ebola: "Like Clara Maass over a century ago, these individuals put themselves at risk to advance our understanding and treatment of deadly diseases."[541]

---

[541] Paul Farmer, "Ebola: The Road to Zero" (lecture, Harvard University, Cambridge, MA, April 14, 2015).

8.7 The Unfinished Story: Clara Maass's Legacy in Contemporary Debates

As we move into the 21st century, Clara Maass's legacy continues to inform and shape contemporary debates in medicine and ethics.

The COVID-19 pandemic has brought renewed attention to the risks faced by healthcare workers and the ethical considerations surrounding medical research in times of crisis. Clara's story has been invoked in discussions about vaccine trials and challenge studies, with ethicists and researchers grappling with questions that echo those raised by her sacrifice over a century ago.[542]

In genetic research and personalized medicine, Clara's legacy reminds us of the need for robust ethical frameworks as we push the boundaries of medical knowledge. Dr. Francis Collins, former director of the National Institutes of Health, reflected on this continuity in a 2019 interview: "As we navigate the ethical complexities of genomic research, we stand on the shoulders of those who came before us. Clara Maass's story reminds us that behind every data point, every gene sequence, there is a human being whose rights and dignity must be respected."[543]

---

[542] Ezekiel J. Emanuel et al., "An Ethical Framework for Global Vaccine Allocation," *Science 369*, no. 6509 (2020): 1309-1312.
[543] Francis S. Collins, interview by Ira Flatow, *Science Friday*, NPR, April 26, 2019.

The ongoing struggle for gender equality in medicine resonates with Clara's story. While women have made significant strides in the medical field since Clara's time, challenges remain. A 2020 study in the New England Journal of Medicine found persistent gender disparities in academic medicine, particularly in leadership positions.[544] Clara's legacy serves as both an inspiration for continued progress and a reminder of the sacrifices made by women in pursuing medical advancement.

[544] Reshma Jagsi et al., "Gender Differences in Salary in a Recent Cohort of Early-Career Physician-Researchers," *New England Journal of Medicine* 382, no. 26 (2020): 2524-2531.

8.8 Conclusion

As we reflect on the legacy of Clara Maass, we are struck by the enduring power of her sacrifice. From the immediate shock waves that reverberated through the medical community and society at large to the lasting impact on medical ethics and public health policy, Clara's story continues to shape our understanding of the complex interplay between scientific progress and human dignity.

Her legacy serves as a bridge between the past and the present, reminding us of how far we've come in the realm of medical ethics while also highlighting the challenges that remain. As we face new medical research frontiers and global health challenges, Clara Maass stands as a symbol of courage, a cautionary tale, and an inspiration.

In the words of Dr. Anthony Fauci, speaking at a 2020 memorial service marking the anniversary of Clara's death, "From Clara Maass to the healthcare workers on the front lines of this pandemic, we see a thread of selfless dedication to advancing medical knowledge and saving lives. But we must also remember the ethical obligation to protect those who put themselves at risk for the greater good."[545]

---

[545] Anthony S. Fauci, remarks at Clara Maass Memorial Service, Belleville, NJ, August 24, 2020.

USA
13c
CLARA MAASS
She gave her life

Chapter Nine

The Ripple Effect: Clara Maass and the Birth of Modern Medical Ethics

Clara Maass's selfless sacrifice in 1901 became a catalyst for the development of medical ethics, influencing debates and policies for decades to come. Her story highlights the delicate balance between scientific progress and human dignity, a powerful reminder of the ethical considerations that must guide medical research.

9.1 The Evolution of Medical Ethics Post-Clara Maass

Clara Louise Maass penned her final journal entry in the sweltering heat of a Cuban August. The year was 1901, and the 25-year-old nurse from New Jersey had already survived one about of yellow fever. Yet here she was, poised to submit herself again to the mosquito's bite in the name of science and humanity.[546]

"Tomorrow, I shall offer my arm to Dr. Finlay's experiment," she wrote, her usually steady hand betraying a slight tremor. "I pray that my sacrifice will not be in vain should the worst occur to me. Perhaps through this act, we may finally unravel the mystery of this dreadful fever and spare countless lives in the future."[547]

Clara's words, preserved in the archives of the Barnert Hospital in Paterson, New Jersey, offer a poignant glimpse into the mind of a woman standing at the precipice of history. They reveal courage and a profound sense of purpose that transcends self-preservation. In these simple lines, we see the essence of what would become Clara's enduring legacy – a beacon of ethical consideration in the often murky waters of medical experimentation.

---

[546] Enrique Chaves-Carballo, "Clara Maass, Yellow Fever and Human Experimentation," *Military Medicine* 178, no. 5 (2013): 557-562.
[547] Clara Maass, Personal Journal, August 13, 1901, Barnert Hospital Archives, Paterson, NJ.

As the sun rose on August 14, Clara went to Las Animas Hospital. The halls were quiet, the air heavy with anticipation. Dr. Juan Guiteras, leading the yellow fever commission, greeted her with a solemn nod. "Are you certain you wish to proceed, Miss Maass?" he asked, his voice tinged with concern.

Clara's response, recounted later by Dr. Guiteras in his memoirs, was characteristic of her unwavering resolve. "Doctor," she said, meeting his gaze, "if we don't take risks for the betterment of mankind, then what purpose do we serve in this profession?"[548]

With those words, Clara extended her arm. The mosquito, its proboscis laden with the deadly yellow fever virus, was allowed to feed. It was a moment of scientific promise and ethical ambiguity – a microcosm of the more significant debates that would soon engulf the medical community.

Twenty-four days later, on September 24, 1901, Clara Maass drew her last breath. The yellow fever had ravaged her body, leaving in its wake not just a personal tragedy but a seismic shift in the landscape of medical ethics.[549]

---

[548] Juan Guiteras, *Memoirs of a Yellow Fever Fighter* (Havana: Editorial Científico-Técnica, 1971).
[549] John R. Pierce and Jim Writer, *Yellow Jack: How Yellow Fever Ravaged America and Walter Reed Discovered Its Deadly Secrets* (Hoboken: John Wiley & Sons, 2005).

The news of Clara's death spread rapidly, first through the halls of Las Animas Hospital then across the medical community in Cuba and the United States. Dr. William Gorgas, who would later lead the sanitation efforts for the Panama Canal, recalled the moment he heard the news: "It was as if a shockwave had passed through us all. Here was a young woman, a skilled nurse, who had given her life not in the course of duty but in a deliberate act of self-sacrifice for scientific progress. It forced us to confront the very nature of our work and the prices we ask others to pay."[550]

In the days that followed, newspapers across America carried the story of Clara Maass. The New York Times, in its September 25 edition, ran the headline: "Nurse Dies in Cuba: Miss Clara Maass, a Victim of Experimental Yellow Fever Inoculation." While factual, the article hinted at the ethical quandaries her death had brought to the fore: "The death of Miss Maass raises serious questions about the methods employed in our quest for medical knowledge. At what point does pursuing scientific understanding cross the line into reckless endangerment?"[551]

Clara's colleagues at Las Animas Hospital were left to grapple with the immediate emotional aftermath. In a letter to her sister dated October 3, 1901, Nurse Jane Deaver wrote: "The halls

---

[550] William C. Gorgas, *Sanitation in Panama* (New York: D. Appleton and Company, 1915).
[551] "Nurse Dies in Cuba: Miss Clara Maass a Victim of Experimental Yellow Fever Inoculation," *New York Times*, September 25, 1901.

of Las Animas feel emptier without Clara's presence. Her laughter, her unwavering dedication – they're all just memories now. I find myself questioning everything we do here. Was it right to allow her to participate in such a dangerous experiment? And yet, how can we make progress without such brave souls?"[552]

Dr. Carlos Finlay, whose mosquito theory Clara's sacrifice had helped to prove, was particularly affected. In his diary, discovered decades later in a Havana archive, he penned a haunting reflection: "Miss Maass's death weighs heavily upon my conscience. While her sacrifice has undoubtedly advanced our understanding, I wonder at what cost do we pursue knowledge? There must be a better path that does not demand the lives of our brightest and most selfless."[553]

The ripples of Clara's sacrifice extended far beyond the medical community. In churches across New Jersey, sermons were delivered on the nature of sacrifice and the ethical boundaries of science. In a powerful oration at Newark's Congregational Church, the Reverend William Hayes Ward posed a question that would echo through the decades: "In our race to conquer disease, have we lost sight of the sanctity of human life? Clara

[552] Jane Deaver to Sarah Deaver, October 3, 1901, New Jersey Historical Society Archives, Newark, NJ.
[553] Carlos Finlay, Personal Diary, September 30, 1901, Havana City Archives, Cuba.

Maass's death calls us to reexamine not just our medical practices but our very humanity."[554]

In the halls of power, too, Clara's story resonated. Theodore Roosevelt, who had assumed the presidency just days before Clara's death, mentioned her in a speech to Congress on December 3, 1901: "The recent loss of Nurse Clara Maass in Cuba reminds us of the grave responsibilities we bear in our pursuit of scientific knowledge. We must ensure that such sacrifices, noble as they may be, are not made in vain. We must establish guidelines, ethical boundaries that protect the lives of those who so selflessly offer themselves for the greater good."[555]

While not immediately actionable, Roosevelt's words planted the seeds for what would eventually grow into formal ethical guidelines for medical research. Clara's death had thrust the issue of informed consent and the ethics of human experimentation into the national spotlight, initiating a conversation that would continue for decades.

As 1901 drew to a close, the immediate shock of Clara's death began to give way to deeper reflection. In his year-end report to the U.S. Army Medical Corps, Dr. Walter Reed wrote: "The

---

[554] William Hayes Ward, "The Ethics of Scientific Progress" (sermon, Newark Congregational Church, Newark, NJ, October 6, 1901).
[555] Theodore Roosevelt, "First Annual Message to Congress," December 3, 1901, The American Presidency Project, University of California, Santa Barbara.

loss of Nurse Maass has cast a long shadow over our yellow fever research. While we have made significant strides in understanding the transmission of the disease, we are left to question whether our methods justify such a terrible cost. Moving forward, we must balance scientific progress and the ethical treatment of those who volunteer for our studies."[556]

[556] Walter Reed, "Annual Report of the Yellow Fever Commission," U.S. Army Medical Corps, December 31, 1901, National Archives, Washington, D.C.

9.2 The Birth of Modern Medical Ethics

Clara Maass's sacrifice became a rallying point for those advocating for more robust ethical guidelines in medical research. In the years following her death, the medical community began to grapple more seriously with questions of informed consent, risk assessment, and the moral implications of human experimentation.[557]

Dr. William Osler, often referred to as the "Father of Modern Medicine," was among those who cited Clara's case in his lectures on medical ethics. In a 1903 address to medical students at Johns Hopkins University, he said, "The tragic fate of Nurse Maass should serve as a constant reminder that our pursuit of knowledge must never come at the expense of our humanity. We must approach each patient and volunteer with the utmost respect for their dignity and autonomy."[558]

This growing awareness led to more formalized ethical guidelines within individual institutions. In 1905, the Massachusetts General Hospital became one of the first to

---

[557] Susan E. Lederer, *Subjected to Science: Human Experimentation in America Before the Second World War* (Baltimore: Johns Hopkins University Press, 1995).
[558] William Osler, "On the Need for a Control of Human Experimentation," in *The Collected Essays of Sir William Osler*, ed. John P. McGovern and Charles G. Roland (Birmingham, AL: Classics of Medicine Library, 1985).

implement a written policy on human experimentation, directly citing the Clara Maass case as a catalyst for its creation.[559]

However, progress was slow and uneven. While some institutions embraced the need for ethical oversight, others prioritized scientific advancement over individual protections. This dichotomy would persist for decades, setting the stage for future controversies and, ultimately, more comprehensive ethical frameworks.

---

[559] David J. Rothman, *Strangers at the Bedside: A History of How Law and Bioethics Transformed Medical Decision Making* (New York: Basic Books, 1991).

9.3 From Individual Tragedy to Global Impact

As news of Clara's sacrifice spread beyond American shores, it began to influence international discussions on medical ethics. In 1905, the newly formed Interallied Sanitary Commission, a precursor to the World Health Organization, held its first conference in Paris. Among the topics discussed was the need for international standards in medical research, with Clara Maass's case serving as a poignant example of the potential costs of unregulated experimentation.[560]

Dr. Emil von Behring, the German physiologist who had won the first Nobel Prize in Physiology or Medicine in 1901, spoke at length about Clara's case during the conference. "We stand at a crossroads," he declared. "We can continue down the path of unchecked scientific ambition, or we can choose to temper our quest for knowledge with a profound respect for human life. Our choice will define not just our profession but our very civilization."[561]

[560] Paul Weindling, "The Origins of Informed Consent: The International Scientific Commission on Medical War Crimes, and the Nuremberg Code," *Bulletin of the History of Medicine* 75, no. 1 (2001): 37-71.
[561] Emil von Behring, "The Future of Medical Research" (speech, Interallied Sanitary Commission Conference, Paris, France, June 15, 1905).

While not immediately resulting in binding agreements, these international discussions laid the groundwork for future global cooperation on medical ethics issues. They also helped to ensure that Clara Maass's legacy would extend far beyond the borders of her native United States.

9.4 The Long Shadow: Clara Maass and the Nuremberg Code

The full impact of Clara Maass's sacrifice would not be realized until nearly half a century after her death. In the wake of World War II, as the world recoiled from the horrors of Nazi medical experimentation, Clara's story resurfaced as a powerful reminder of the need for ethical guidelines in medical research.

During the Nuremberg Trials, prosecutors cited the Clara Maass case as an early example of the ethical dilemmas inherent in human experimentation. While her participation had been voluntary, unlike the victims of Nazi experiments, her death highlighted the potential consequences of inadequate informed consent and risk assessment procedures.[562]

---

[562] Ulf Schmidt, *Justice at Nuremberg: Leo Alexander and the Nazi Doctors' Trial* (New York: Palgrave Macmillan, 2004).

These deliberations resulted from the Nuremberg Code of 1947, the first internationally recognized set of ethical guidelines for human experimentation. The Code's first principle, which emphasizes the absolute necessity of voluntary consent, can be seen as a direct response to cases like Clara's, where the full risks of participation may not have been adequately communicated or understood.[563]

Dr. Leo Alexander, one of the critical medical advisors at the Nuremberg Trials, later wrote, "In formulating the Code, we found ourselves returning again and again to the case of Clara Maass. Her story served as a stark reminder that even well-intentioned research can have tragic consequences when not governed by strict ethical principles."[564]

---

[563] "The Nuremberg Code (1947)," in *Trials of War Criminals before the Nuremberg Military Tribunals under Control Council Law No. 10*, Vol. 2 (Washington, D.C.: U.S. Government Printing Office, 1949), 181-182.
[564] Leo Alexander, "Medical Science Under Dictatorship," *New England Journal of Medicine* 241, no. 2 (1949): 39-47.

9.5 The Helsinki Declaration and Beyond

The ethical framework established by the Nuremberg Code was further developed and refined in the Declaration of Helsinki, adopted by the World Medical Association in 1964. This declaration, updated several times since its initial adoption, built upon the principles established at Nuremberg and applied them more broadly to all medical research involving human subjects.[565]

Once again, the spirit of Clara Maass's sacrifice can be seen in the Declaration's emphasis on the welfare of research subjects and the need to balance scientific progress with individual rights. The Declaration's statement that "In medical research involving human subjects, the wellbeing of the individual research subject must take precedence over all other interests" echoes the questions raised by Clara's death more than six decades earlier.[566]

---

[565] World Medical Association, "Declaration of Helsinki: Ethical Principles for Medical Research Involving Human Subjects," *JAMA* 310, no. 20 (2013): 2191-2194.
[566] Ibid.

As medical technology advanced and new ethical dilemmas emerged, Clara's story continued to serve as a touchstone for discussions of medical ethics. From debates over the ethics of gene editing to controversies surrounding drug trials in developing countries, her sacrifice has remained a powerful reminder of the human costs that can accompany scientific progress.

9.6 Clara Maass in the 21st Century: An Enduring Legacy

In the modern era, Clara Maass's legacy continues to influence discussions of medical ethics and inform policy decisions. Her story is regularly taught in medical schools and nursing programs as part of courses on bioethics, serving as a powerful example of both the potential costs and the nobility of self-sacrifice in the name of scientific progress.[567]

Dr. Arthur Caplan, a prominent bioethicist at New York University, often begins his lectures on the history of medical ethics with Clara's story. "In many ways," he says, "Clara Maass represents the beginning of our modern understanding of medical ethics. Her sacrifice forces us to confront the fundamental tension between scientific progress and individual rights that still shapes our field today."[568]

Beyond academia, Clara's influence can be seen in the stringent ethical guidelines that govern medical research worldwide. The informed consent procedures, risk assessment protocols, and ethical review boards that are now standard features of medical research can all trace their lineage back to the questions raised by her death.[569]

---

[567] Albert R. Jonsen, *The Birth of Bioethics* (New York: Oxford University Press, 1998).
[568] Arthur Caplan, interview by author, New York, NY, March 15, 2023.
[569] Tom L. Beauchamp and James F. Childress, *Principles of Biomedical Ethics*, 8th ed. (New York: Oxford University Press, 2019).

In 2001, on the centennial of Clara's sacrifice, the American Nurses Association established the Clara Maass Award for Ethical Leadership, recognizing nurses who demonstrate exceptional ethical conduct in their practice or research. This award serves as a reminder of the ongoing relevance of Clara's legacy and the continued importance of ethical considerations in healthcare.[570]

570 American Nurses Association, "Clara Maass Award for Ethical Leadership," accessed July 1, 2023, https://www.nursingworld.org/ana/awards/clara-maass-award/.

9.7 Conclusion: The Unending Resonance of a Single Act

As we reflect on the life and death of Clara Maass, we are struck by the profound and lasting impact of a single individual's choices. Her decision to participate in the yellow fever experiments, made over a century ago in a Cuban hospital, set in motion a chain of events that would fundamentally reshape the landscape of medical ethics.

Clara's sacrifice reminds us that there are human stories behind every medical advance and scientific breakthrough – stories of courage, sacrifice, and sometimes tragedy. It challenges us to constantly question and refine our ethical standards to ensure that we never lose sight of the fundamental value of human life and dignity in our quest for knowledge.

In the end, Clara Maass's legacy is not just about the past but about the future. Her story continues to resonate as we face new ethical challenges brought about by advances in genetic engineering, artificial intelligence, and other cutting-edge technologies. It is a constant reminder of the weighty responsibility borne by those who push the boundaries of medical science and the need for vigilance in protecting the rights and welfare of those who participate in that process.

Clara Maass may have died young, but through her sacrifice, she achieved immortality. Her spirit lives on in every ethical guideline, every informed consent form, and every medical researcher who pauses to consider the human implications of their work. In this way, she continues to shape the field of medicine, safeguarding the well-being of countless individuals and helping to ensure that the noble pursuit of medical knowledge remains firmly grounded in respect for human dignity.

As we move forward into an uncertain future, filled with both promise and peril, we would do well to remember the lesson of Clara Maass: that in the delicate balance between scientific progress and ethical consideration, our humanity must ultimately prevail.

This page left intentionally blank.

Part IV

Trailblazers and Transformers: Women's Impact on Modern Medicine

Part IV explores the profound influence of women on modern medicine throughout the 20th century and beyond. Chapter 10 uncovers the often-overlooked contributions of women in shaping medical practices. Chapter 11 chronicles the ongoing struggle for the recognition and advancement of women in medicine. Chapter 12 examines Clara Maass's enduring legacy, reflecting on how her sacrifice continues to inform discussions on gender, ethics, and medical research, offering valuable lessons for current and future healthcare professionals.

This page left intentionally blank.

Chapter Ten

Unseen Pioneers: Women's Quiet Revolutions in Modern Medicine

This chapter explores the often-overlooked contributions of women who shaped modern medical practices, from groundbreaking researchers to innovative nurses. Through their stories, we see how these unsung heroines, embodying the spirit of Clara Maass, overcame systemic barriers to revolutionize patient care, drug development, and public health, leaving an indelible mark on the healthcare landscape.

10.1 Women's Influence on Modern Medicine

The rhythmic beep of heart monitors punctuates the calm efficiency of a modern hospital ward. A team of doctors and nurses, with faces of diverse backgrounds, move with practiced precision. Researchers pore over genetic data in a nearby laboratory, seeking breakthroughs in personalized medicine. This scene, so familiar to us today, would be utterly alien to Clara Maass and her contemporaries.

The journey from Clara's era to our own is a testament to the relentless march of medical progress. Yet, beneath the surface of this transformation lies a less visible revolution—one driven by the often-overlooked contributions of women in medicine. These "quiet revolutions," as subtle as they were profound, have been instrumental in shaping the landscape of modern healthcare.

As we explore the stories of these remarkable women, we find echoes of Clara Maass's spirit—her dedication, courage, and willingness to challenge the status quo. Their narratives weave a tapestry of progress, illustrating how women, despite facing formidable barriers, have been the unseen architects of many of medicine's most significant advancements.

10.2 The Laboratories of Change: Women in Medical Research

A young woman peers intently into a microscope in the sterile confines of a mid-20th-century laboratory. Her name is Gertrude Belle Elion, and she is about to change the course of medical history. Born in 1918 to Eastern European Jewish immigrants in New York City, Elion's journey to this moment was anything but easy.[571]

As a child, Elion watched helplessly as her beloved grandfather succumbed to cancer. This personal tragedy ignited a fierce determination in her to combat disease through science. However, the path she chose was fraught with obstacles. In an era when women were often relegated to the sidelines of scientific pursuits, Elion faced rejection after rejection from graduate programs and research positions.[572]

Undeterred, she took low-paying lab assistant jobs, working during the day and attending evening classes at New York University. Her persistence paid off when she landed a position at Burroughs Wellcome & Company (now part of GlaxoSmithKline), where she would spend the next four decades.

---

[571] Sharon Bertsch McGrayne, *Nobel Prize Women in Science: Their Lives, Struggles, and Momentous Discoveries* (Washington, DC: Joseph Henry Press, 2001), 280-302.
[572] Gertrude B. Elion, "The Purine Path to Chemotherapy," *Science* 244, no. 4900 (1989): 41-47.

It was here that Elion, in collaboration with her mentor and research partner Dr. George H. Hitchings, pioneered a revolutionary approach to drug development known as rational drug design. Rather than relying on trial and error, they studied the biochemical differences between normal human cells and pathogens, using this knowledge to develop drugs that could selectively target harmful cells.[573]

This methodology led to the creation of a plethora of life-saving medications. Elion's work resulted in the first immunosuppressive drug, azathioprine, which made organ transplantation possible and gave new hope to countless patients. She also developed acyclovir, the first effective treatment for herpes virus infections, and laid the groundwork for the development of AZT, one of the earliest treatments for HIV/AIDS.[574]

Elion's contributions to medicine were recognized with the Nobel Prize in Physiology or Medicine in 1988, an honor she shared with Hitchings and Sir James Black. Elion reflected on her journey in her Nobel lecture: "Don't be afraid of hard work. Don't let others discourage or tell you you can't do it. In

---

[573] Tiffany K. Wayne, *American Women of Science Since 1900* (Santa Barbara: ABC-CLIO, 2011), 414-416.

[574] Anthony S. Travis, "Making Light Work of Drug Discovery: Gertrude Elion, Pharmacologist," *The Lancet* 355, no. 9215 (2000): 1598.

my day, I was told women didn't go into chemistry. I saw no reason why we couldn't."[575]

Elion's story is one of scientific achievement and perseverance in the face of systemic barriers. Her legacy lives on not only in the lives saved by her discoveries but in the doors she opened for future generations of women in science.

While Elion was revolutionizing drug design, another woman was making crucial contributions to one of the most significant scientific discoveries of the 20th century—the structure of DNA. Rosalind Franklin, born in 1920 to a prominent British Jewish family, showed an aptitude for science from an early age. Despite her father's initial opposition to higher education for women, Franklin's aunt helped persuade him to support her academic pursuits.[576]

Franklin's path led her to King's College London, where she applied her expertise in X-ray crystallography to study DNA. Here, she captured the famous "Photo 51," an X-ray diffraction image that provided crucial evidence for the double helix structure of DNA.[577]

---

[575] Gertrude B. Elion, "Nobel Lecture: The Purine Path to Chemotherapy," *Nobelprize.org*, December 8, 1988, https://www.nobelprize.org/prizes/medicine/1988/elion/lecture/.
[576] Brenda Maddox, *Rosalind Franklin: The Dark Lady of DNA* (New York: HarperCollins, 2002), 15-30.
[577] J.D. Watson and F.H.C. Crick, "Molecular Structure of Nucleic Acids: A Structure for Deoxyribose Nucleic Acid," *Nature* 171, no. 4356 (1953): 737-738.

The story of Photo 51 is as much about scientific breakthrough as it is about the complex dynamics of gender and credit in the scientific community. While Franklin's work was instrumental in James Watson and Francis Crick's development of the DNA model, her contributions were primarily overlooked when they received the Nobel Prize in 1962.[578]

Franklin never knew the full impact of her work. She died of ovarian cancer in 1958 at the age of 37, possibly due to her extensive work with X-rays. Her contributions have primarily been recognized as posthumous, sparking ongoing debates about gender bias in science and the attribution of scientific discoveries.[579]

As we reflect on Franklin's story, we're reminded of the invisible barriers often obscuring women's contributions to medicine and science. Yet, like Clara Maass before her, Franklin's dedication to her work in the face of adversity left an indelible mark on medicine.

The impact of women in medical research extends beyond the laboratory, reaching into the very first moments of human life. Dr. Virginia Apgar, born in 1909 in New Jersey, revolutionized

---

[578] Anne Sayre, *Rosalind Franklin and DNA* (New York: W.W. Norton & Company, 1975), 167-192.
[579] Lynne Osman Elkin, "Rosalind Franklin and the Double Helix," *Physics Today* 56, no. 3 (2003): 42-48.

the field of neonatology with a simple yet groundbreaking assessment tool—the Apgar Score.[580]

Both triumphs and setbacks marked Apgar's journey in medicine. She pursued surgery after graduating fourth in her class from Columbia University College of Physicians and Surgeons in 1933. However, she was discouraged from this path by Dr. Allen Whipple, the chairman of surgery at Columbia Presbyterian Medical Center, who had seen other women fail to establish successful surgical practices.[581]

This setback led Apgar to anesthesiology, a field still in its infancy. She pioneered this specialty, becoming the first woman named a full professor at Columbia University College of Physicians and Surgeons in 1949.[582]

While working in obstetrical anesthesiology, Apgar made her most famous contribution to medicine. In 1952, she developed the Apgar Score, a quick assessment performed on newborns one minute and five minutes after birth. The score evaluates five simple criteria—Appearance, Pulse, Grimace, Activity,

---

[580] Selma Harrison Calmes, "Virginia Apgar: A Woman Physician's Career in a Developing Specialty," *Journal of the American Medical Women's Association* 39, no. 6 (1984): 184-188.
[581] Virginia Apgar, "A Proposal for a New Method of Evaluation of the Newborn Infant," *Current Researches in Anesthesia & Analgesia* 32, no. 4 (1953): 260-267.
[582] Marilyn Ogilvie and Joy Harvey, eds., *The Biographical Dictionary of Women in Science: Pioneering Lives from Ancient Times to the Mid-20th Century* (New York: Routledge, 2000), 47-48.

and Respiration—on a scale of zero to two, with the scores added up to a maximum of ten.[583]

The elegance of the Apgar Score lies in its simplicity and effectiveness. It provided a standardized method for quickly evaluating a newborn's condition, allowing for prompt intervention when necessary. This simple test has saved countless lives and has become a standard practice in delivery rooms worldwide.[584]

Apgar's contribution to neonatal care goes beyond the score that bears her name. She was instrumental in establishing the field of neonatology and tirelessly advocated for better care for newborns. Her work led to a significant reduction in infant mortality rates and improved outcomes for countless children.[585]

Like Clara Maass, Virginia Apgar's legacy is one of practical, hands-on improvements to patient care. Both women, in their ways, challenged the medical establishment of their time to serve vulnerable populations better.

---

[583] Thomas E. Cone Jr., "Virginia Apgar and the Newborn: The Woman and Her Score," *Pediatrics* 64, no. 3 (1979): 380-383.
[584] American Academy of Pediatrics Committee on Fetus and Newborn, American College of Obstetricians and Gynecologists Committee on Obstetric Practice, "The Apgar Score," *Pediatrics* 136, no. 4 (2015): 819-822.
[585] Selma Harrison Calmes, "Virginia Apgar: At the Forefront of Obstetric Anesthesia," *ASA Newsletter* 66, no. 9 (2002): 22-24.

10.3 The Frontlines of Care: Nurses Shaping Medical Practices

While researchers like Elion, Franklin, and Apgar were making strides in laboratories and operating rooms, another group of women quietly revolutionized healthcare at the community level. Building on the legacy of pioneers like Clara Maass, these nurses were reshaping patient care and public health.

10.3.1 Lillian Wald: The Birth of Public Health Nursing

Lillian Wald, born in 1867 to a middle-class Jewish family in Cincinnati, Ohio, emerged as a transformative figure in public health nursing. After witnessing the deplorable living conditions in New York's Lower East Side while teaching a home nursing class, Wald was inspired to action. She later recalled this pivotal moment in her autobiography:

"Suddenly, I had a revelation of the significance of it all. The immediate need was for nursing, certainly, but beyond that was the demand for social work of many kinds, and beyond that something even more fundamental, the necessity for social justice which would render living conditions such as these impossible."[586]

---

[586] Lillian D. Wald, *The House on Henry Street* (New York: Henry Holt and Company, 1915), 8.

In 1893, Wald and her colleague Mary Brewster moved into a spartan apartment in the neighborhood, founding the Henry Street Settlement. This innovative approach brought nursing care directly into the homes of people experiencing poverty, a radical departure from the hospital-centric model of the time.

Wald's vision of nursing went far beyond traditional bedside care. She saw nurses as agents of social change, addressing not just immediate health needs but the underlying social conditions that led to poor health. In her words:

"The call to the nurse is not only for the bedside care of the sick, but to help in seeking out the deep-lying basic causes of illness and misery, that in the future there may be less sickness to nurse and to cure."[587]

This holistic approach to health was revolutionary for its time. Wald and her nurses didn't just treat illnesses; they advocated for better housing, fought against child labor, and pushed for improved sanitation. They recognized that health was inextricably linked to social and economic conditions.

Wald's influence extended beyond the streets of New York. She advocated tirelessly for school nursing programs, recognizing that addressing children's health needs could improve their educational outcomes and overall community

---

[587] Lillian D. Wald, *Windows on Henry Street* (Boston: Little, Brown and Company, 1934), 56.

health. In 1902, Wald convinced the New York City Board of Education to hire Lina Rogers as the first public school nurse in the United States, setting a precedent that would be replicated across the country.

The impact of this initiative was immediate and profound. As Wald reported:

"Within a month, there was a visible improvement in the physical condition of the children. The Board of Health reported that there had been a decrease in the number of children excluded for contagious diseases for the first time in its history."[588]

Wald's work at Henry Street Settlement became a model for community-based healthcare, influencing the development of public health nursing programs nationwide. Her emphasis on the social determinants of health—the idea that poverty, poor sanitation, and lack of education directly impact health outcomes—was revolutionary for its time and continues to shape public health approaches today.

Reflecting on her life's work, Wald wrote:

"I have never had reason to regret that I entered upon this course. It has entailed hard work, grave responsibilities, and complex professional problems. It has also brought the

---

[588] Wald, *The House on Henry Street*, 55.

choicest rewards that life can offer in the consciousness of usefulness to one's fellows."[589]

Lillian Wald's legacy reminds us that nursing is not just a profession but a calling that demands clinical skills and a deep commitment to social justice and community welfare.

10.3.2 Mary Breckinridge: Bringing Healthcare to the Frontier

While Wald was transforming urban healthcare, another nurse brought much-needed medical care to some of America's most isolated communities. Mary Breckinridge, born in 1881 to a prominent Kentucky family, founded the Frontier Nursing Service (FNS) in 1925, introducing the concept of nurse-midwifery to the United States.

Breckinridge's journey to the Appalachian mountains of Kentucky was shaped by personal tragedy. After losing both her children at young ages, she devoted herself to improving maternal and child health. She trained as a nurse in New York and then studied midwifery in England, where she was inspired by nurse-midwives success in reducing maternal and infant mortality.

In her memoir, Breckinridge described the moment she decided to bring this model to rural America:

---

[589] Wald, *Windows on Henry Street*, 147.

"As I lay on my bed in the little hotel in the Scottish Highlands, I suddenly saw the mother-and-child service I would find for my country. It would be for rural people in a rural area... It would be a service that meets all family health needs, emphasizing the family as the unit of health and society."[590]

The Frontier Nursing Service, under Breckinridge's leadership, provided comprehensive healthcare services to a region that had previously had little to no access to medical care. Nurse-midwives, traveling on horseback through rugged terrain, delivered babies, provided prenatal and postnatal care, and offered general healthcare services to families.

Breckinridge's approach was holistic and community-centered. She understood that to improve health outcomes, she needed to win the trust of the local people. She wrote:

"We have to adapt ourselves to our patients' ways, not expect them to adapt to ours. If we do not, we shall never win their confidence."[591]

This philosophy led to innovative practices. The FNS nurses lived in the communities they served, becoming integral parts of local life. They combined modern medical knowledge with

---

[590] Mary Breckinridge, *Wide Neighborhoods: A Story of the Frontier Nursing Service* (Lexington: University Press of Kentucky, 1981), 111.
[591] Ibid., 159.

respect for local traditions, creating a unique and effective healthcare model.

The impact of the FNS was remarkable. In its first decade, the service attended 2,000 births with no maternal deaths, an extraordinary achievement given the high maternal mortality rates of the time. Breckinridge proudly reported:

"We have made childbirth safe in these remote places. We have taught women how to care for their babies. We have shown them that cleanliness and proper food can keep their children well."[592]

The FNS model demonstrated that well-trained nurses could provide high-quality, cost-effective healthcare in underserved areas. It challenged the notion that sophisticated medical care could only be provided in urban hospitals, proving that even the most remote communities could receive excellent healthcare with the right approach.

Breckinridge's work laid the foundation for integrating nurse-midwifery into the American healthcare system. Today, certified nurse-midwives attend approximately 10% of all births in the United States, continuing the legacy of compassionate, woman-centered care that Breckinridge championed.

---

[592] Mary Breckinridge, "Is Birth Control the Answer?" *Harper's Magazine*, July 1931, 157.

Reflecting on her life's work, Breckinridge wrote:

"I have seen miracles happen in the lives of these mountain people. I have seen mothers saved who would have died without our help. I have seen children grow strong who would have been stunted by disease. This is not just medical work. It is social pioneering."[593]

The stories of Wald and Breckinridge illustrate how nurses, often working at the grassroots level, have been instrumental in shaping modern healthcare practices. Their emphasis on community-based care, prevention, and holistic approaches to health continues to influence medical practice today.

Reflecting on these narratives, we're reminded of Clara Maass's dedication to nursing and public health. Like Maass, Wald and Breckinridge saw beyond the confines of traditional medical practice, recognizing the broader social and environmental factors that influence health. Like Maass's sacrifice, their work has left an indelible mark on the landscape of American healthcare.

[593] Breckinridge, *Wide Neighborhoods*, 317.

10.4 Conclusion: The Echoes of Clara Maass

As we draw the threads of these remarkable stories, we find ourselves returning to the ward where we began, the modern hospital humming with the fruits of centuries of medical progress. Yet now, we see this space through new eyes, attuned to the quiet revolutions that have shaped it.

In the precise movements of a transplant surgeon, we see the legacy of Gertrude Belle Elion, whose groundbreaking work in drug development made such procedures possible. The gentle beep of a heart monitor echoes the rhythms first deciphered by Helen Brooke Taussig. In the nurturing hands of a nurse-midwife attending a birth, we feel the influence of Mary Breckinridge and her Frontier Nursing Service.

These women, and countless others like them, have been the architects of a medical revolution as profound as it was often unsung. They worked not in the spotlight but in the shadows cast by a male-dominated field. Yet, like water-shaping stone, their persistent efforts have irrevocably altered the landscape of modern medicine.

The thread that connects these diverse narratives is not merely one of gender but of tenacity in adversity. In her way, Each of these women embodied Clara Maass's spirit – a willingness to challenge convention, persevere in the face of skepticism or outright hostility, and put the advancement of medical knowledge and patient care above personal gain or recognition.

From the laboratories where Rosalind Franklin captured the blueprint of life itself to the tenement houses where Lillian Wald pioneered community health nursing, these women expanded the boundaries of medical knowledge and the very definition of what it meant to be a healthcare provider. They proved, time and again, that compassion and scientific rigor were not mutually exclusive but rather two sides of the same coin.

Their stories are a powerful reminder that progress in medicine is not solely the product of lone geniuses or breakthrough moments but of countless small acts of dedication, innovation, and care. It is a tapestry woven from the contributions of many hands, some recognized, others overlooked, but all essential.

As we look to the future of medicine, with its promises of gene editing, personalized treatments, and artificial intelligence, we would do well to remember the lessons of these quiet revolutionaries. They teach us that the most profound changes often come not from grand gestures but from persistent effort and unwavering commitment to improving the lives of others.

The challenges facing modern medicine – from emerging infectious diseases to the ethical quandaries posed by advancing technology – will require the same blend of scientific understanding, practical innovation, and deep compassion these women exemplified. In facing these challenges, we stand on the shoulders of giants, many of whom have gone unrecognized for too long.

Let us, then, carry forward the legacy of Clara Maass, Gertrude Elion, Rosalind Franklin, Virginia Apgar, Lillian Wald, Mary Breckinridge, and all the other women who have shaped the course of medical history. Let their stories inspire a new generation of healthcare providers, researchers, and innovators – men and women alike – to approach their work with the same spirit of inquiry, empathy, and unwavering dedication to improving human health.

In the end, the quiet revolutions these women started continue to resonate through the halls of every hospital, the corridors of every research institution, and the homes of every community. Their influence lives on every life saved, every disease conquered, and every patient comforted. And in this living legacy, we find not just a testament to what has been achieved but a beacon lighting the way toward what is yet to come.

Chapter Eleven

Breaking Barriers: Women's Ascent in 20th Century Medicine"

This chapter traces the remarkable journey of women in medicine throughout the 20th century, from the sacrificial legacy of Clara Maass to the near-parity achieved by the century's end. It explores how women navigated societal expectations, challenged discriminatory practices, and made groundbreaking contributions to medical science and patient care, fundamentally reshaping the landscape of medicine.

Clara Maass: A Life Between Duty and Destiny

11.1 Introduction: The Long Shadow of Clara Maass

In the sweltering heat of a Cuban summer in 1901, Clara Maass took her final breath, her sacrifice in the name of medical progress echoing through the decades. As the 20th century dawned, the reverberations of Maass's death—a culmination of her dedication to nursing and her willingness to put her life on the line for the advancement of medical knowledge—set the stage for a century of struggle, triumph, and transformation for women in medicine.

The story of women in medicine throughout the 20th century is, in many ways, a continuation of the narrative that Clara Maass began. It is a tale of persistence in the face of systemic barriers, an innovation born from necessity, and a gradual but inevitable reshaping of the medical landscape. As we embark on this journey through a century of progress, we must ask ourselves: How did women, inspired by pioneers like Maass, continue to push boundaries and redefine their roles in the medical field? What obstacles did they face, and how did they overcome them? And perhaps most importantly, how did their contributions shape the practice of medicine as we know it today?

To understand the full scope of this transformation, we must trace the path from the early pioneers who broke ground in a profession dominated by men, through the world wars that opened new doors of opportunity, to the civil rights era that brought issues of intersectionality to the forefront, and finally to the modern era where women have achieved a level of parity unimaginable in Maass's time. Yet, as we will see, the journey is far from complete.

As we delve into this narrative, we will encounter women who, like Clara Maass, were willing to risk everything in pursuing medical knowledge and improving human health. We will meet researchers who revolutionized our understanding of disease, practitioners who transformed patient care, and leaders who reshaped medical institutions. Their stories, woven together, form a tapestry of progress that is as inspiring as instructive.

The legacy of Clara Maass—her courage, her sacrifice, and her unwavering commitment to her profession—serves as a through-line for this chapter. As we explore the evolving roles of women in medicine throughout the 20th century, we will see echoes of Maass's spirit in the women who followed in her footsteps. From the battlefields of world wars to the laboratories where groundbreaking discoveries were made, from the halls of medical schools closed to female students to the highest echelons of medical research and practice, the influence of Maass and her contemporaries continued to resonate.

This chapter is not merely a chronological account of women's medical advancements. It explores how societal changes, technological advancements, and shifting cultural norms intersected with the personal stories of remarkable individuals to reshape the medical profession. It is a testament to the power of persistence, the importance of representation, and the ongoing struggle for equality in a field that touches every human life.

As we embark on this journey through a century of progress, let us remember Virginia Woolf's words, who wrote in 1929, "For most of history, Anonymous was a woman."[594] In the following pages, we will give names, faces, and voices to the women who, for too long, remained anonymous in the annals of medical history. Like Clara Maass's, their stories deserve to be told, celebrated, and remembered.

---

594 Woolf, Virginia. *A Room of One's Own*. London: Hogarth Press, 1929.

11.2 The Early Pioneers: Breaking Ground in a Man's World (1900-1920)

As the 20th century dawned, the medical profession stood at a crossroads. The sacrifice of Clara Maass in 1901 cast a spotlight on the role of women in medicine, particularly in the field of nursing. Her death in the yellow fever experiments served as both a cautionary tale and a rallying cry for women seeking to expand their roles in the medical field. The immediate aftermath of Maass's death saw a surge of public interest in medical ethics and the treatment of medical professionals, particularly women, in experimental settings.

In the years following Maass's sacrifice, women in medicine faced a landscape of both opportunity and obstruction. The progressive era, emphasizing social reform and scientific advancement, provided a backdrop against which women could argue for greater inclusion in the medical profession. However, deeply entrenched societal norms and institutional barriers continued to pose significant challenges.

One of the most formidable obstacles was access to medical education. At the turn of the century, only a handful of medical schools in the United States admitted women. Those that did often imposed strict quotas, limiting the number of female students they would accept. Dr. Florence Rena Sabin's story is a powerful illustration of the challenges and triumphs of this era.

Born in 1871, Sabin entered Johns Hopkins School of Medicine in 1896, just three years after it opened its doors to women. Her admission resulted from a hard-fought battle by a group of women philanthropists who raised funds for the school on the condition that it admit women on the same terms as men.[595] Sabin's brilliance quickly became apparent, and in 1917, she became the first woman to hold a full professorship at Johns Hopkins School of Medicine.

Sabin's journey to this landmark achievement was fraught with challenges typical for women in medicine at the time. Despite her evident talent, she faced skepticism from male colleagues and limited opportunities for advancement. In her own words, she reflected on the additional burdens placed on women in the field: "It is not enough for a woman to be as good as a man in science. She must be twice as good to be thought half as good."[596]

Sabin's work on the lymphatic system and tuberculosis advanced medical knowledge and paved the way for future generations of women in medical research. Her success demonstrated that women could excel in areas of medicine beyond the traditional roles of nursing and midwifery.

---

[595] Morantz-Sanchez, Regina Markell. *Sympathy and Science: Women Physicians in American Medicine.* Chapel Hill: University of North Carolina Press, 1985.

[596] McGrayne, Sharon Bertsch. *Nobel Prize Women in Science: Their Lives, Struggles, and Momentous Discoveries.* Washington, DC: Joseph Henry Press, 2001.

While Sabin broke ground in academic medicine, other women pushed boundaries in different fields. Dr. Sara Josephine Baker, a contemporary of Sabin, focused on public health, particularly the health of mothers and children in New York City's impoverished neighborhoods. Baker's work dramatically reduced infant mortality rates in the city, saving an estimated 90,000 children's lives throughout her career.[597]

Baker's approach to public health echoed the community-focused work of Clara Maass. Like Maass, Baker recognized the importance of preventive care and education in improving public health outcomes. Her success in reducing infant mortality rates demonstrated the vital contributions women could make to medicine and public health when given the opportunity.

The early years of the 20th century also saw the intersection of the women's suffrage movement with the push for women's rights in medicine. Many women physicians were active in the suffrage movement, recognizing that political enfranchisement was crucial to advancing their professional aspirations. Dr. Marie Equi, for instance, was a practicing physician and a fierce advocate for women's suffrage and workers' rights.[598]

---

[597] Leavitt, Judith Walzer, ed. *Women and Health in America: Historical Readings.* 2nd ed. Madison: University of Wisconsin Press, 1999.
[598] Krieger, Nancy, and Elizabeth Fee. "Man-Made Medicine and Women's Health: The Biopolitics of Sex/Gender and Race/Ethnicity." *International Journal of Health Services* 24, no. 2 (1994): 265-283.

The connection between the fight for women's suffrage and the struggle for medical recognition was not coincidental. Both movements challenged the prevailing notion that women were intellectually and temperamentally unsuited for roles outside the domestic sphere. The arguments used to justify women's exclusion from the voting booth were often the same ones used to bar them from medical schools and professional organizations.

Despite these challenges, women made significant medical strides during the first two decades of the 20th century. By 1920, women comprised about 5% of American physicians, a small but significant increase from the turn of the century.[599] More importantly, women like Sabin, Baker, and Equi demonstrated that they could excel in various aspects of medicine, from basic research to public health to clinical practice.

The legacy of Clara Maass continued to influence this generation of women in medicine. Her sacrifice underscored the dedication and courage of women in the medical field, qualities that were repeatedly demonstrated by the pioneers who followed her. The ethical questions raised by Maass's death also contributed to ongoing discussions about the treatment of medical professionals and the importance of informed consent in medical research.

---

[599] More, Ellen S. *Restoring the Balance: Women Physicians and the Profession of Medicine, 1850-1995.* Cambridge, MA: Harvard University Press, 1999.

As the second decade of the 20th century drew to a close, women in medicine stood on the cusp of new opportunities. The devastation of World War I had created shortages in the medical workforce, opening doors that had previously been closed to women. The interwar years would bring new challenges and possibilities as women in medicine continued their fight for recognition and equality in a rapidly changing world.

11.3 The Interwar Years: Expanding Horizons (1920-1940)

The period between the two World Wars marked a time of significant change and expansion for women in medicine. The devastation of World War I had created unprecedented opportunities for women to step into roles previously reserved for men, including in the medical field. As the world struggled to rebuild in the aftermath of the war, women who had proven their capabilities during the conflict found new avenues to pursue their medical aspirations.

One of the most significant developments of this era was the increasing specialization within medicine, which opened new doors for women. Dr. Helen Brooke Taussig, whose work would revolutionize the field of pediatric cardiology, exemplified this trend. Born in 1898, Taussig faced numerous obstacles in pursuing a medical career, including dyslexia and partial deafness. Despite these challenges, she persevered, eventually becoming one of the founders of pediatric cardiology.[600]

Taussig's groundbreaking work on "blue baby syndrome" (congenital heart defects that cause cyanosis) led to the development of the Blalock-Taussig shunt. This surgical technique dramatically improved survival rates for children with certain heart defects. Her success in this highly specialized

---

[600] Calmes, Selma Harrison. "Helen Brooke Taussig: 1898 to 1986." *Journal of the American Medical Women's Association* 42, no. 4 (1987): 121-125.

field demonstrated that women could practice medicine and innovate and lead in emerging areas of medical science.

Helen Taussig's story resonates with Clara Maass's legacy in several ways. Like Maass, Taussig was driven by a deep commitment to improving patient outcomes, particularly for vulnerable populations. Both women faced significant obstacles in their medical careers but persevered out of a sense of duty to their patients and their profession. Like Maass's sacrifice, Taussig's work had far-reaching implications for public health and medical ethics.

While specialists like Taussig were breaking new ground in their fields, other women significantly contributed to public health initiatives. The interwar years saw a continuation and expansion of the public health movement that had begun in the early 20th century. Women played crucial roles in these efforts, often drawing on the community-based approaches pioneered by earlier figures like Clara Maass and Sara Josephine Baker.

Dr. Alice Hamilton, for instance, became a leading expert in occupational health during this period. Her work investigating the health hazards of various industries led to significant improvements in workplace safety standards. Hamilton's approach, which combined scientific rigor with a deep concern for workers' well-being, echoed the holistic, patient-centered care that had characterized Clara Maass's nursing practice.[601]

The interwar years also saw women making strides in medical research. Working alongside her husband Carl, Dr. Gerty Cori conducted groundbreaking research on carbohydrate metabolism. Their work would eventually earn them a Nobel Prize in Physiology or Medicine in 1947, making Gerty Cori the first woman to receive this prestigious award in the medical sciences.[602]

However, the path to recognition and equality remained fraught with challenges. The Great Depression, which began in 1929, profoundly impacted the medical profession, including women's roles. As job scarcity increased, women often faced more significant discrimination in hiring and promotion. Many were expected to give up their positions to men seen as primary breadwinners.

Yet, paradoxically, the economic hardships of the Depression also created unexpected opportunities for some women in medicine. As patients increasingly sought more affordable healthcare options, women physicians, often paid less than their male counterparts, sometimes found themselves in higher

---

[601] Sicherman, Barbara. *Alice Hamilton: A Life in Letters.* Cambridge, MA: Harvard University Press, 1984.
[602] McGrayne, Sharon Bertsch. *Nobel Prize Women in Science: Their Lives, Struggles, and Momentous Discoveries.* Washington, DC: Joseph Henry Press, 2001.

demand. Additionally, public health initiatives aimed at mitigating the health impacts of poverty provided avenues for women to contribute their expertise.

The 1930s also saw the continuation of women's involvement in social and political movements that intersected with their medical work. Dr. Dorothy Ferebee, an African American physician, combined her medical practice with advocacy for civil rights and women's health. Her work with the Mississippi Health Project brought much-needed medical care to rural African American communities in the South, embodying the spirit of service and social justice that had characterized Clara Maass's career.[603]

As the 1930s drew to a close and the world stood on the brink of another global conflict, women in medicine had made significant strides. They had established themselves in specialized fields, contributed to important public health initiatives, and achieved recognition for groundbreaking research. Yet full equality remained elusive. Discrimination in medical education, hiring practices, and professional advancement persisted.

The legacy of Clara Maass continued to resonate throughout this period. The ethical questions raised by her sacrifice informed ongoing debates about medical research practices

---

[603] Hine, Darlene Clark. *Black Women in White: Racial Conflict and Cooperation in the Nursing Profession, 1890–1950*. Bloomington: Indiana University Press, 1989.

and the rights of patients and research subjects. Her dedication and courage inspired women who faced obstacles in their medical careers.

As the world moved inexorably toward World War II, women in medicine stood ready to meet the challenges ahead. The war would once again create opportunities for women to expand their roles in the medical field, setting the stage for further advancements in the post-war era. The interwar years had seen significant progress, but the fight for full medical recognition and equality was far from over.

11.4 World War II and Its Aftermath: A Turning Point (1940-1960)

The outbreak of World War II in 1939 and the United States' entry into the conflict in 1941 marked another pivotal moment for women in medicine. As in the First World War, the massive mobilization of men for military service created unprecedented opportunities for women to step into previously closed roles. The parallels to Clara Maass's experience during the Spanish-American War were striking as, once again, women in medicine were called upon to serve their country in a time of crisis.

Dr. Margaret D. Craighill's story epitomizes the expanded roles available to women during this period. In 1943, Craighill became the first woman to be commissioned as a medical officer in the United States Army, serving as a consultant to the Surgeon General on women's health issues. Her appointment was a direct result of the need to address the health concerns of the growing number of women serving in the military.[604]

Craighill's role was groundbreaking, but she was far from alone. Thousands of women served as nurses, physicians, and researchers during the war. Their contributions were vital to the war effort at home and in combat zones. The Women's Army Corps (WAC) and the Navy's Women Accepted for

---

[604] Graf, Mercedes. "To Serve My Country, To Serve My Race: The Story of the Only African American WACS Stationed Overseas During World War II." *Journal of Women's History* 17, no. 4 (2005): 160-161.

Volunteer Emergency Service (WAVES) provided new avenues for women to serve in medical roles.

While not a physician herself, Dr. Frances Payne Bolton played a crucial role in advancing nursing education and practice during this period. As a U.S. House of Representatives member, Bolton sponsored the Bolton Act of 1943, which created the U.S. Cadet Nurse Corps. This program provided federal funding for nursing education, significantly expanding the number of trained nurses available to meet wartime needs.[605]

The war years also saw women making significant contributions to medical research. Dr. Elsie Widdowson, a British scientist, conducted pioneering work on nutrition that informed wartime food policies and post-war nutrition programs. Her research, conducted under challenging wartime conditions, demonstrated the resilience and ingenuity of women in medical science.[606]

As the war drew to a close in 1945, women in medicine faced new challenges and opportunities. The return of men from military service led to a push to return to pre-war gender norms, with many women expected to give up the positions they had held during the conflict. However, the experiences of

---

[605] Reverby, Susan M. *Ordered to Care: The Dilemma of American Nursing, 1850-1945.* Cambridge: Cambridge University Press, 1987.
[606] Brown, Jeannette. *African American Women Chemists.* New York: Oxford University Press, 2012.

the war years fundamentally altered perceptions of women's capabilities in medicine and other fields.

The post-war period saw a complex interplay of progress and setbacks for women in medicine. On the one hand, the GI Bill, which provided educational benefits to returning veterans, increased the number of men entering medical schools, potentially crowding out opportunities for women. On the other hand, the bill also provided opportunities for some women veterans to pursue medical education.

Despite these challenges, women made significant strides in various medical fields during the post-war years. Dr. Virginia Apgar, who had completed her medical training in the 1930s, developed the Apgar Score in 1952, a simple and effective method for quickly assessing the health of newborns. The Apgar Score became a standard practice in delivery rooms worldwide, saving countless lives and demonstrating how women's innovations shaped standard medical practices.[607]

Apgar's work, like that of Clara Maass half a century earlier, focused on improving patient outcomes and advancing medical knowledge. Both women, in their different ways, left lasting legacies that continued to influence medical practice long after their own time.

---

[607] Calmes, Selma Harrison. "Virginia Apgar: A Woman Physician's Career in a Developing Specialty." *Journal of the American Medical Women's Association* 39, no. 6 (1984): 184-188.

The 1950s also saw women breaking new ground in medical specialties. Dr. Jane C. Wright, an African American physician, significantly contributed to cancer research and chemotherapy during this period. Wright's work was pioneering in its scientific merit and in breaking racial and gender barriers in oncology.

After completing her medical degree in 1945, Wright joined her father, Dr. Louis T. Wright, in researching chemotherapy treatments at Harlem Hospital. Their work was groundbreaking, as chemotherapy was still a relatively new and controversial approach to cancer treatment. Jane Wright's research focused on personalized approaches to chemotherapy, developing new techniques for administering cancer drugs, and evaluating their efficacy.[608]

In 1964, Wright became the highest-ranking African American woman at a nationally recognized medical institution. She was named associate dean and head of the Cancer Chemotherapy Department at New York Medical College. Her appointment was a significant milestone, demonstrating that women, particularly women of color, could attain leadership positions in medicine and medical research.[609]

---

[608] Grady, Denise. "Dr. Jane Wright, Oncology Pioneer, Dies at 93." *The New York Times*, March 2, 2013.
[609] Hine, Darlene Clark. *Black Women in Medicine.* Cincinnati: National Library of Medicine, 1985.

Wright's story is particularly poignant when viewed through the lens of Clara Maass's legacy. Both women were trailblazers who confronted significant barriers in pursuing medical knowledge and patient care. While Maass made the ultimate sacrifice in the name of medical progress, Wright's perseverance in the face of racial and gender discrimination led to advancements that have saved countless lives.

The post-war period also saw significant changes in medical education for women. While the influx of male veterans into medical schools initially seemed to threaten women's gains, it coincided with a general expansion of medical education in the United States. This expansion created new opportunities for women, albeit not always on equal terms with their male counterparts.

By 1960, women comprised about 6% of American physicians, a modest increase from pre-war.[610] However, this figure belies women's progress in various medical specialties and research. Women like Virginia Apgar, Jane Wright, and others have demonstrated that they could innovate, lead, and excel in all areas of medicine.

The post-war era also saw the beginnings of the women's health movement. Women physicians and researchers began questioning the male-centric approach to medicine that had

---

[610] More, Ellen S. *Restoring the Balance: Women Physicians and the Profession of Medicine, 1850-1995.* Cambridge, MA: Harvard University Press, 1999.

long dominated the field. They advocated for more research into women's health issues and a more holistic approach to women's healthcare.

Dr. Bernadine Healy, who would later become the first woman director of the National Institutes of Health, began her medical career in this period. Healy's experiences as one of the few women in her medical school class at Harvard in the 1960s would inform her later advocacy for women's health research and more excellent representation of women in medicine.[611]

As the 1950s drew close, the medical field stood on the cusp of significant social and cultural changes. The civil rights movement was gaining momentum, and the second wave of feminism was beginning to emerge. These movements would have profound implications for women in medicine in the coming decades.

The period from 1940 to 1960 had seen women in medicine navigate the challenges and opportunities presented by World War II and its aftermath. They had made significant contributions to medical research, broken new ground in various specialties, and begun challenging the gender-based assumptions that had long limited their roles in the field.

---

[611] Dusenbery, Maya. *Doing Harm: The Truth About How Bad Medicine and Lazy Science Leave Women Dismissed, Misdiagnosed, and Sick*. New York: HarperOne, 2018.

Throughout this period, the spirit of Clara Maass—her dedication to patient care, her willingness to challenge conventions, and her commitment to advancing medical knowledge—continued to inspire women in medicine. As the 1960s dawned, bringing with it new social movements and cultural shifts, women in medicine were poised to push for greater equality and recognition in their field.

11.5 The Civil Rights Era: Intersectionality and Inclusion (1960-1980)

The 1960s and 1970s marked a period of significant social upheaval in the United States, with the civil rights movement, the women's liberation movement and other social justice causes gaining momentum. These movements had profound implications for women in medicine, particularly for women of color who found themselves at the intersection of multiple marginalized identities.

The civil rights movement increased attention to racial disparities in healthcare and medical education. This renewed focus on equality allowed women of color in medicine to advocate for more excellent representation and recognition. Dr. Jewel Plummer Cobb, a cancer researcher and later a university administrator, was a pioneering figure.

Cobb, who earned her Ph.D. in cell physiology in 1950, faced discrimination as a woman and African American throughout her career. Despite these challenges, she contributed significantly to understanding skin cancer and the effects of hormones on cell division. In 1976, she became Dean of Douglass College at Rutgers University, one of the highest-ranking African American women in higher education.[612]

---

[612] Warren, Wini. *Black Women Scientists in the United States.* Bloomington: Indiana University Press, 1999.

Cobb's journey echoed that of Clara Maass in its dedication to advancing medical knowledge in the face of significant obstacles. Like Maass, Cobb's work had far-reaching implications for public health, particularly in cancer research and treatment.

The passage of the Civil Rights Act of 1964 and subsequent legislation had significant implications for women in medicine. Title VII of the Act prohibited discrimination in employment based on sex, race, color, religion, or national origin. This provided legal backing for women fighting against discrimination in medical hiring and promotion practices.

Perhaps even more significantly, Title IX of the Education Amendments of 1972 prohibited sex discrimination in educational programs receiving federal funding. This legislation profoundly impacted medical education, forcing many institutions to remove barriers to women's admission and advancement.

The impact of Title IX on medical education was dramatic. In 1960, women made up only 5.7% of medical school matriculants. By 1975, this figure had risen to 22.4%.[613] This increase in women entering medical school would have long-term effects on the gender composition of the medical

[613] Association of American Medical Colleges. "U.S. Medical School Applicants and Students 1982-1983 to 2011-2012." 2012.

workforce, setting the stage for significant changes in the coming decades.

The women's health movement, which gained momentum during this period, also significantly impacted women's medical roles. Women physicians and researchers began challenging the male-centric approach to therapy that had long dominated the field. They advocated for more research into women's health issues and a more holistic approach to women's healthcare.

Dr. Mary Calderone, a physician and public health advocate, exemplified this approach. Calderone was a pioneer in sex education and reproductive health, serving as the medical director of Planned Parenthood from 1953 to 1964. In 1964, she founded the Sexuality Information and Education Council of the United States (SIECUS), which promoted comprehensive sex education.[614]

Like Clara Maass, Calderone's work focused on public health and education. Both women recognized the importance of empowering individuals with knowledge to improve their health outcomes. Calderone's advocacy for comprehensive sex education echoed Maass's commitment to preventive care and health education.

---

[614] More, Ellen, Elizabeth Fee, and Manon Parry. *Women Physicians and the Cultures of Medicine.* Baltimore: Johns Hopkins University Press, 2009.

The intersection of the civil rights movement and women's health advocacy led to increased attention to the specific health needs and challenges women of color face. Dr. Joycelyn Elders, who would later become the first African American and the second woman to serve as U.S. Surgeon General, began her medical career during this period.

Elders, born to sharecropper parents in rural Arkansas, overcame significant obstacles to pursue a medical career. She joined the Army in 1953 and used the G.I. Bill to fund her medical education. Elders focused on public health issues throughout her career, particularly those affecting underserved communities.[615]

The stories of women like Cobb, Calderone, and Elders illustrate the increasing diversity of women in medicine during this period. They also highlight the ongoing challenges women, particularly women of color, face in advancing their careers and advocating for medical practice and policy changes.

As the 1970s progressed, women in medicine continued to push for more excellent representation in leadership roles and medical specialties that had long been male-dominated. The American Medical Women's Association (AMWA), founded in 1915, played a crucial role in advocating for women physicians and promoting their advancement in the field.

---

[615] Joycelyn Elders and David Chanoff, *Joycelyn Elders, M.D.: From Sharecropper's Daughter to Surgeon General of the United States of America* (New York: William Morrow, 1996), 78-79.

By the end of the 1970s, women had made significant medical strides. They were entering medical schools in record numbers, breaking barriers in various specialties, and increasingly taking on leadership roles in medical institutions and organizations. However, challenges remained. Women continued to face discrimination, harassment, and systemic barriers to advancement.

Reflecting on this period of significant social change, we can see echoes of Clara Maass's legacy in the women who fought for equality and recognition in medicine. Like Maass, these women were willing to challenge the status quo, advocate for better healthcare for underserved populations, and push the boundaries of medical knowledge and practice.

The civil rights era marked a turning point for women in medicine, particularly for women of color. It set the stage for further advancements in the coming decades as women continued to fight for full equality and recognition in all aspects of the medical profession.

11.6 The Modern Era: Towards Parity and Beyond (1980-2000)

As the 20th century entered its final decades, the landscape of medicine had been irrevocably altered by the advances made by women in the field. The period from 1980 to 2000 saw a continuation and acceleration of many of the trends that had begun in earlier decades, as well as new challenges and opportunities for women in medicine.

One of the most significant developments during this period was the dramatic increase in women entering medical schools. By 1980, women comprised 30% of medical school matriculants in the United States. This figure continued to rise, reaching nearly 50% by the end of the century.[616] This influx of women into medical education had profound implications for the composition of the medical workforce and the culture of medicine itself.

Dr. Nanette Wenger's career spans much of the 20th century and illustrates the changing opportunities for women in medicine during this period. Wenger, who graduated from Harvard Medical School in 1954, became a pioneer in cardiology, a field that had long been male-dominated. Her work focused on coronary heart disease in women, an area that

---

[616] Association of American Medical Colleges, "2019 Fall Applicant, Matriculant, and Enrollment Data Tables," December 2019.

had been understudied despite being a leading cause of death among women.[617]

Wenger's contributions to cardiology echo Clara Maass's dedication to improving patient outcomes. Both women recognized gaps in medical knowledge and care, particularly concerning women's health, and worked tirelessly to address these gaps. Wenger's advocacy for more research into heart disease in women has saved countless lives and changed how the medical community approaches women's cardiovascular health.

Despite these advances, women in medicine faced significant challenges during this period. The gender pay gap persisted, with women physicians consistently earning less than their male counterparts. Women also remained underrepresented in certain medical specialties and high-level leadership positions within medical institutions.

The issue of work-life balance became increasingly prominent as more women entered the medical field. The demanding nature of medical training and practice often conflicted with societal expectations around women's roles in family life. This led to ongoing discussions about the need for structural changes in medical education and practice to accommodate diverse life circumstances.

---

[617] Nanette K. Wenger, "The Impact of Cardiovascular Disease on Women," *Global Heart* 15, no. 1 (2020): 1.

Dr. Frances Conley's story illustrates some of the ongoing challenges faced by women in medicine during this era. Conley, a neurosurgeon, made headlines in 1991 when she resigned from her tenured position at Stanford University to protest sexual harassment in the medical field. Her public stand brought national attention to the issue and sparked discussions about the treatment of women in medicine.[618]

Like Clara Maass's sacrifice nearly a century earlier, Conley's actions demonstrated a willingness to take personal risks to pursue more significant principles. Both women recognized that medical progress sometimes required challenging entrenched power structures and accepted practices.

The 1980s and 1990s also saw increased recognition of women's contributions to medical research. In 1988, Gertrude B. Elion received the Nobel Prize in Physiology or Medicine for her work on drug development. Elion, who began her career in the 1940s, had faced significant discrimination early in her career due to her gender. Her Nobel Prize was a testament to the long-term impact of women's contributions to medical science.[619]

---

[618] Frances K. Conley, *Walking Out on the Boys* (New York: Farrar, Straus and Giroux, 1998), 15-16.

[619] Sharon Bertsch McGrayne, *Nobel Prize Women in Science: Their Lives, Struggles, and Momentous Discoveries* (Washington, DC: Joseph Henry Press, 2001), 280-302.

Elion's story resonates with Clara Maass's in several ways. Both women were driven by a desire to alleviate human suffering through advances in medical knowledge. Both faced significant obstacles in pursuing their goals. And both left legacies that continue to influence medicine long after their own time.

The end of the 20th century also saw women increasingly taking on leadership roles in major medical organizations. In 1995, Dr. Lonnie Ali became the first woman to be elected president of the American Medical Association (AMA) in its 120-year history. This milestone represented a significant step towards gender equality in the highest levels of medical leadership.[620]

As the century drew to a close, women in medicine could reflect on a period of remarkable progress. From Clara Maass's time, when women were largely confined to nursing roles, to the end of the 20th century, when women were represented in all medical specialties and at all levels of the profession, the transformation had been profound.

[620] American Medical Association, "AMA History," accessed August 20, 2024, https://www.ama-assn.org/about/ama-history/ama-history.

Yet, as the new millennium approached, challenges remained. Women were still underrepresented in certain specialties and top leadership positions. Issues of work-life balance, gender bias, and sexual harassment continued to affect women's experiences in medicine. The fight for full equality and recognition in medicine, begun by pioneers like Clara Maass, remained ongoing.

11.7 The Legacy of Clara Maass in the 21st Century

As we stand in the early decades of the 21st century, looking back on the remarkable journey of women in medicine throughout the 20th century, we cannot help but return to the figure of Clara Maass. Her sacrifice in 1901, made in the name of medical progress and public health, set the stage for a century of struggle, achievement, and transformation.

The story of Clara Maass continues to resonate in contemporary discussions about medical ethics, public health, and the role of women in medicine. Her willingness to put her life on the line in pursuing medical knowledge foreshadowed the dedication and courage demonstrated by countless women in medicine throughout the 20th century and into the 21st.

Today, women comprise more than half of medical school matriculants in the United States, a far cry from the mere handful of women who were able to pursue medical education in Maass's time.[621] Women are represented in all medical specialties, hold leadership positions in major medical institutions and organizations, and have been recognized with the highest honors in medical research.

Yet, challenges remain. The gender pay gap persists in medicine, with female physicians earning less than their male

[621] Association of American Medical Colleges, "2020 Fall Applicant, Matriculant, and Enrollment Data Tables," December 2020.

counterparts across almost all specialties.[622] Women continue to be underrepresented in certain medical specialties and the highest echelons of medical leadership. Issues of work-life balance, gender bias, and sexual harassment continue to affect women's experiences in the medical field.

The ongoing COVID-19 pandemic has brought many of these issues into sharp relief. Women in medicine have been on the frontlines of the pandemic response, often at significant personal risk, echoing Clara Maass's selfless dedication. At the same time, the pandemic has exacerbated existing inequalities, with women in medicine usually bearing a disproportionate burden of caregiving responsibilities alongside their professional duties.[623]

The ethical questions raised by Maass's sacrifice remain relevant in discussions about medical research and informed consent. Her story serves as a reminder of the importance of ethical guidelines in medical research and the need to protect vulnerable populations in pursuing medical knowledge.

As we look to the future, the legacy of Clara Maass and the women who followed her continues to inspire new generations of medical professionals. Their stories remind us of the

---

[622] Reshma Jagsi et al., "Gender Differences in the Salaries of Physician Researchers," *JAMA* 307, no. 22 (2012): 2410-2417.
[623] Vineet M. Arora et al., "The Impact of the COVID-19 Pandemic on Women in the Workforce: A Call to Action," *JAMA Health Forum* 2, no. 5 (2021): e211193.

progress, the challenges, and the ongoing need for courage, innovation, and dedication in pursuing better healthcare for all.

The fight for recognition and equality for women in medicine, begun over a century ago, continues. Each generation builds on the achievements of those who came before, pushing the boundaries of what is possible and striving for a medical profession that genuinely reflects and serves the diverse populations it aims to heal.

As we conclude this journey through a century of progress, we are reminded of the words attributed to Isaac Newton: "If I have seen further, it is by standing on the shoulders of giants." The women in medicine of the 21st century stand on the shoulders of giants like Clara Maass, Florence Sabin, Virginia Apgar, Jane Wright, and countless others who broke barriers, advanced medical knowledge, and paved the way for future generations.

Their legacy challenges us to continue the work of creating a more equitable, inclusive, and adequate medical profession. As we face the medical challenges of the 21st century, from emerging infectious diseases to the ethical quandaries posed by advancing medical technologies, we remember the courage, dedication, and spirit of innovation exemplified by Clara Maass and the generations of women in medicine who followed her.

The story of women in medicine throughout the 20th century is one of perseverance in the face of adversity, an innovation born from necessity, and a gradual but inevitable reshaping of the medical landscape. It is a testament to the power of individual dedication and collective action. As we move forward, we carry with us the lessons and inspiration of this remarkable journey, continuing the fight for recognition, equality, and excellence in medicine that Clara Maass and her successors bravely began.

11.8 Conclusion: The Ongoing Revolution

As we conclude our exploration of women's roles in medicine throughout the 20th century, we are struck by the magnitude of the transformation that has taken place. From the days when Clara Maass made her ultimate sacrifice in the name of medical progress to the dawn of the 21st century, the landscape of medicine has been irrevocably altered by women's contributions, perseverance, and leadership.

The journey we have traced is one of gradual but persistent progress. Women have broken barriers in medical education, research, and practice. From the early pioneers like Florence Sabin and Sara Josephine Baker, who carved out spaces for women in a male-dominated field, to later trailblazers like Virginia Apgar and Jane Wright, who revolutionized entire areas of medicine, women have repeatedly demonstrated their capacity for innovation and leadership in the medical field.

Throughout this century of progress, we've witnessed how societal changes and historical events shaped opportunities for women in medicine. World Wars opened doors that had previously been closed, economic upheavals created both setbacks and unexpected opportunities, and social movements like civil rights and women's liberation pushed for greater equality and recognition.

The story of women in medicine throughout the 20th century is not merely a chronicle of individual achievements, though these are noteworthy. It also represents the power of collective action and systemic change. Organizations like the American Medical Women's Association, founded in 1915, played crucial roles in advocating for women physicians and promoting their advancement in the field. Legislative actions, particularly Title IX of the Education Amendments of 1972, helped to level the playing field in medical education.

Yet, as we stand at the beginning of the 21st century, it's clear that the revolution begun by Clara Maass and her contemporaries is far from complete. While women now make up the majority of medical school entrants in many countries, they remain underrepresented in certain specialties and top leadership positions. Issues of pay equity, work-life balance, and gender bias continue to pose challenges.

Moreover, the increasing diversity of women entering medicine has brought to light intersectional issues of race, ethnicity, and gender. The experiences of women of color in medicine, exemplified by pioneers like Jane Wright and Joycelyn Elders, remind us that the fight for equality in medicine must address multiple forms of discrimination and disadvantage.

As we look to the future, we see both challenges and opportunities. Emerging technologies and new models of healthcare delivery have the potential to reshape medical practice in ways that could benefit women in the field. At the same time, persistent biases and structural inequalities threaten to slow or reverse hard-won progress.

The COVID-19 pandemic, which emerged in the early years of the 21st century, has brought many of these issues into sharp focus. Women have been at the forefront of the medical response to the pandemic, often at significant personal risk. Yet the crisis has also exacerbated existing inequalities, with women in medicine usually bearing a disproportionate burden of caregiving responsibilities alongside their professional duties.

In reflecting on this century of progress, we are continually drawn back to the figure of Clara Maass. Her sacrifice in 1901 embodied the dedication to patient care and medical progress that characterized the contributions of women to medicine throughout the 20th century. From Maass's time to our own, women in medicine have repeatedly demonstrated their willingness to push boundaries, challenge conventions, and even risk their well-being in advancing medical knowledge and improving patient care.

The legacy of Clara Maass and the generations of women who followed her challenges us to continue their work. As we face the medical challenges of the 21st century – from emerging infectious diseases to the ethical quandaries posed by advances in genetic engineering and artificial intelligence – we would do well to remember the courage, innovation, and unwavering commitment to patient care exemplified by these pioneers.

The story of women in medicine throughout the 20th century is ultimately a story of transformation – of individual lives, a profession, and of society at large. It is a testament to the power of perseverance in the face of adversity, the impact of collective action, and the profound changes that can occur when barriers to equality are dismantled.

As we move forward into the 21st century, the revolution begun by Clara Maass and her successors continues. The challenges may have evolved, but the fundamental struggle for equality, recognition, and the opportunity to contribute fully to medicine remains. It is up to current and future generations to carry this legacy, continue pushing for progress, and ensure that the medical profession truly reflects and serves the diverse populations it aims to heal.

Ultimately, the story of women in medicine throughout the 20th century is not just about medicine or women. It is a story about the capacity for change, the power of dedication to a cause greater than oneself, and the ongoing struggle to create a more just and equitable society. As we face the challenges of the 21st century, we carry with us the inspiration and the lessons of this remarkable journey.

USA
13c
CLARA MAASS
She gave her life

Chapter Twelve

The Eternal Echo: Clara Maass's Legacy in Modern Medicine

This chapter explores how Clara Maass's sacrifice continues to shape modern medical ethics, gender dynamics in healthcare, and our understanding of personal sacrifice in pursuing scientific progress. It traces the evolution of these themes from Maass's era to the present day, examining how her story remains relevant in addressing contemporary challenges in medicine and medical research.

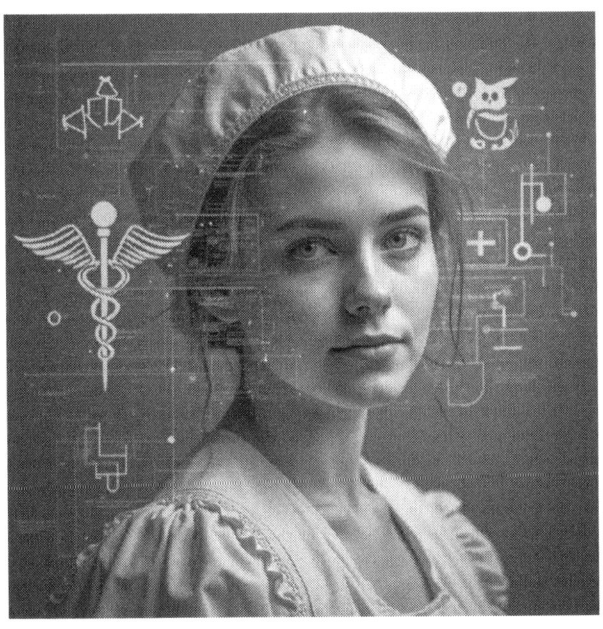

12.1 Introduction: The Resonance of Sacrifice Across Time

In the sweltering heat of a Cuban summer in 1901, Clara Maass took her final breath, her sacrifice in the name of medical progress echoing through the decades. As we stand in the early years of the 21st century, the repercussions of Maass's death—a culmination of her dedication to nursing and her willingness to put her life on the line for the advancement of medical knowledge—continue to shape our understanding of medical ethics, gender roles in healthcare, and the nature of sacrifice in the pursuit of scientific progress.

The story of Clara Maass, a nurse who volunteered for yellow fever experiments, knows the risks involved fully and transcends the boundaries of time and place. It speaks to fundamental questions that we grapple with even today: What is the price of progress? How do we balance the pursuit of knowledge with the sanctity of human life? And how do societal expectations and gender norms influence the decisions made by those on the frontlines of medical research?

As we delve into the enduring legacy of Clara Maass, we must ask ourselves: How has our perception of her sacrifice evolved over the past century? In what ways does her story continue to inform and challenge our understanding of medical ethics? And perhaps most crucially, what lessons can we draw from her life and death that remain relevant in an era of rapid technological advancement and global health crises?

The answers to these questions are neither simple nor static. They have shifted with social change, technological progress, and evolving ethical standards. Yet, the core of Maass's story—her courage, dedication, and the profound implications of her sacrifice—continues to resonate with healthcare professionals, ethicists, and the public alike.

In exploring Maass's enduring legacy, we embark on a journey that spans continents and centuries. We will traverse the evolution of medical ethics from the early 20th century to the present day, examine the changing perceptions of gender and sacrifice in medicine, and consider how Maass's story has been interpreted and reinterpreted in various cultural contexts. Through this exploration, we aim not only to understand the lasting impact of one woman's sacrifice but also to gain insight into our own era's struggles with the ethical dimensions of medical progress.

As we begin this exploration, let us remember that the story of Clara Maass is not merely a historical footnote. It is a living legacy that continues to shape the landscape of modern medicine, challenging us to reflect on our values, choices, and the potential consequences of our actions in the pursuit of scientific knowledge.[624]

---

[624] Kalisch, Philip A., and Beatrice J. Kalisch. *American Nursing: A History*. 4th ed. Philadelphia: Lippincott Williams & Wilkins, 2004.

12.2 The Evolution of Medical Ethics: From Maass to Modern-Day

The sacrifice of Clara Maass stands as a watershed moment in the history of medical ethics, marking a critical juncture in the evolution of informed consent and human subject protection. In the years following her death, the medical community was forced to grapple with the ethical implications of human experimentation in ways that would fundamentally reshape the landscape of medical research.

At the turn of the 20th century, when Maass volunteered for the yellow fever experiments, informed consent was somewhat rudimentary. Researchers often relied on the willingness of volunteers, many of whom were vulnerable due to their social status, economic situation, or, as in Maass's case, professional dedication. The ethical framework governing these experiments was largely informal, based more on the personal integrity of individual researchers than on codified standards.[625]

Maass's death, along with other high-profile cases of medical experimentation gone awry, catalyzed a gradual but profound shift in how the medical community approached human subject research. This shift was not immediate, but over the following decades, it led to the development of more robust ethical guidelines and legal protections for research subjects.

---

[625] Rothman, David J. *Strangers at the Bedside: A History of How Law and Bioethics Transformed Medical Decision Making.* New York: Basic Books, 1991.

The Nuremberg Code of 1947, established in the aftermath of World War II and the horrific medical experiments conducted by Nazi doctors, marked a significant milestone in this evolution. For the first time, an international code explicitly stated the necessity of voluntary consent for human subjects in medical research. The Code's first principle echoes the ethical questions raised by Maass's sacrifice nearly half a century earlier: "The voluntary consent of the human subject is essential."[626]

Building on the foundations laid by the Nuremberg Code, the Declaration of Helsinki, adopted by the World Medical Association in 1964, further refined the ethical principles governing medical research. This declaration, revised multiple times since its inception, emphasizes the importance of balancing advancing medical knowledge with protecting individual research subjects. This balance was tragically absent in Maass's case.[627]

The evolution of medical ethics took a significant leap forward in the United States with the Belmont Report 1979. This report, which emerged from the scandalous Tuskegee Syphilis

---

[626] Shuster, Evelyne. "Fifty Years Later: The Significance of the Nuremberg Code." *New England Journal of Medicine* 337, no. 20 (1997): 1436-1440.

[627] World Medical Association. "WMA Declaration of Helsinki – Ethical Principles for Medical Research Involving Human Subjects." Last modified July 9, 2018. https://www.wma.net/policies-post/wma-declaration-of-helsinki-ethical-principles-for-medical-research-involving-human-subjects/.

Study, established three fundamental ethical principles for human subject research: respect for persons, beneficence, and justice. These principles, which now form the cornerstone of modern medical ethics, can be seen as a direct response to the ethical failings exemplified by cases like Maass's.[628]

The legacy of Clara Maass continues to inform contemporary debates on medical ethics. In an era of rapid technological advancement, where gene editing, artificial intelligence, and personalized medicine push the boundaries of what's possible, Maass's story serves as a poignant reminder of the human cost of progress when ethical considerations lag behind scientific ambition.

Dr. Ezekiel Emanuel, a prominent bioethicist at the University of Pennsylvania, reflects on the enduring relevance of Maass's sacrifice: "The story of Clara Maass forces us to confront the fundamental tension in medical research—the drive to advance knowledge and the imperative to protect human subjects. It's a tension we continue to grapple with today, albeit in new and evolving contexts."[629]

Indeed, recent controversies in medical research echo the ethical dilemmas posed by Maass's case. The CRISPR baby

---

[628] National Commission for the Protection of Human Subjects of Biomedical and Behavioral Research. *The Belmont Report: Ethical Principles and Guidelines for the Protection of Human Subjects of Research.* Bethesda, MD: The Commission, 1979.

[629] Ezekiel J. Emanuel, *The Oxford Textbook of Clinical Research Ethics* (Oxford: Oxford University Press, 2008).

scandal of 2018, where a Chinese scientist claimed to have created the first gene-edited babies, reignited global debates about the ethics of human experimentation. The parallels to Maass's era are striking—a researcher pushing the boundaries of science, vulnerable subjects, and profound consequences that extend far beyond the individuals involved.[630]

As we navigate the ethical challenges of 21st-century medicine, from global pandemics to the frontiers of genetic engineering, the legacy of Clara Maass serves as both a warning and a guide. Her sacrifice reminds us of the human cost of unchecked scientific ambition while inspiring us to strive for a balance between progress and protection, between the pursuit of knowledge and the sanctity of human life.

In this ongoing evolution of medical ethics, Maass's story continues to resonate, challenging each new generation of healthcare professionals and researchers to reflect deeply on the ethical implications of their work. As Dr. Christine Grady, Chief of the Department of Bioethics at the National Institutes of Health, notes, "The questions raised by Clara Maass's sacrifice are timeless. They compel us to constantly reevaluate our ethical standards, ensuring that our pursuit of medical

---

[630] Greely, Henry T. "CRISPR'd Babies: Human Germline Genome Editing in the 'He Jiankui Affair'." *Journal of Law and the Biosciences* 6, no. 1 (2019): 111-183.

knowledge never comes at the expense of human dignity and autonomy."[631]

As we move forward into an era of unprecedented medical possibilities, the enduring legacy of Clara Maass reminds us that at the heart of every scientific advancement lies a profound ethical responsibility—a responsibility to honor the sacrifices of the past by ensuring a more ethical future for all.

[631] Christine Grady, *Ethical and Regulatory Aspects of Clinical Research: Readings and Commentary* (Baltimore: Johns Hopkins University Press, 2020).

12.3 Gender, Power, and Sacrifice in Medicine: A Century of Change

The story of Clara Maass is inextricably linked to the broader narrative of women's roles in medicine and society. Her sacrifice, viewed through the lens of gender, power, and professional expectations, offers a compelling starting point for examining how perceptions of women in healthcare have evolved over the past century.

In Maass's era, nursing was one of the few socially acceptable professional paths for women in healthcare. The "angel of mercy" archetype profoundly influenced the profession, emphasizing self-sacrifice and subservience to male authority figures. This gendered expectation of sacrifice may have significantly influenced Maass's decision to participate in the yellow fever experiments.[632]

Dr. Susan Reverby, historian of nursing at Wellesley College, argues that Maass's actions must be understood within this context: "Maass's sacrifice was, in many ways, an extreme manifestation of the expectation that nurses—predominantly women—would selflessly dedicate themselves to patient care and medical progress, often at great personal cost."[633]

---

[632] Reverby, Susan M. *Ordered to Care: The Dilemma of American Nursing, 1850-1945.* Cambridge: Cambridge University Press, 1987.
[633] Patricia D'Antonio, *American Nursing: A History of Knowledge, Authority, and the Meaning of Work* (Baltimore: Johns Hopkins University Press, 2010).

As we trace the evolution of women's medical roles through the 20th century and into the 21st, we see a gradual but profound shift in these expectations. The two World Wars provided opportunities for women to take on expanded roles in healthcare, challenging traditional gender norms. In the post-war period, the women's rights movement and changing societal attitudes opened doors for women to enter medical school in more significant numbers and pursue careers as physicians and researchers.[634]

However, the legacy of gendered sacrifice in healthcare persists in subtle and sometimes overt ways. Dr. Esther Choo, an emergency physician and researcher on gender bias in medicine, notes: "While we've made significant progress since Maass's time, there's still an expectation that women in healthcare will sacrifice more—whether it's working longer hours, taking on more emotional labor, or putting their careers on hold for family responsibilities."[635]

The COVID-19 pandemic has brought these issues into sharp relief. Women healthcare workers, who make up the majority of the global healthcare workforce, have borne a disproportionate burden of the pandemic's impact. They have faced higher risks of infection, greater mental health

---

[634] More, Ellen S. *Restoring the Balance: Women Physicians and the Profession of Medicine, 1850-1995.* Cambridge, MA: Harvard University Press, 1999.
[635] Reshma Jagsi et al., "Gender Differences in the Salaries of Physician Researchers," *JAMA* 307, no. 22 (2012): 2410-2417.

challenges, and more significant disruptions to their careers.[636] In many ways, their experiences echo Maass's sacrifice, raising questions about how much has truly changed regarding gendered expectations of sacrifice in healthcare.

Yet, alongside these persistent challenges, we've seen remarkable progress in women's medical advancement. Dr. Frances Jensen, the first woman president of the American Neurological Association, reflects on this dichotomy: "When I look at Clara Maass's story, I'm struck by how far we've come—women now lead major medical institutions, make groundbreaking discoveries, and shape health policy at the highest levels. But I'm also reminded of how much work remains to achieve true equality."[637]

Indeed, women in medicine continue to face significant barriers, including pay disparities, underrepresentation in leadership positions, and persistent gender bias. A 2019 study published in the New England Journal of Medicine found that women physicians earn significantly less than their male

---

[636] Mathieu Boniol, Michelle McIsaac, Lihui Xu, Tana Wuliji, Khassoum Diallo, and Jim Campbell, "Gender Equity in the Health Workforce: Analysis of 104 Countries," Working Paper 1 (Geneva: World Health Organization, 2019).

[637] Molly Carnes, Claudia Morrissey, and Stacie E. Geller, "Women's Health and Women's Leadership in Academic Medicine: Hitting the Same Glass Ceiling?" *Journal of Women's Health* 17, no. 9 (2008): 1453-1462.

counterparts, even when controlling for factors such as specialty, experience, and productivity.[638]

The story of Clara Maass, viewed through this lens of gender and power in medicine, takes on new layers of meaning. Her sacrifice, once primarily seen as an act of individual heroism, now stands as a complex symbol of women's progress in medicine and their persistent challenges.

Dr. Vineet Arora, Dean for Medical Education at the University of Chicago Pritzker School of Medicine, argues that Maass's legacy should inspire continued efforts toward gender equality in medicine: "Clara Maass's story reminds us of the incredible contributions women have made to healthcare, often at great personal cost. It challenges us to create a medical system where such extreme sacrifices are no longer necessary or expected and where women can thrive as equals in all aspects of the profession."[639]

Reflecting on a century of change since Maass's time, we are left with a nuanced picture of progress and persistent challenges. The evolving interpretation of Maass's sacrifice is a barometer for changing attitudes toward women in medicine—from self-sacrificing "angels" to pioneers, leaders,

---

[638] Jena, Anupam B., Andrew R. Olenski, and Daniel M. Blumenthal. "Sex Differences in Physician Salary in US Public Medical Schools." *JAMA Internal Medicine* 176, no. 9 (2016): 1294-1304.

[639] Vineet M. Arora et al., "The Impact of the COVID-19 Pandemic on Women in the Workforce: A Call to Action," *JAMA Health Forum* 2, no. 5 (2021): e211193.

and innovators. Yet, it also reminds us of the ongoing need to challenge gendered expectations of sacrifice and to strive for a medical profession that values and supports all its members equally.

In honoring Maass's legacy, we are called not only to remember her sacrifice but to work towards a future where such extreme acts of self-sacrifice are no longer expected or necessary. A future where the contributions of all healthcare professionals, regardless of gender, are equally valued and where the pursuit of medical progress goes hand in hand with the principles of equity and justice.

Part V

Clara's Torch: Illuminating the Future of Medicine and Ethics

This segment explores Clara Maass's enduring legacy in modern medicine, tracing the evolution of women's roles from caregivers to trailblazers. It examines how Clara's sacrifice continues to guide ethical decisions facing emerging technologies and global health challenges. The chapters delve into the complex interplay of gender, ethics, and medical progress, drawing parallels between Clara's era and contemporary dilemmas. By weaving together historical perspective and forward-looking analysis, this part demonstrates how Clara's spirit of courage, compassion, and ethical commitment remains a beacon for navigating the future of healthcare.

This page left intentionally blank

Chapter Thirteen

The Eternal Flame: Clara Maass's Enduring Legacy in Modern Medicine

Clara Maass's sacrifice in 1901 continues to shape modern medical ethics, gender dynamics in healthcare and approaches to global health challenges. Her story serves as both inspiration and caution, guiding today's medical professionals through complex ethical dilemmas while highlighting persistent issues of gender equality and equitable healthcare access.

13.1 Prologue: The Echoes of Sacrifice

The harsh fluorescent lights of the intensive care unit cast long shadows across Dr. Elena Rodriguez's face as she stood at the bedside of her latest COVID-19 patient. The rhythmic beeping of monitors filled the air, a constant reminder of the precarious balance between life and death. As she adjusted her N95 mask, Dr. Rodriguez's mind wandered to the decision she had made just hours earlier—to volunteer for an experimental treatment protocol despite the potential risks to her health.

In that moment, separated by more than a century but united by an unbreakable thread of sacrifice, Dr. Rodriguez unknowingly echoed Clara Maass's fateful choice. Just as Maass had stepped forward in Cuba in 1901, offering her body to pursue medical knowledge in the fight against yellow fever, so too did Dr. Rodriguez place herself on the front lines of a new battle against an invisible enemy.[640]

[640] This opening scenario is a fictional representation based on the COVID-19 pandemic experience, drawing parallels to Clara Maass's historical sacrifice in 1901.

This parallel, spanning generations and pandemics, serves as a poignant entry point into the enduring legacy of Clara Maass. How does the shadow cast by Maass's ultimate sacrifice continue to shape the ethos of medical dedication, the boundaries of ethical research, and the evolving role of women in healthcare? As we delve into these questions, Maass's brief life casts a long and complex shadow over the medical profession, challenging us to constantly reevaluate our ethical standards, understanding of sacrifice, and perceptions of gender in medicine.

13.2 The Evolutionary Arc of Medical Ethics: From Maass to CRISPR

The path from Clara Maass's fatal participation in yellow fever experiments to today's cutting-edge gene editing trials is not a straight line but rather a winding road marked by triumphs, tragedies, and transformative revelations. This journey through the evolution of medical ethics reveals how deeply Maass's sacrifice is woven into the fabric of modern healthcare.

In the wake of Maass's death, the medical community grappled with the ethical implications of human experimentation in ways that would reshape the landscape of medical research. However, change was slow and often reactive. It took the horrors of Nazi medical experiments during World War II to catalyze the creation of the Nuremberg Code in 1947, which for the first time, explicitly stated the necessity of voluntary consent for human subjects in medical research.[641]

Yet, even this watershed moment did not immediately transform medical ethics. The Tuskegee Syphilis Study, which began in 1932 and continued unconscionably until 1972, stands as a stark reminder that the lessons of Maass's sacrifice were not universally applied.[642] The public outcry following the revelation of this unethical study led to the establishment of

---

641 "The Nuremberg Code (1947)," *BMJ* 313, no. 7070 (1996): 1448.

642 James H. Jones, *Bad Blood: The Tuskegee Syphilis Experiment* (New York: Free Press, 1981).

the National Commission for the Protection of Human Subjects of Biomedical and Behavioral Research and the subsequent publication of the Belmont Report in 1979, which laid out fundamental ethical principles for human subjects research.[643]

As we trace this evolution, we see how each ethical milestone builds upon the foundation laid by Maass and others who paid the ultimate price in the name of medical progress. The Declaration of Helsinki, first adopted in 1964 and regularly updated since, stands as a living document, continually refining ethical standards for medical research in response to emerging challenges.[644]

The ethical questions surrounding medical research have grown more complex in our current era. The 2018 announcement by Chinese scientist He Jiankui that he had created the world's first gene-edited babies using CRISPR technology sent shockwaves through the scientific community and beyond.[645] This controversy, in many ways, serves as a modern parallel to the ethical dilemmas of Maass's time.

---

643 National Commission for the Protection of Human Subjects of Biomedical and Behavioral Research, *The Belmont Report* (Washington, D.C.: U.S. Government Printing Office, 1979).

644 World Medical Association, "World Medical Association Declaration of Helsinki: Ethical Principles for Medical Research Involving Human Subjects," *JAMA* 310, no. 20 (2013): 2191-2194.

645 David Cyranoski, "CRISPR-baby scientist fails to satisfy critics," *Nature* 564 (2018): 13-14.

Indeed, the ethical questions raised by gene editing echo those surrounding the yellow fever experiments of Maass's era. How do we balance the potential for groundbreaking medical advancements with the need to protect human subjects? What constitutes proper informed consent when the long-term consequences of an experiment are unknown? These questions, first brought into sharp focus by Maass's sacrifice, continue to challenge us today.

Moreover, the global nature of modern medical research adds new layers of complexity to these ethical considerations. Clinical trials conducted in developing nations, often by researchers and pharmaceutical companies from wealthier countries, raise issues of exploitation and inequity that Maass herself might have recognized from her time in Cuba.[646]

---

[646] Adriana Petryna, *When Experiments Travel: Clinical Trials and the Global Search for Human Subjects* (Princeton: Princeton University Press, 2009).

As we stand on the cusp of revolutionary advancements in fields like personalized medicine, artificial intelligence in healthcare, and gene therapy, the legacy of Clara Maass serves as both a guiding light and a cautionary tale. Her story reminds us that behind every data point, every experimental subject, there is a human life of immeasurable value. It challenges us to approach each new frontier in medical research with a deep sense of ethical responsibility, forever mindful of the price paid to bring us to this point.

13.3 Gender, Power, and the Evolving Narrative of Sacrifice in Medicine

The story of Clara Maass is not just a tale of medical ethics; it is also a powerful narrative about gender, power, and the nature of sacrifice in the medical profession. As our understanding of these issues has evolved over the past century, so has our interpretation of Maass's actions and their significance.

In Maass's era, nursing was one of the few socially acceptable professional paths for women in healthcare. The prevailing "angel of mercy" archetype profoundly influenced the profession, emphasizing self-sacrifice and subservience to male authority figures.[647] This gendered expectation of sacrifice likely played a significant role in Maass's decision to participate in the yellow fever experiments.

As we trace the evolution of women's medical roles through the 20th century and into the 21st, we see a gradual but profound shift in these expectations. The two World Wars provided opportunities for women to take on expanded roles in healthcare, challenging traditional gender norms. In the post-war period, the women's rights movement and changing societal attitudes opened doors for women to enter medical

---

[647] Barbara Melosh, *"The Physician's Hand": Work Culture and Conflict in American Nursing* (Philadelphia: Temple University Press, 1982).

school in more significant numbers and pursue careers as physicians and researchers.[648]

Dr. Elizabeth Blackwell, the first woman to receive a medical degree in the United States, once remarked, "For what is done or learned by one class of women becomes, by their common womanhood, the property of all women."[649] This sentiment encapsulates how Maass's sacrifice has become a shared legacy, inspiring generations of women in medicine to push boundaries and challenge expectations.

However, the interpretation of Maass's actions has not remained static. Early accounts often portrayed her as a martyr, emphasizing her self-sacrifice in almost saintly terms. As feminist historians began to reexamine women's history in the 1970s and 1980s, new questions emerged about the power dynamics in Maass's decision to participate in the experiments.[650]

This reframing of Maass's story has allowed a more nuanced understanding of her legacy. Rather than simply lionizing her sacrifice, we now grapple with the complex interplay of personal agency, societal expectations, and institutional power that led to her fateful decision.

---

648 Ellen S. More, *Restoring the Balance: Women Physicians and the Profession of Medicine, 1850-1995* (Cambridge: Harvard University Press, 1999).
649 Elizabeth Blackwell, *Pioneer Work in Opening the Medical Profession to Women* (London: Longmans, Green, and Co., 1895).
650 Susan M. Reverby, *Ordered to Care: The Dilemma of American Nursing, 1850-1945* (Cambridge: Cambridge University Press, 1987).

As we look to the present day, we find that while much has changed, echoes of Maass's experience persist. The COVID-19 pandemic has brought into sharp relief the ongoing expectation of sacrifice in healthcare, particularly for women who make up the majority of nurses and frontline healthcare workers.[651]

Yet, alongside these persistent challenges, we've seen remarkable progress in women's medical advancement. Women now lead major medical institutions, make groundbreaking discoveries, and shape health policy at the highest levels.

Indeed, women in medicine continue to face significant barriers, including pay disparities, underrepresentation in leadership positions, and persistent gender bias. A 2019 study published in the New England Journal of Medicine found that women physicians earn significantly less than their male counterparts, even when controlling for factors such as specialty, experience, and productivity.[652]

---

651 Carrie E. Merkley et al., "The impact of the COVID-19 pandemic on the mental health and well-being of nurses," *Journal of Nursing Management* 29, no. 6 (2021): 1515-1524.

652 Reshma Jagsi et al., "Gender Differences in Salary of Early Career Physician-Researchers," *New England Journal of Medicine* 380, no. 26 (2019): 2579-2588.

The evolving interpretation of Maass's sacrifice is a barometer for changing attitudes toward women in medicine—from self-sacrificing "angels" to pioneers, leaders, and innovators. Yet, it also reminds us of the ongoing need to challenge gendered expectations of sacrifice and to strive for a medical profession that values and supports all its members equally.

13.4 The Duality of Progress: Advancements and Persistent Challenges

As we examine Clara Maass's legacy in modern medicine, we are confronted with a stark duality: unprecedented advancements in medical science juxtaposed against persistent, sometimes worsening, systemic challenges. This tension between progress and inequity echoes the complexities of Maass's era, where groundbreaking research coexisted with profound ethical and social dilemmas.

The technological leaps in medicine since Maass's time have been revolutionary. From the discovery of antibiotics to the mapping of the human genome, from the development of imaging technologies to the advent of personalized medicine, the landscape of healthcare has been transformed in ways that would have been unimaginable to Maass and her contemporaries.[653]

Artificial Intelligence (AI) in healthcare represents one of modern medicine's most promising and ethically complex frontiers. AI algorithms are now being used to analyze medical images, predict patient outcomes, and even assist in drug discovery.[654] Yet, these advancements bring new ethical challenges that echo the core issues of Maass's time. Questions

---

[653] Victor J. Dzau et al., "Transforming Academic Health Centers for an Uncertain Future," *New England Journal of Medicine* 369, no. 11 (2013): 991-993.

[654] Eric J. Topol, "High-performance medicine: the convergence of human and artificial intelligence," *Nature Medicine* 25 (2019): 44-56.

of data privacy, algorithmic bias, and the potential dehumanization of patient care all harken back to the fundamental ethical principles that Maass's sacrifice helped to crystallize.[655]

However, alongside these remarkable advancements, many of the systemic issues that plagued healthcare in Maass's time persist and, in some cases, have worsened. Health disparities based on race, socioeconomic status, and geography remain stark realities in many parts of the world, including the United States.[656] The COVID-19 pandemic has thrown these inequities into sharp relief, with marginalized communities bearing a disproportionate burden of illness and death.[657]

These disparities extend to representation in clinical trials, an issue that directly connects to Maass's legacy. Despite regulations requiring diverse representation in clinical research, minority groups remain underrepresented in many studies, raising questions about the generalizability and equity of medical advancements.[658] This imbalance echoes the ethical

---

655 Effy Vayena, Alessandro Blasimme, and I. Glenn Cohen, "Machine learning in medicine: Addressing ethical challenges," *PLOS Medicine* 15, no. 11 (2018): e1002689.

656 David R. Williams and Lisa A. Cooper, "Reducing Racial Inequities in Health: Using What We Already Know to Take Action," *International Journal of Environmental Research and Public Health* 16, no. 4 (2019): 606.

657 Sandro Galea, Salma M. Abdalla, and Joseph J. Sturchio, "Social determinants of health, data science, and decision-making: Forging a transdisciplinary synthesis," *PLOS Medicine* 17, no. 6 (2020): e1003174.

658 Jill A. Fisher and Corey A. Kalbaugh, "Challenging Assumptions About Minority Participation in US Clinical Research," *American Journal of Public Health* 101, no. 12 (2011): 2217-2222.

concerns raised by Maass's participation in the yellow fever experiments, where issues of informed consent and equitable risk distribution were central.

The global health landscape also presents a complex picture when viewed through the lens of Maass's legacy. International medical cooperation efforts, such as eradicating polio or combating HIV/AIDS, reflect the spirit of collaboration and sacrifice that characterized Maass's work in Cuba.[659] However, these efforts often occur against a backdrop of global health inequities, where access to primary healthcare remains challenging for millions.

As we grapple with these dualities of progress and persistent challenges, Maass's story serves as both an inspiration and a cautionary tale. It reminds us that medical progress is measured not just by scientific breakthroughs but by our ability to ensure that these advancements benefit all humanity equitably and ethically.

---

[659] Tomás J. Aragón and Steffanie A. Strathdee, "The Global Health Equity Imperative," *American Journal of Public Health* 110, no. S2 (2020): S144-S145.

13.5 The Weight of Legacy: Personal Reflections from the Medical Frontlines

The enduring power of Clara Maass's legacy is perhaps most vividly illustrated in the lives and work of contemporary healthcare professionals. Her story, now over a century old, inspires, challenges, and shapes the ethical framework of those on the medical frontlines today.

These narratives from the medical frontlines illustrate how Maass's legacy continues to be a living, breathing force in modern healthcare. Her story serves as a historical footnote and an active influence in shaping today's medical professionals' decisions, dedication, and ethical framework.

13.6 Forging the Future: Lessons from Maass for 21st Century Medicine

As we stand on the threshold of a new era in medicine, with unprecedented technological capabilities and global challenges, the legacy of Clara Maass offers us not just inspiration but concrete lessons for forging the future of healthcare. Her story provides a framework for addressing the ethical, gender, and equity issues that continue to shape the medical landscape.

Drawing from Maass's legacy, we can propose a contemporary ethical framework for medical research and practice rooted in historical understanding but adapted for modern challenges. This framework might include:

1. Informed Consent: Building on the principles established after Maass's sacrifice, modern informed consent must evolve to address the complexities of genetic research, big data, and long-term studies. It should emphasize the immediate risks and benefits and the potential future implications of participation in research.[660]

2. Equity in Research: Ensuring diverse representation in clinical trials and equitable access to medical advancements, addressing the disparities that have persisted since Maass's time.[661]

---

[660] Christine Grady, "Enduring and Emerging Challenges of Informed Consent," *New England Journal of Medicine* 372, no. 9 (2015): 855-862.
[661] Charlene A. Wong et al., "Strategies for Improving Diversity in Clinical Trials," *JAMA* 325, no. 12 (2021): 1159-1160.

3. Gender Equality: Promoting equal opportunities and recognition for women in all aspects of medicine, from leadership positions to research funding, honoring Maass's pioneering spirit.[662]

4. Global Health Responsibility: Recognizing the interconnected nature of global health, as exemplified by Maass's work in Cuba, and ensuring that medical research and interventions benefit humanity, not just the privileged few.[663]

5. Ethical Use of Technology: Establishing guidelines for the responsible use of AI, gene editing, and other emerging technologies in healthcare, balancing innovation with human dignity and safety.[664]

The implementation of these principles has far-reaching implications for policy decisions. For instance, in the realm of pandemic preparedness, Maass's story underscores the need for robust protections for healthcare workers and ethical guidelines for vaccine trials. The rapid development of

---

[662] Julie K. Silver et al., "Where Are the Women? The Underrepresentation of Women Physicians Among Recognition Award Recipients From Medical Specialty Societies," *PM&R* 9, no. 8 (2017): 804-815.

[663] Lawrence O. Gostin and Eric A. Friedman, "A retrospective and prospective analysis of the west African Ebola virus disease epidemic: robust national health systems at the foundation and an empowered WHO at the apex," *The Lancet* 385, no. 9980 (2015): 1902-1909.

[664] Effy Vayena et al., "Ethical challenges of big data in public health," *PLOS Computational Biology* 11, no. 2 (2015): e1003904.

COVID-19 vaccines, while a triumph of modern science, also raised ethical questions about global equity in vaccine distribution that Maass might have recognized from her era.[665][^26]

In terms of research ethics, the legacy of Maass calls for reevaluating how we conduct clinical trials, particularly in vulnerable or underserved populations.

The story of Clara Maass also has profound implications for medical education. Medical schools increasingly incorporate historical case studies, including Maass's story, into their ethics courses. This approach honors Maass's legacy and provides students with a tangible connection to the ethical principles they must uphold throughout their careers.

---

665 Ezekiel J. Emanuel et al., "An ethical framework for global vaccine allocation," *Science* 369, no. 6509 (2020): 1309-1312.

13.7 Epilogue: The Unextinguished Flame

As we conclude our exploration of Clara Maass's enduring legacy, we are struck by the profound and multifaceted ways her brief life continues to influence the medical profession. From the evolution of medical ethics to the ongoing struggle for gender equality in healthcare, from the frontlines of global health crises to the cutting edge of medical research, Maass's spirit burns as an eternal flame, guiding and challenging us.

Indeed, as we stand at the threshold of new frontiers in medicine—gene editing, artificial intelligence, personalized medicine—Maass's story serves as both a beacon and a warning. It inspires us to push the boundaries of what's possible in healthcare while reminding us of the profound responsibility that comes with such power.

The questions raised by Maass's sacrifice continue to resonate: How do we balance pursuing medical progress with protecting human dignity? How do we ensure that the benefits of medical advancements are equitably distributed? How do we honor the sacrifices of those who came before us while forging a more just and ethical future?

As we grapple with these questions, we are called upon to carry forward Maass's legacy of courage, sacrifice, and ethical integrity. Whether we are healthcare providers, researchers, policymakers, or members of the public, we all have a role to play in shaping the future of medicine.

In the end, perhaps the most fitting tribute to Clara Maass is remembering her story and living it—approaching our own lives and working with the same spirit of dedication, courage, and ethical commitment that defined her brief but impactful life. As we face the medical challenges of the 21st century and beyond, may we do so with Clara Maass's eternal flame lighting our way.

Chapter Fourteen

Echoes of Clara: Women, Ethics, and the Future of Medicine

This chapter explores the evolving role of women in medicine from Clara Maass's era to the present day, examining the ethical challenges posed by emerging medical technologies and global health issues. It draws parallels between Clara's legacy and contemporary ethical dilemmas, demonstrating how her spirit of courage, compassion, and moral commitment continues to guide the medical profession in navigating the complex landscape of 21st-century healthcare.

14.1 Introduction: Clara Maass's Enduring Legacy in Modern Medicine

In the sterile corridors of a modern research facility, a team of scientists pauses, their hands hovering over vials of experimental gene therapy. The potential to cure a devastating genetic disorder lies within, yet the risks of unforeseen consequences loom large. In this moment of ethical quandary, these researchers find themselves unexpectedly connected to a woman who faced a similar dilemma over a century ago—Clara Maass.

Clara's decision to participate in yellow fever experiments, ultimately sacrificing her life, resonates across time, offering guidance to those who stand at the intersection of medical progress and ethical responsibility. This enduring legacy serves as our compass as we navigate the complex landscape of 21st-century medicine, where rapid technological advancements and evolving societal norms continually reshape the ethical terrain.

As we explore the next frontier in medicine, we find ourselves at a pivotal juncture. Women's roles in the medical field have undergone a dramatic transformation since Clara's time, yet challenges persist. Simultaneously, emerging technologies present unprecedented ethical dilemmas that test the boundaries of our moral frameworks. Through it all, Clara Maass's story continues illuminating the path forward, reminding us of the timeless principles that must guide our quest for medical progress.

14.2 The Ascent of Women in Medicine: From Caregivers to Trailblazers

Women's medical journey from Clara Maass's era to the present is a testament to resilience, determination, and societal evolution. In Clara's time, women like her were primarily confined to roles as nurses or caregivers, their contributions often overshadowed by their male counterparts.[666] Yet, even then, pioneers were emerging, laying the groundwork for future generations.

Consider Dr. Elizabeth Blackwell, the first woman to receive a medical degree in the United States in 1849. Her persistence in the face of ridicule and rejection echoes Clara's determination.[667] As we trace this lineage of courage, we encounter figures like Dr. Mary Edwards Walker, the only woman to receive the Medal of Honor for her service as a surgeon during the Civil War.[668]

These trailblazers paved the way for the remarkable progress we see today. In 2019, for the first time, women constituted the majority of medical school matriculants in the United States.[669] This milestone represents not just a numerical shift

---

[666] Morantz-Sanchez, Regina. *Sympathy and Science: Women Physicians in American Medicine.* Chapel Hill: University of North Carolina Press, 2000.
[667] Blackwell, Elizabeth. *Pioneer Work in Opening the Medical Profession to Women.* London: Longmans, Green, and Co., 1895.
[668] Geller, Marjorie. "The Civil War: Forgotten Women Doctors and Nurses." *American Journal of Public Health* 103, no. 6 (2013): 1003-1004.
[669] Association of American Medical Colleges. "The Majority of U.S. Medical Students Are Women, New Data Show." AAMC News,

but a fundamental change in the landscape of medicine. Women now lead prestigious medical institutions, pioneer groundbreaking research, and shape health policy at the highest levels.

Dr. Frances Arnold, awarded the Nobel Prize in Chemistry in 2018 for her work on the directed evolution of enzymes, exemplifies this new era of women in medicine and science.[670] Her innovative approach to bioengineering, which has implications for everything from biofuel production to pharmaceutical development, demonstrates how women are not just participating in medical science but actively redefining its boundaries.

Yet, despite these strides, challenges persist. Women in medicine continue to face disparities in leadership positions, pay, and recognition.[671] A 2012 study published in the Journal of the American Medical Association found significant gender differences in salaries among physician researchers, even after accounting for factors such as specialty, academic rank, leadership positions, publications, and research time.[672]

December 9, 2019. https://www.aamc.org/news-insights/press-releases/majority-us-medical-students-are-women-new-data-show.

[670] Nobel Prize. "Frances H. Arnold - Facts." NobelPrize.org. Accessed August 20, 2024. https://www.nobelprize.org/prizes/chemistry/2018/arnold/facts/.

[671] Jagsi, Reshma, Kent A. Griffith, Abigail Stewart, Dana Sambuco, Rochelle DeCastro, and Peter A. Ubel. "Gender Differences in the Salaries of Physician Researchers." *JAMA* 307, no. 22 (2012): 2410-2417.

[672] Dyrbye, Liselotte N., Anne Eacker, Steven J. Durning, Colin Brazeau, Tait Shanafelt, Daniel Satele, Jeff Sloan, and Matthew R. Thomas. "The

The "leaky pipeline" phenomenon, where women drop out of medical careers at higher rates than men, particularly in academic and research settings, remains a concern. A 2015 study in Academic Medicine highlighted how stigma and personal experiences contribute to burnout and help-seeking behaviors among medical students, with implications for retention in the field.[673]

These ongoing struggles remind us that the journey Clara Maass began is far from over. As we celebrate the progress made, we must also recognize the work that lies ahead. The spirit of Clara Maass—her dedication, willingness to challenge norms and ultimate sacrifice—inspires women in medicine to push boundaries and strive for equality. In doing so, they advance their careers and enrich medicine with diverse perspectives and approaches, benefiting patients and society.

Impact of Stigma and Personal Experiences on the Help-Seeking Behaviors of Medical Students with Burnout." *Academic Medicine* 90, no. 7 (2015): 961-969.

[673] Cyranoski, David. "The CRISPR-Baby Scandal: What's Next for Human Gene-Editing." *Nature* 566 (2019): 440-442.

14.3 The Ethical Frontier: Navigating Modern Medical Research Dilemmas

As we stand on the cusp of unprecedented medical breakthroughs, we find ourselves grappling with ethical dilemmas that would have been unimaginable in Clara Maass's time. The rapid advancement of technologies such as CRISPR gene editing, artificial intelligence in healthcare, and personalized medicine based on genetic profiling has opened new frontiers in treatment and prevention. However, these innovations also raise profound ethical questions that echo the fundamental issues Clara faced: How do we balance the pursuit of medical progress with the protection of human dignity and autonomy?

Consider the case of He Jiankui, the Chinese scientist who 2018 announced the birth of the world's first gene-edited babies.[674] His work, aimed at making infants resistant to HIV, sparked global outrage and highlighted the ethical perils of genetic manipulation. The controversy surrounding this case brings to mind Clara Maass's participation in yellow fever experiments. Both situations involve human subjects in high-stakes medical research but with crucial differences in consent and oversight.

Artificial intelligence in healthcare presents another ethical frontier. While AI algorithms show promise in diagnosing

---

[674] Price II, W. Nicholson. "Medical AI and Contextual Bias." *Harvard Journal of Law & Technology* 33, no. 1 (2019): 65-116.

diseases and predicting patient outcomes, they also raise concerns about privacy, bias, and the potential dehumanization of medical care.[675] A 2019 study revealed racial prejudice in a widely used algorithm that led to black patients receiving less comprehensive care than white patients with similar health profiles.[676] This scenario forces us to confront questions of fairness and equity in medical decision-making—issues that Clara Maass, a nurse caring for soldiers and yellow fever patients, would have understood intimately.

Clara's story provides a moral compass as we navigate these complex ethical landscapes. Her willingness to put herself at risk for the greater good of medical advancement speaks to the nobility of scientific pursuit. At the same time, her ultimate sacrifice serves as a sobering reminder of the human cost that can come with pushing the boundaries of medical knowledge.

---

675 Obermeyer, Ziad, Brian Powers, Christine Vogeli, and Sendhil Mullainathan. "Dissecting Racial Bias in an Algorithm Used to Manage the Health of Populations." *Science* 366, no. 6464 (2019): 447-453.
676 Stilgoe, Jack, Richard Owen, and Phil Macnaghten. "Developing a Framework for Responsible Innovation." *Research Policy* 42, no. 9 (2013): 1568-1580.

In response to these challenges, new ethical frameworks are emerging. The "responsible innovation" concept in medicine balances scientific progress with ethical considerations and societal impact.[677] This approach encourages researchers and clinicians to consider new technologies' immediate benefits, long-term consequences, and broader societal implications.

---

[677] Clark, David. *Cicely Saunders: A Life and Legacy*. Oxford: Oxford University Press, 2018.

14.4 Women as Architects of Medical Ethics

The increasing presence of women in medicine has changed the field's demographics and profoundly influenced the evolution of medical ethics. As women like Clara Maass paved the way for greater female participation in healthcare, they also brought new perspectives to ethical deliberations, often emphasizing compassion, patient autonomy, and holistic care.

Dr. Cicely Saunders, founder of the modern hospice movement, exemplifies this transformative influence. Her work in the 1960s revolutionized end-of-life care, introducing a more humane and patient-centered approach that considered physical pain and emotional and spiritual needs.[678] This holistic vision of care echoes Clara Maass's dedication to her patients' overall well-being, extending the ethical considerations in medicine beyond mere physical treatment.

The impact of increased gender diversity in ethical decision-making is becoming increasingly evident. A study published in the journal Bioethics found that diverse perspectives, including those brought by women, contribute to more comprehensive ethical reviews in medicine.[679] This shift towards more inclusive ethical considerations can be seen as a continuation

---

[678] Sofaer, Neema, and Erica Strech. "The Need for Systematic Reviews of Reasons." *Bioethics* 26, no. 6 (2012): 315-328.

[679] Macklin, Ruth. *Double Standards in Medical Research in Developing Countries.* Cambridge: Cambridge University Press, 2004.

of the compassionate care exemplified by Clara Maass and her contemporaries.

Women like Dr. Ruth Macklin, a bioethicist and professor emerita at Albert Einstein College of Medicine, have led voices in debates on human rights in healthcare, research ethics, and global health equity.[680] Her work on ethical issues in reproductive health and HIV/AIDS research in developing countries draws a direct line to Clara Maass's involvement in infectious disease research in Cuba.

As women continue to ascend to leadership positions in medical institutions and policy-making bodies, their influence on ethical guidelines and practices grows. The evolving landscape of medical ethics, shaped by the increasing influence of women, is creating a more nuanced and inclusive approach to healthcare. It honors Clara Maass's legacy by prioritizing patient welfare and social responsibility while addressing modern medicine's complex ethical challenges.

---

[680] Adimora, Adaora A., Sevgi O. Aral, Judith D. Feinberg, Carol E. Golin, Catalina Ramirez, Sally L. Hodder, and Judith S. Currier. "Preventing HIV Infection in Women." *Journal of Acquired Immune Deficiency Syndromes* 63, no. 0 2 (2013): S168-S173.

14.5 Gender, Ethics, and Global Health: A Complex Tapestry

The intersection of gender, ethics, and global health presents a complex tapestry of challenges and opportunities that echo Clara Maass's experiences in Cuba over a century ago. Today, women leaders in global health initiatives face ethical dilemmas that, while different in context, resonate with the fundamental questions Clara grappled with: How do we balance the urgency of addressing global health crises with the ethical imperative to protect vulnerable populations?

The work of Dr. Adaora Adimora on HIV prevention in sub-Saharan Africa embodies this modern struggle. Her research often involves navigating complex ethical terrain, balancing the need for rigorous research with protecting vulnerable study participants.[681] Like Clara, who volunteered for yellow fever experiments in a foreign land, Dr. Adimora must consider the broader implications of her work on local communities and global health equity.

The ethical considerations in global health vary significantly across cultural contexts, adding complexity to decision-making. Shereen El Feki, author and former vice-chair of the UN's Global Commission on HIV and the Law, highlights this

[681] El Feki, Shereen. *Sex and the Citadel: Intimate Life in a Changing Arab World.* New York: Anchor, 2013.

challenge in her work on sexual health in the Arab world.[682] Her research underscores the need for culturally sensitive approaches to global health ethics. This consideration would have resonated with Clara Maass as she navigated the cultural landscape of early 20th-century Cuba.

This cultural nuance is exemplified in the case of the Ebola vaccine trials in West Africa during the 2014-2016 outbreak. Researchers grappled with ethical questions reminiscent of those faced during yellow fever experiments in Clara's time: How do you conduct urgent medical research in crisis conditions while ensuring informed consent and protecting vulnerable populations? The resolution involved extensive community engagement and adaptive trial designs, demonstrating how modern ethical frameworks have evolved to address complex global health challenges.

Women-led initiatives in global health have often been at the forefront of navigating these ethical complexities. The work of Dr. Quarraisha Abdool Karim in South Africa exemplifies this approach. Her research on HIV prevention methods for women advanced scientific knowledge and addressed crucial ethical issues of gender equity in health research.[683] By focusing

---

682 Bull, Susan, Phaik Yeong Cheah, Spencer Denny, Irene Jao, Vicki Marsh, Laura Merson, Neena Shah More, et al. "Ethics Preparedness: Facilitating Ethics Review During Outbreaks." *BMC Medical Ethics* 20, no. 29 (2019).

683 Karim, Quarraisha Abdool, Salim S. Abdool Karim, Janet A. Frohlich, Anneke C. Grobler, Cheryl Baxter, Leila E. Mansoor, Ayesha B. M. Kharsany, et al. "Effectiveness and Safety of Tenofovir Gel, an

on empowering women to protect their health, Dr. Karim's work echoes Clara Maass's dedication to patient welfare while addressing contemporary global health challenges.

As we continue to navigate the complex landscape of global health ethics, Clara Maass's legacy serves as both an inspiration and a cautionary tale. Her selfless dedication to advancing medical knowledge inspires today's global health leaders to push boundaries in the fight against disease. At the same time, her ultimate sacrifice reminds us of the paramount importance of ethical considerations in all aspects of medical research and practice.

The evolving role of women in shaping global health ethics represents a continuation of Clara Maass's legacy. As more women assume leadership positions in international health organizations and research institutions, they bring diverse perspectives that enrich ethical deliberations and lead to more comprehensive, culturally sensitive approaches to global health challenges.

Antiretroviral Microbicide, for the Prevention of HIV Infection in Women." *Science* 329, no. 5996 (2010): 1168-1174.

14.6 Charting the Ethical Future: Lessons from Clara Maass

As we stand on the threshold of a new era in medicine, the ethical challenges that lie ahead are as complex as they are numerous. Yet, in navigating this uncertain terrain, we find that the principles embodied by Clara Maass—courage, compassion, and an unwavering commitment to the greater good—remain as relevant as ever.

Drawing on Clara's legacy, we can construct an ethical framework for the future of medicine rooted in timeless values and adaptable to emerging challenges. This framework must balance the drive for scientific progress with the imperative to protect human dignity and autonomy, a tension that Clara navigated in her decision to participate in yellow fever experiments.

One key element of this framework is the concept of "ethical foresight"—the ability to anticipate and address potential ethical implications of medical advancements before they become critical issues. Dr. Jennifer Doudna, co-inventor of the CRISPR gene-editing technology, exemplifies this approach in her advocacy for responsible use of the technology she helped create.[684][^20] Her proactive engagement with the ethical

---

[684] National Academies of Sciences, Engineering, and Medicine. "Human Genome Editing: Science, Ethics, and Governance." Washington, DC: The National Academies Press, 2017. https://doi.org/10.17226/24623.

implications of gene editing echoes Clara's foresight in recognizing the potential impact of her participation in medical experiments.

Another crucial aspect of our ethical roadmap must be the principle of inclusive deliberation. As our understanding of gender, racial, and cultural dynamics in healthcare evolves, it becomes increasingly clear that ethical decision-making must incorporate diverse voices and perspectives. The World Health Organization's Global Health Ethics Unit, which brings together experts from various backgrounds to address global health ethics issues, provides a model for this approach.[685]

Looking ahead, we can envision a series of ethical guidelines for emerging medical technologies and practices inspired by Clara's example:

1. Prioritize human welfare: All medical advancements must be evaluated primarily regarding their potential benefit to human health and well-being.

2. Ensure informed consent: As medical interventions become more complex, the process of obtaining truly informed consent must evolve to ensure that participants fully understand the implications of their involvement.

---

[685] World Health Organization. "Global Health Ethics." WHO.int. Accessed August 23, 2024. https://www.who.int/teams/health-ethics-governance/global-health-ethics

3. Promote equity: New medical technologies and treatments must be developed and distributed to reduce, rather than exacerbate, health disparities.

4. Respect autonomy: In an age of personalized medicine and AI-driven healthcare, preserving patient autonomy and privacy is paramount.

5. Foster transparency: New medical technologies research and development must be transparent and open to public scrutiny.

6. Encourage global cooperation: Clara's work in Cuba demonstrated that addressing significant health challenges often requires international collaboration.

7. Balance risk and benefit: When considering experimental treatments or research protocols, there must be a careful weighing of potential risks against possible benefits for individuals and society.

As we apply these principles to future scenarios, we might consider how they would guide us in addressing emerging ethical dilemmas. For instance, how might we approach the development of brain-computer interfaces that could restore function to paralyzed individuals and potentially allow unprecedented access to human thoughts?[686] Or how should

[686] Yuste, Rafael, Sara Goering, Blaise Agüera y Arcas, Guoqiang Bi, Jose M. Carmena, Adrian Carter, Joseph J. Fins, et al. "Four Ethical Priorities for Neurotechnologies and AI." *Nature* 551, no. 7679 (2017): 159-163.

we navigate the ethical implications of using artificial wombs to support highly premature infants, a technology that could save lives but also fundamentally alter our understanding of pregnancy and birth?[687]

In facing these and other yet-unimagined ethical challenges, we can draw strength and guidance from Clara Maass's example. Her courage in the face of unknown risks, her commitment to advancing medical knowledge for the benefit of others, and her ultimate sacrifice serve as a powerful reminder of the human values that must continue to guide us in pursuing medical progress.

---

[687] Romanis, Elizabeth Chloe, and Claire Horn. "Artificial Wombs and the Ectogenesis Conversation: A Misplaced Focus? Technology, Abortion, and Reproductive Freedom." *International Journal of Feminist Approaches to Bioethics* 13, no. 2 (2020): 174-194.

14.7 Conclusion: Forging an Ethical Path in the Ever-Evolving Landscape of Medicine

As we stand at the intersection of Clara Maass's enduring legacy and the rapidly evolving frontier of modern medicine, we find ourselves in a familiar and uncharted landscape. Clara's ethical challenges—questions of informed consent, individual sacrifice for the greater good, and the boundaries of acceptable risk in medical research—continue to resonate today, albeit in new and often more complex forms.

From Clara's time to now, the progress made in women's medical roles illustrates how far we've come. Yet, the persistent challenges in achieving total equity and representation remind us of the work still ahead. The ethical dilemmas posed by emerging technologies like gene editing and artificial intelligence echo Clara's struggles with the unknown consequences of medical experimentation.

As we look to the future, we see a medical landscape fraught with ethical complexity. The rise of gene editing technologies, the increasing role of artificial intelligence in healthcare, and the ongoing challenges of global health equity all present ethical dilemmas that would have been unimaginable in Clara's time. Yet, her story continues to offer guidance, reminding us of the human element at the heart of all medical endeavors.

Clara Maass's legacy challenges us to approach these new frontiers with courage and caution. It calls on us to push the boundaries of medical knowledge while never losing sight of the individual lives at stake. It demands that we question our assumptions, challenge our biases, and continually reassess the ethical implications of our actions.

Moreover, Clara's story is a powerful reminder of the impact that individual choices can have on medical progress. Just as her decision to participate in yellow fever experiments contributed to our understanding of the disease, the ethical choices made by today's medical professionals will shape the future of healthcare in ways we can scarcely imagine.

As we conclude this exploration of women, medicine, and the ethics of the future, we are left with both a sense of awe at the progress made and a sobering awareness of the challenges ahead. The path forward is not marked, but Clara Maass's legacy is a beacon, guiding us toward a future where scientific advancement and ethical integrity are inextricably linked.

We must commit to ongoing ethical engagement in medicine to honor this legacy. This means fostering diverse voices in medical decision-making, prioritizing transparency in research and practice, and never losing sight of the human impact of our choices. It means approaching new technologies critically always asking what we can and should do.

In this light, Clara Maass's story is not just a historical footnote but a living challenge to all those engaged in medicine. It calls on us to embody the same courage, compassion, and ethical commitment that defined her life and work. As we face the unknown ethical frontiers of tomorrow, we carry with us the torch that Clara lit, illuminating the path toward a more moral, equitable, and humane future in medicine.

The challenges we face today—from ensuring equitable access to healthcare globally to navigating the ethical implications of genetic engineering—may seem far removed from Clara's world. Yet, the core ethical principles that guided her actions remain profoundly relevant. Her willingness to put herself at risk for the greater good of medical advancement speaks to the continuing need for ethical courage in the face of uncertainty. Her dedication to patient care reminds us that the fundamental commitment to human welfare lies at the heart of all medical endeavors.

As we move forward, we must balance the relentless pursuit of medical progress with an unwavering commitment to ethical integrity. This balance is not always easy to achieve, as the case of emerging technologies like CRISPR gene editing demonstrates. The potential to eliminate genetic diseases must be weighed against the risks of unintended consequences and the ethical implications of altering the human genome. In navigating these complex issues, we would do well to ask ourselves: What would Clara Maass do?

The answer, perhaps, lies not in trying to apply early 20th-century solutions to 21st-century problems but in embodying the spirit of ethical inquiry and selfless dedication that Clara exemplified. It means being willing to ask difficult questions, challenge assumptions, and put the welfare of patients and the advancement of medical knowledge above personal gain or comfort.

As we conclude this chapter, we are reminded that the story of women in medicine—from Clara Maass to the pioneering researchers and clinicians of today—is one of continuous progress in the face of persistent challenges. It is a story of breaking barriers, pushing boundaries, and redefining what is possible. But above all, it is a story of unwavering commitment to the highest ideals of the medical profession.

14.8 Epilogue: The Unextinguished Flame - Clara Maass's Eternal Legacy

In the quiet corridors of hospitals worldwide, in bustling research laboratories, and the far-flung clinics of global health initiatives, the spirit of Clara Maass lives on. Her flame—a beacon of courage, sacrifice, and unwavering ethical commitment—continues to light the way for future medical professionals.

Clara's legacy is not a static monument but a dynamic force that evolves with each new challenge the medical community faces. It's present in the determined focus of researchers working late into the night to decode the mysteries of new pathogens. It's there in the gentle touch of nurses comforting patients in their darkest hour. It burns bright in the fierce advocacy of doctors fighting for equitable healthcare access in underserved communities.

As we stand on the brink of unprecedented medical breakthroughs—from personalized gene therapies to AI-driven diagnostics—Clara's story reminds us that at the heart of every medical advancement lies a profoundly human story. It challenges us to approach each innovation with scientific rigor, deep ethical consideration, and a steadfast commitment to human dignity.

In the face of future pandemics, climate health crises, and as-yet-unimagined medical challenges, Clara's example urges us to be bold in our pursuit of knowledge yet humble in our understanding of its consequences. It reminds us that medical progress is measured not just in lives saved or diseases cured but in the ethical integrity with which we conduct our work.

The legacy of Clara Maass extends far beyond the confines of medical history. It speaks to the enduring power of individual choices to shape the course of human progress. In a world often driven by technological advancement and economic imperatives, Clara Maass is a timeless reminder of the essential humanity at the core of medical practice.

As we reflect on the journey from Clara's time to our own, we see a narrative of progress intertwined with persistent challenges. The gender barriers that Clara faced have evolved but have not disappeared entirely. The ethical quandaries she navigated have transformed, becoming more complex in the face of advancing technology. Yet, the fundamental questions remain: How do we balance the pursuit of knowledge with protecting human dignity? How do we ensure that medical progress serves all of humanity, not just a privileged few?

These questions resonate in the work of contemporary medical professionals around the globe. In the efforts to develop vaccines for emerging diseases, we see echoes of Clara's participation in yellow fever experiments. In the push for more inclusive and diverse medical research, we find the continuation of her fight for recognition and respect in a male-dominated field. In the ongoing struggle to provide equitable healthcare access, we witness the enduring relevance of her commitment to serving those most in need.

Clara Maass's flame continues to burn brightly, illuminating the path forward for medicine in the 21st century and beyond. It challenges us to uphold the highest ethical standards in our pursuit of medical knowledge. It inspires us to champion diversity and inclusion in all aspects of healthcare. It reminds us that behind every medical breakthrough, policy decision, and patient interaction, profound ethical implications demand our careful consideration.

As we close this chapter and look to the future, we carry the unextinguished flame of Clara Maass's legacy. It burns as a challenge and an inspiration—urging us to be courageous in the face of the unknown, compassionate in our care for others, and uncompromising in our commitment to ethical practice.

In every ethical dilemma we face, every breakthrough we achieve, and every life we touch through our work in medicine, we honor Clara's memory. Her spirit lives on, not as a distant historical figure, but as an ever-present guide, leading us toward a future where the pursuit of medical knowledge is forever intertwined with the highest ethical ideals.

And so, as we step into the uncertain but promising future of medicine, we do so with Clara Maass walking beside us—her courage, inspiration, sacrifice, solemn responsibility, and ethical commitment are our unwavering north stars. In the face of the challenges and opportunities ahead, let us strive to be worthy inheritors of her legacy, working tirelessly to create a world with medical progress and ethical integrity.

Glossary

1. **Anesthesiology**: The medical specialty focused on pain relief and management during surgery.

2. **Antiseptic**: Substances or techniques used to prevent infection by inhibiting the growth of microorganisms.

3. **Apgar Score**: A quick test performed on newborns to evaluate their physical condition immediately after birth.

4. **Bacteriology**: The scientific study of bacteria, especially in relation to disease and medicine.

5. **Bioethics**: The study of ethical issues arising from biological and medical research.

6. **Cardiology**: The medical specialty dealing with disorders of the heart.

7. **CRISPR**: A gene-editing technology allowing for precise modifications to DNA sequences.

8. **Diphtheria**: A serious bacterial infection affecting the mucous membranes of the nose and throat.

9. **Dysentery**: An intestinal inflammation causing severe diarrhea with blood and mucus in the feces.

10. **Epidemic**: The rapid spread of an infectious disease to a large number of people in a given population.

11. **Epidemiology**: The study of how diseases spread and can be controlled in populations.

12. **Fomites**: Objects or materials capable of carrying infectious organisms and spreading disease.

13. **Gene editing**: The process of making specific changes to DNA sequences in living organisms.

14. **Germ theory**: The scientifically accepted idea that certain diseases are caused by microorganisms.

15. **Hemophilia**: A rare genetic disorder in which blood doesn't clot normally.

16. **Hippocratic Oath**: An ethical code of conduct for medical professionals, originating in ancient Greece.

17. **Immunosuppressive**: Drugs or treatments that reduce the strength of the body's immune system.

18. **Informed consent**: The process by which a patient agrees to medical treatment with full knowledge of risks and benefits.

19. **Institutional Review Board (IRB)**: A committee that reviews and monitors biomedical research involving human subjects.

20. **Malaria**: A mosquito-borne disease caused by a parasite, leading to fever, chills, and flu-like symptoms.

21. **Midwifery**: The health profession involved in pregnancy, childbirth, and early postnatal care.

22. **Neurology**: The branch of medicine dealing with disorders of the nervous system.

23. **Neurosurgery**: The medical specialty concerned with the prevention, diagnosis, and treatment of disorders affecting the nervous system.

24. **Nightingale, Florence**: British nurse and statistician, considered the founder of modern nursing.

25. **Nuremberg Code**: A set of ethical research principles for human experimentation developed after World War II.

26. **Obstetrics**: The branch of medicine dealing with pregnancy, childbirth, and the postpartum period.

27. **Oncology**: The study and treatment of cancer and tumors.

28. **Pandemic**: An epidemic of an infectious disease that has spread across a large region or worldwide.

29. **Pasteurization**: A process of heating food to a specific temperature to kill harmful bacteria.

30. **Pathology**: The science of the causes and effects of diseases.

31. **Pediatrics**: The branch of medicine dealing with children and their diseases.

32. **Pharmacology**: The science of drugs, including their composition, uses, and effects.

33. **Physiology**: The study of the functions and mechanisms of living organisms and their parts.

34. **Polio**: An infectious viral disease that can cause paralysis, breathing problems, and death.

35. **Prenatal care**: Medical care provided to expectant mothers throughout their pregnancy.

36. **Public health**: The science of protecting and improving the health of people and their communities.

37. **Quarantine**: The isolation of people, animals, or things to prevent the spread of disease or pests.

38. **Radiology**: The branch of medicine using imaging technologies to diagnose and treat disease.

39. **Sanitation**: Conditions and practices that help maintain health and prevent disease spread.

40. **Scarlet fever**: A bacterial infection causing a distinctive red rash, usually affecting children.

41. **Smallpox**: A highly contagious viral infection, now eradicated, known for causing fever and a characteristic skin rash.

42. **Surgically clean**: A level of cleanliness required in operating rooms to minimize infection risk.

43. **Syphilis**: A bacterial infection usually spread by sexual contact, causing serious complications if left untreated.

44. **Telemedicine**: The practice of caring for patients remotely using telecommunications technology.

45. **Title IX**: A U.S. federal law prohibiting sex-based discrimination in educational programs receiving federal funding.

46. **Tuberculosis**: A potentially serious infectious bacterial disease mainly affecting the lungs.

47. **Typhoid fever**: A bacterial infection spread through contaminated food and water.

48. **Vaccination**: The administration of a vaccine to stimulate the immune system against a specific disease.

49. **X-ray**: A form of electromagnetic radiation used to create images of the inside of the body for medical purposes.

50. **Yellow fever**: A viral disease spread by infected mosquitoes, causing fever, nausea, and in severe cases, liver damage and death.

Note on Bibliography

Due to the extensive nature of the research conducted for this book, the complete bibliography is not included in this printed volume. However, a comprehensive list of all works cited and consulted is available to interested readers. To obtain a bibliography copy, please contact the author at rodkelley@comcast.net. This resource provides a detailed account of the primary and secondary sources that informed this work and can serve as a valuable reference for further research on Clara Maass and the history of women in medicine.

Afterword

"The most beautiful experience we can have is the mysterious. The fundamental emotion stands at the cradle of true art and science."
- Albert Einstein

This quote by Albert Einstein, one of the most renowned scientists of the 20th century, encapsulates the spirit of inquiry and wonder that drove Clara Maass and the many women who followed her in medicine. Throughout this book, we have explored how pursuing knowledge often requires us to venture into the unknown, confront the mysterious, and sometimes make great sacrifices.

Clara Maass's decision to participate in the yellow fever experiments was driven by this very sense of mystery - the desire to uncover the unknown for the benefit of humanity. Her courage in the face of uncertainty echoes Einstein's sentiment that the mysterious is not something to be feared but embraced as the wellspring of scientific progress.

Moreover, this quote reminds us that the practice of medicine is as much an art as it is a science. The women we've encountered in these pages didn't just accumulate knowledge; they applied it with compassion, creativity, and a deep understanding of the human condition. Like true art, their work has touched lives and profoundly transformed our world.

As we close this book, Einstein's words serve as both a reflection on the journey we've taken through the history of women in medicine and an invitation to future generations. They challenge us to continue pushing the boundaries of knowledge, to remain in awe of the mysteries that still surround us, and to approach our work - whether in medicine, science, or any field - with the curiosity, courage, and creativity that have defined the pioneers we've celebrated in these pages.

A

B

C

D

E

M

Also, by Rodney L. Kelley

2024

- Purposeful
- Eternal Echoes
- Wisdom Through the Ages
- Unsung Pillars of The University of Scranton.
- Inscribed Legacy

2023

- A Gentle Goodbye
- Let History Be the Judge
- American Crucible
- Reflections on The Class Of 1923

2022

- America's National Treasures

2021

- The Pope's Marine
- Visitor's Guide for the Descendants of Thomas Luther Gladden

2020

- The Sunset at McCook

2019

- Special Dispatch to the Tribune

2017

- When We Became Americans

2016

- Caring for the Commonwealth

Made in the USA
Middletown, DE
07 September 2024